The Politics of the Personal in Feminist Family Therapy: International Examinations of Family Policy

The Politics of the Personal in Feminist Family Therapy: International Examinations of Family Policy has been co-published simultaneously as *Journal of Feminist Family Therapy*, Volume 17, Numbers 3/4 2005.

The Politics of the Personal in Feminist Family Therapy: International Examinations of Family Policy

Anne M. Prouty Lyness
Editor

The Politics of the Personal in Feminist Family Therapy: International Examinations of Family Policy has been co-published simultaneously as *Journal of Feminist Family Therapy*, Volume 17, Numbers 3/4 2005.

NEW YORK AND LONDON

First published 2005 by The Haworth Press, Inc.

This edition published 2014 by Routledge
711 Third Avenue, New York, NY 10017, USA
27 Church Road, Hove, East Sussex BN3 2FA

Routledge is an imprint of the Taylor & Francis Group, an informa business

The Politics of the Personal in Feminist Family Therapy: International Examinations of Family Policy has been co-published simultaneously as *Journal of Feminist Family Therapy*™, Volume 17, Numbers 3/4 2005.

©2005 by The Haworth Press, Inc. All rights reserved. No part of this work may be reproduced or utilized in any form or by any means, electronic or mechanical, including photocopying, microfilm and recording, or by any information storage and retrieval system, without permission in writing from the publisher.

The development, preparation, and publication of this work has been undertaken with great care. However, the publisher, employees, editors, and agents of The Haworth Press and all imprints of The Haworth Press, Inc., including The Haworth Medical Press® and Pharmaceutical Products Press®, are not responsible for any errors contained herein or for consequences that may ensue from use of materials or information contained in this work. With regard to case studies, identities and circumstances of individuals discussed herein have been changed to protect confidentiality. Any resemblance to actual persons, living or dead, is entirely coincidental.

The Haworth Press is committed to the dissemination of ideas and information according to the highest standards of intellectual freedom and the free exchange of ideas. Statements made and opinions expressed in this publication do not necessarily reflect the views of the Publisher, Directors, management, or staff of The Haworth Press, Inc., or an endorsement by them.

Cover design by Lora Wiggins

Library of Congress Cataloging-in-Publication Data

The politics of the personal in feminist family therapy : international examinations of family policy / Anne M. Prouty Lyness, editor.
 p. cm.
 "Co-published simultaneously as Journal of Feminist Family Therapy, Volume 17, Numbers 3/4 2005."
 Includes bibliographical references and index.
 ISBN-13: 978-0-7890-3399-4 (hard cover : alk. paper)
 ISBN-10: 0-7890-3399-2 (hard cover : alk. paper)
 ISBN-13: 978-0-7890-3400-7 (soft cover : alk. paper)
 ISBN-10: 0-7890-3400-X (soft cover : alk. paper)
 1. Feminist therapy–Cross-cultural studies. 2. Family psychotherapy–Cross-cultural studies. 3. Family policy–Cross-cultural studies. 4. Social policy–Cross-cultural studies. I. Prouty Lyness, Anne M. II. Journal of feminist family therapy.
RC488.5.P64 2005
616.89'156–dc22

2006004465

The Politics of the Personal in Feminist Family Therapy: International Examinations of Family Policy

CONTENTS

ABOUT THE CONTRIBUTORS — xv

Editor's Foreword — xix
   Anne M. Prouty Lyness

FEMINIST EXAMINATIONS OF FAMILY POLICY

The Morphing of Family Therapy and Family Support: How British Social Policy and Feminist Practice Are Interacting — 1
   Steven Walker

The Notion of Interdependence and Its Implications for Child and Family Policy — 23
   Susan Brooks
   Ya'ir Ronen

Babies and Bosses: Family Policy Directions in the OECD — 47
   Celia Briar

A Response to the Babies and Bosses Report: The Effects of Policies on Therapy and the Influence of Therapists on Politics — 67
   Markie Twist

Aging Societies and Intergenerational Equity Issues: Beyond Paying for the Elderly, Who Should Care for Them? — 79
   Steven K. Wisensale

Wisensale's Analysis: Thoughts from a Feminist Family Therapist   105
   Scott Johnson

FEMINIST RESEARCH OF WOMEN'S EXPERIENCES

Counter-Spaces as Resistance in Conflict Zones:
  Palestinian Women Recreating a Home   109
   Nadera Shalhoub-Kevorkian

Puerto Rican and Dominican Women's Perceptions
  of Divorced Women   143
   Joyce A. Arditti
   Nancy P. Lopéz

Index   175

ABOUT THE EDITOR

Anne M. Prouty Lyness, PhD, LMFT, is Associate Professor and Director of Clinical Training in the Marriage and Family Therapy program within the Department of Applied Psychology at Antioch New England Graduate School in Keene, New Hampshire. Anne earned her masters degree in Marriage and Family Therapy from East Carolina University and her doctorate from Purdue University. She has a lifelong interest in feminism and her writing reflects her clinical and research interests in women's health and the importance of focusing on human diversity and marginalized voices in therapy, training, and research. This is her third year as Editor of the *Journal of Feminist Family Therapy*, and she is honored to be able to work with such distinguished and dedicated feminist activists such as the authors in this very special volume.

About the Contributors

Joyce Arditti, PhD, is Associate Professor in Family Studies within the Department of Human Development at Virginia Polytechnic Institute and State University in Blacksburg, Virginia. She earned her PhD from the University of North Carolina at Greensboro. Her areas of research include: Criminal Justice and Families, Divorce, and Family Policy, and has numerous publications in these areas of expertise. She is the current Editor of the journal entitled *Family Relations: Interdisciplinary Journal of Applied Family Studies*, on the Editorial Boards of the *Journal of Divorce & Remarriage* and *Marriage and the Family*, and has served for several years on the University Human Subjects Review Committee.

Celia Briar, PhD, is Senior Lecturer within the School of Sociology, Department of Social Policy and Social Work at Massey University, Palmerston North, New Zealand. Her interests include the feminist research and analysis of women, work and welfare policies, family policy, on Universal Basic Income and other policies to prevent poverty amongst women and children. She has a particular focus on strategies to assist lone mothers. She is currently doing research and writing on gender and occupational health. Publications include the book *Working for Women?* (1997) and numerous book chapters and articles. She has two sons, now both adults. In her spare time Celia plays Celtic harp and has made four CDs.

Susan L. Brooks, JD, (BA 1983, MA (Social Work) 1984, University of Chicago; JD New York University, 1990) joined the law faculty as a clinical professor in 1993. Currently, she directs the Child and Family Policy Clinic, in which law students engage in micro- and macro-level advocacy on behalf of vulnerable children and families. Because of her interdisciplinary training, she has brought substantial innovations to the Law School and the University. She has also served as a consultant to the Tennessee Supreme Court on a study of children in foster care and has spearheaded two successful legislative initiatives related to kinship care in Tennessee. In addition to her responsibilities in the Child and Family Policy Clinic, Professor Brooks teaches Children and the Law and Child Welfare: Law and Policy. She has numerous professional publications and has been involved in co-editing three books: *Family Systems and the Law* (forthcoming); *Creative Child Advocacy: Global Perspectives*; and *Clinical Anthology: Readings for Live-Client Clinics*. Professor Brooks especially enjoys outdoor activities, including cycling and camping with her family, which includes her husband Brian, and three-year-old son, Sam.

Scott Johnson, PhD, LMFT, is Associate Professor and Director of the Marriage and Family Therapy doctoral program at Virginia Polytechnic Institute and State University in Blacksburg, Virginia. He holds bachelors degrees in English Literature and Classic Guitar, and a masters degree in creative writing. He taught college English for many years before earning his PhD in Marriage and Family Therapy from Virginia Tech in 1991. His academic interests include Family Systems Theory in the larger world, and the arts in psychotherapy. He has numerous publications and presentations in both areas, in addition to training and supervision in Family Therapy. He is a Clinical Member, Approved Supervisor, former Treasurer, and current President Elect of the American Association for Marriage and Family Therapy. He is a JMFT Advisory Editor and an active Editorial Board Member for JFFT. He enjoys canoeing and travel with his daughter Mara and his wife, Anna Beth.

Nancy P. López, MA, earned her MA in Area Studies: Latin American Studies, at Virginia Polytechnic Institute and State University, in Blacksburg, Virginia in 2004. Her thesis was entitled, "Latin American Women's Perceptions of Divorce: An Exploratory Study of the Situation and Image of Divorced Women in Puerto Rico and the Dominican Republic." She holds a Bachelor Degree in Law from the Dominican Republic, where she lived until 1991 and worked as a Lawyer in a Commercial Law firm. She is currently a Spanish instructor within the Department of Foreign Languages and Literatures at Virginia Polytechnic Institute and State University in Blacksburg, Virginia. She works also as an independent translator, interpreter, and cultural consultant, and is a member of several International Students Associations. She has two children.

Ya'ir Ronen, PhD, earned a doctorate in law and a masters in education. Dr. Ronen is a lecturer at Ben Gurion University's Department of Social Work and holds teaching positions at Bar Ilan University's Faculty of Law and Ramat Gan's College of Law. He has written and taught on children's rights, identity, human rights advocacy, social justice and social exclusion and is the author of a book in Hebrew entitled, *The Child's Participation in the Determination of His Guardianship*. He has been involved in law reform efforts in Israel for more than thirteen years. Ya'ir's wife, Gila, is a social worker and family therapist in training. He is the father of three girls: Tay, Noa and Shir.

Nadera Shalhoub-Kevorkian, PhD, is affiliated with the Faculty of Law and the School of Social Work, Hebrew University, Jerusalem. She is an active Palestinian feminist who, among others, initiated the first hotline in Palestine for abused females; lobbied and participated in women campaigns to gender-desensitize the criminal justice system and the legislative council in Palestine; assisted abused women; and has extensive activism in various human rights, feminist, and civil society organizations inside Israel. Her main theoretical and research interest has focused on the study of women in Palestine, Jordan, and Israel focusing on women's victimization and agency, women and law, and female child sexual abuse. Her research in the past five years has examined the crime of femicide; the criminalization of sexual abuse in both Palestine and Jordan, and among Palestinians in Israel. Her recent study on women victims of war crimes and the effect of militarization on violence against women made her develop particular therapeutic models of intervention (Social Service Review, 2005), and discuss the effect of occupation on gender and education (Social Identities, 2005; American Behavioral Scientist Queries, in press). She also has collaborated on three books in Arabic on the Trauma of Loss in Conflict Zones, The Parallel Legal System, and Space as Race and Racism in Arab Jerusalem.

Markie Twist, MA, MEd, is a student in the Human Development and Family Studies doctoral program at Iowa State University in Ames, Iowa, specializing in Marriage and Family Therapy. She earned her Masters of Arts in Marriage and Family Therapy from the University of Louisiana at Monroe in 2002 and her Masters in Education from Northern Arizona University at Flagstaff in 1998. Her academic interests include: GLBT studies and issues, social justice, human sexuality, therapeutic program evaluation, and prevention of adolescent high-risk behaviors. She is a two-time recipient of the Alice M. Ford Scholarship and was named the 2005 Outstanding Graduate Student of the Year by the Iowa Association for Marriage and Family Therapy. She currently teaches, is a member of a research team involving a partnership between the university and the Iowa Department of Health and Human Services. She has also worked in various therapy contexts over the last 6 years. She hails from Alaska and in her leisure time enjoys traveling, skiing, running, and cheerleading activities, as well as spending time with her animal companion, Dax.

Steven Walker, BA (Hons), MSc, CQSW, Dip FT, studied Social Work and Social Policy at the London School of Economics, is faculty in the Mental Health and Learning Disability Department, in the Institute of Health and Social Care of Anglia Ruskin University in Chelmsford, Essex, United Kingdom. He has worked in voluntary and statutory social work contexts for 15 years in generic and specialist settings with older people, adult mental health and children and families work. Dr. Walker has specialized in child protection and child and adolescent mental health practice qualifying as a UKCP registered family psychotherapist in 1992 after post-graduate training at the Institute of Family Therapy, and the Tavistock Institute, London. He teaches Mental Health Assessment, Therapeutic Intervention, and Family Therapy, and has research interests in child and adolescent mental health which have generated numerous national and international conference presentations and publications including his recent books: *Social Work* and *Child and Adolescent Mental Health; Applying Family Therapy;* and *Culturally Competent Therapy*. He is currently Programme Leader in child and adolescent mental health for post-qualifying multi-disciplinary students up to Masters Degree level. He is also a Standards and Ethics Board member of the British Association of Social Workers, an Editorial Board member of the *British Journal of Social Work* and a member of the Essex Coalition of Disabled People, North Essex Stronger Together mental health advocacy organization, the Association for Family Therapy and Systemic Practice and the Higher Education Academy. Steven's work and home life are heavily informed by a feminist perspective. He works part-time, and enjoys writing, music and film. Steven does most of the cooking, cleaning and ironing and shares equally in the care of his daughter Rose with his wife Isobel.

Steven Wisensale, PhD, is Professor of Public Policy in the School of Family Studies at the University of Connecticut, Storrs, CT. He earned his PhD in Social Welfare Policy from the Heller School at Brandeis University in 1983. He holds a master's in education from Temple University and a master's in liberal studies from Wesleyan University. In 1973 he earned a Graduate Diploma in Comparative Government and Social Welfare Policy from the University of Stockholm in Sweden. His primary research interests include Social Welfare Policy, Family Leave Policy, and Aging Policy. He has published more than 50 professional papers and two books, including *Family Leave Policy: The Political Economy of Work and Family in America*. In 1999 he was a special consultant to the United Nations on world population aging. A recipient of a university-wide teaching award, his teaching responsibilities include courses in family policy, family law, comparative family policy, and aging policy. He is a former Acting Dean of the School of Family Studies and twice chaired the School's graduate program. A former Gerontology Research Fellow and Health Policy Research Fellow, he also received two Fulbright Fellowships to teach and conduct research in Germany and the Czech Republic. He is the former chair of the family policy section of the National Council on Family Relations and currently sits on the Board of Directors of the Council on Contemporary Families. He and his wife Nan and their two dogs, Zephyr and Rainbow, reside in Essex, Connecticut.

Editor's Foreword

Politics are always very personal. People are ignored, neglected or harmed by social and family policy. Other policies reflect attempts to make family life safer, more accessible, and more inclusive. As a feminist family therapist and trainer, I deeply believe that family policy trends around the world affect the daily routines and choices of women and their families. The world is too small to think that war, deprivation, or violence in one country is an isolated event–we are all affected in ways that we may or may not ever know or understand, because we are all connected as a global community. Family policy trends reflect competing human and cultural values. Feminist family therapists are clinicians, activists, trainers, researchers, and members of families and communities. The more we understand and collaborate with others interested in people and families, especially those without power and a voice, the stronger our communities and the world community can become. We cannot save the world, but we can compassionately participate in it. We can participate in supporting, even demanding, more humane, inclusive, and respectful local and international family social policies.

This very special volume is a collection of work focusing on several important issues of family policy that affect women and their families around the world. The call for papers for this collection went out in the spring and summer of 2004; all of the submissions went through a peer review process by members of *The Journal of Feminist Family Therapy's* Editorial Board. The authors whose work appears in this volume come from several countries and disciplines, and all have been working and writing in their specialty areas for many years. This collection reflects a beginning answer to the question: What is happening in interna-

---

[Haworth co-indexing entry note]: "Editor's Foreword." Lyness, Anne M. Prouty. Co-published simultaneously in *Journal of Feminist Family Therapy* (The Haworth Press, Inc.) Vol. 17, No. 3/4, 2005, pp. xxiii-xxv; and: *The Politics of the Personal in Feminist Family Therapy: International Examinations of Family Policy* (ed: Anne M. Prouty Lyness) The Haworth Press, Inc., 2005, pp. xix-xxi. Single or multiple copies of this article are available for a fee from The Haworth Document Delivery Service [1-800-HAWORTH, 9:00 a.m. - 5:00 p.m. (EST). E-mail address: docdelivery@haworthpress.com].

© 2005 by The Haworth Press, Inc. All rights reserved.

tional family policy about which feminist family therapists should be aware? How should we be integrating these issues into our professional and personal lives?

In the first section, Steven Walker explores how Britain's social policies and feminist family therapy have been co-evolving; how family policy often sustains limited and dominant gender roles and family constructs; and how feminist-informed family therapy and family support are influencing change. Susan Brooks and Ya'ir Ronen examine how the construct of interdependence could transform family law into a more respectful and empowering system. They discuss how including the lenses of culture, family systems, therapeutic jurisprudence, and prevention law could promote societal empathy and promote individual, family and community well-being. Celia Briar discusses the Organisation for Economic Cooperation and Development's Babies and Bosses report and how it might actually affect mothers and children, as well as women's economic options for working outside the home while caring for their children. Markie Twist then follows up with a reflection on the Babies and Bosses report from a feminist family therapy perspective. This section is concluded with Steven Wisensale's thoughtful analysis of family policies in several countries regarding the costs of caring for our aging family members and the values inferred by the choices made in current policy. Scott Johnson provides a reflection from a therapist on Wisensale's comparative analysis.

The second section brings us two qualitative studies of women's experiences of family policies. The first is brought to us by Nadera Shalhoub-Kevorkian. She brings us the voices of Palestinian women whose homes were being bulldozed. In her research, she focuses on women's resiliency as women persevere to create hope and a sense of a family home, with whatever they can. The women provide photographs so readers have a view of their world. This research reminds us that no matter where one's sympathies may lie in any armed conflict, we must listen to and learn from the stories of women from all sides, if we are to have any hope of creating a meaningful, lasting, and peaceful coexistence. The second is a study by Joyce Arditti and Nancy Lopéz of Latin American women's perspectives on divorce and what it means to them and how they are reconstructing meaning for themselves. I applaud the participants in both of these studies who bravely shared their experiences with the world so as to fight the silence that is used to disempower them. There are women all over the world whose voices are not being heard.

I applaud and thank all of the researchers, activists, and clinicians who work in the arena of family public policy. I thank all of the authors, reviewers, and my Editorial Assistant, Jeremiah Brown, who contributed their work and time to this special volume. I hope that this present collection provides one more step in promoting human empathy and understanding of the families themselves and for all who work for promoting healthy families. And, I hope that future submissions' authors can educate us about family policy in more areas of the globe, including Asia and Africa, and facilitate more in-depth examinations of how family policies affect the lives of families with lesbian, gay, bisexual, and transgendered members. Politics are always very personal.

Anne M. Prouty Lyness

FEMINIST EXAMINATIONS OF FAMILY POLICY

The Morphing of Family Therapy and Family Support: How British Social Policy and Feminist Practice Are Interacting

Steven Walker

SUMMARY. This paper focuses on contemporary British public policy and how social policies and feminist-informed family therapy are influencing and challenging each other. The concept and practice of family support is evaluated in terms of the central political role it fulfils in replicating stereotyped gender roles and normative family constructs. It is argued that family support and family therapy are morphing as government policies encourage more voluntary sector services, presenting feminist

Address correspondence to: Dr. Steven Walker, Anglia Ruskin University, Institute of Health and Social Care, Bishop Hall Lane, Chelmsford CM1 1SQ Essex, United Kingdom.

[Haworth co-indexing entry note]: "The Morphing of Family Therapy and Family Support: How British Social Policy and Feminist Practice Are Interacting." Walker, Steven. Co-published simultaneously in *Journal of Feminist Family Therapy* (The Haworth Press, Inc.) Vol. 17, No. 3/4, 2005, pp. 1-22; and: *The Politics of the Personal in Feminist Family Therapy: International Examinations of Family Policy* (ed: Anne M. Prouty Lyness) The Haworth Press, Inc., 2005, pp. 1-22. Single or multiple copies of this article are available for a fee from The Haworth Document Delivery Service [1-800-HAWORTH, 9:00 a.m. - 5:00 p.m. (EST). E-mail address: docdelivery@haworthpress.com].

© 2005 by The Haworth Press, Inc. All rights reserved.
doi:10.1300/J086v17n03_01

family therapists with both challenges and opportunities to influence social policy. *[Article copies available for a fee from The Haworth Document Delivery Service: 1-800-HAWORTH. E-mail address: <docdelivery@haworthpress.com> Website: <http://www.HaworthPress.com> © 2005 by The Haworth Press, Inc. All rights reserved.*

KEYWORDS. British public policy, family public policy, systems theory, feminist family therapy, family support, social policy, service design, service delivery, child mental health, adolescent mental health, early intervention, early prevention

INTRODUCTION

Current British public policy aspires to promote and support the interests of families by developing a range of general fiscal, tax and employment measures combined with new child and family support services specifically targeted on socially disadvantaged communities in economically deprived areas. These initiatives mirror the broader government strategy to liberalise the economy for private enterprise to take over former state-run transport, utility and health care infrastructure. Voluntary social care agencies are encouraged to fill the gap where private companies cannot make profits and the statutory sector access threshold is drawn. Thus, generally speaking, family support is being undertaken in the voluntary sector while family therapy is offered in statutory and private services. The result is the emergence of a mosaic of family support services inspired by local community action to meet the needs of a variety of families in diverse circumstances. They offer a range of services including parenting groups, child care, single parent support, welfare advice, information, practical help and counseling/therapeutic services (Utting, 1995; Tunstill, 1996; Thoburn et al., 1998; Statham, 2000).

One of the defining characteristics of the systemic theory underpinning a family therapy approach is the need to take account of this wider socioeconomic context of family experience. This means keeping in mind those external forces influencing intra-familial patterns of relationships. Family support policies and services are therefore very important variables for feminist family therapists to consider when assessing where and how to help. This is particularly the case when there is evidence of therapeutic work already being undertaken within family support services which utilise systems theory and family therapy approaches (Coleman et al., 1997; Crisp, 1994; Walker & Akister, 2004; Walker, 2005). Social care professionals with family therapy training and skills are increasingly being employed in these settings where the work is appealing, rewarding and less constrained than in statutory agencies. This is leading to a morphing of specific family therapy concepts and practices with generic family support approaches.

Feminist theory explains the critically important context of masculine privileging and how this affects gender behaviour and the role of power in family organisation (Pilatis & Anderton, 1986; Goldner, 1991; Hare-Mustin, 1991; Dallos & Draper, 2000; Walker & Akister, 2004). Combining these two concepts in feminist-informed family therapy provides an important framework within which to empower women inside their families and outside in patriarchal society. Using this knowledge in family and couple therapy means opening up the subject of power in relationships rather than colluding with its denial. This is an example of how a *meta* theoretical context frames the *micro* context of intimate therapeutic work. Using this combined systemic and feminist conceptual tool enables us to take account of the multiple influences on modern British family therapy practice. Recent social policies and the current economic and political agenda of the early 21st century can thus be seen to affect the macro family structure and micro gender relationships.

In Europe several meta contexts are influencing family life and therefore shaping the way a feminist-informed family therapy practice can develop. The latter part of the 20th century witnessed the collapse of orthodox Communism symbolized by the toppling of the Berlin Wall followed by emerging multi-party democracies in former Eastern bloc states. Enlargement of the European Union continued with the original West European core embracing less-developed Southern European countries and preparing to admit former communist regimes. These enormous political and economic changes pose challenges for those involved in the task of defining social policy in the enlarged European Union and those seeking to regulate and codify family therapy practice across national boundaries.

In the short term the consequences of these geopolitical shifts have resulted in war and conflict in the Balkans incarnating deep ethnic and religious rivalries that cross physical and cultural boundaries. In addition, the growing gap between the wealthier industrially developed nations and the poorer former soviet economies as well as the chronic poverty in Africa has produced a rapid increase in emigration into Europe. Whole nations are thus in transition with communities split in two and families disintegrating as a human tide of refugees, asylum seekers and economic migrants is displaced and searches for refuge in the Western-developed countries. Further tensions can be detected where there is a strong seam of Nationalist public opinion that believes the public policy of closer European economic integration could undermine individual national sovereignty and further immigration will dilute the sense of national personal identity (Walker, 2003a).

This is causing public policy tensions as legislators governed by patriarchal ideologies use prevailing national and international policies to manage the quantitative pressures of housing, welfare and work, while feminist-inspired family practitioners attempt to meet the qualitative emotional and psychological needs of families. Family support is steadily percolating into political consciousness as the generic vehicle for a raft of fiscal, tax, and employment public policies with the ostensible aim of helping modern families. It is also increasingly apparent that refugee and asylum-seeking families with diverse cultural characteristics, religious traditions, relationship patterns and structures cannot be helped using a homogeneous or one-dimensional approach.

Family support as a quasi-professional social care practice is thus morphing with family therapy, reflecting many of the characteristics of planned therapeutic intervention. This is creating challenges and opportunities particularly for feminist-informed family therapy, as a rapidly changing economic and social system requires an isomorphic response in order to ensure an empowering therapeutic stance. This makes the task of identifying best practice and designing appropriate family support policies and practice across Europe a challenging one for feminist family therapists keen to employ feminist values of connectedness, cooperation, community and the equalization of power.

PART ONE: ORGANISATIONAL CONTEXT

Service Design and Delivery

Both family support and family therapy use the word "family" that can in itself be misleading if there are a number of assumptions about what a family is and how services can be designed and delivered to help it. Traditional definitions were very narrow and reflected an era when a heterosexual couple married, had children, and lived under the same roof. Nowadays this nuclear family stereotype is surprisingly resilient in British public policy despite evidence of the diversity of different forms of family life. This is a popular conception of how the family is constituted that is more a reflection of how some traditionalists believe sexual, emotional and parental relationships ought to be structured (Walters et al., 1988; Perelberg & Miller, 1990).

In contemporary multicultural society with a rich tapestry of ethnic diversity combined with rapid sociological transformations there are a wide and complex variety of "families" such as extended, kin group, and lone parent. These can be further distinguished by parental partnerships that are same sex couples, cohabiting, adoptive, fostering, separated, divorced, remarried, and stepparents (Eliason, 1996; Salmon, 1999). Stretching the definition of family further can include the important role peers, friends and local community figures perform in shaping and influencing family patterns of behaviour. We can therefore see that apparently simple concepts such as family and support/therapy are more complex the closer we examine them.

This is important in the context of finding ways of working, using a feminist perspective, that are relevant and acceptable to service users. Family support has, for example, had to adapt its historical focus on the traditional nuclear family model. Whereas the more recent practice of family therapy has had to consider the effectiveness of culturally competent methods of working with different family forms, rather than trying to defend its focus on systems rather than individuals whilst using a normative family model (Walker, 2005). Indeed there is a creative body of literature developing that illustrates how family therapy concepts can be adapted for work with individuals or couples (Dallos & Draper, 2000).

The diverse nature of family life in contemporary Britain and in other European societies therefore requires sophisticated analysis of the broad trends reported in social surveys; otherwise abrupt policy changes can fail to address fully the needs of every family requiring support. Racist and cultural patriarchal stereotypes of the role played by extended families, for example, distort the picture of unique family situations which are complex and fluid, and inhibit proper assessment of the needs of black and other ethnic minority families, travelers, and refugee families. These families all face additional problems in the context of prejudice, institutional racism and discrimination, which can all find expression in child care and adult mental health problems where family therapy can offer help (Dominelli, 1999; Kiddle, 1999; Vostanis & Cumella, 1999).

It is crucial for the future development of family life that support services are designed and delivered in the most appropriate, effective and accessible way possible (Holterman, 1995). Feminist-informed family therapy can bring an understanding of the gendered context impacting different organisational cultures, professional knowledge and theories used by a range of practitioners in order to integrate and coordinate help for children and families. Services geared towards the needs of specific age groups of children or young people, or adults can determine the type of help offered and whether it is perceived as family or individual support. This becomes particularly important in the area of child and family work where the initial assessment of the presenting problem could be formulated on an individual or family basis. Feminist family therapists are particularly alert to the potential for scapegoating individual children or women within family systems functioning in negative and punitive ways (Gorrell Barnes, 1998).

Assessment methodology designed around the needs of bureaucratic systems intent on rationing and restricting access to support services in this context tends to remain rooted in psychiatric diagnostic models. Psycho-social factors are embraced as risk factors reflecting negative, deficit indicators, rather than a more holistic feminist approach seeking to identify and amplify strengths, coping strategies, alternative community resources, and user perceptions. Handled carefully, assessment itself can be an empowering experience for women and children oppressed and embedded in a culture of blame and fault.

The creation of Children's Trusts in which previously separate education, social and health services are joined organizationally, and in some cases into multidisciplinary services, represent structural attempts to better coordinate services and meet the needs of children. The implications for practice with families highlight the need to ensure a family therapy approach that provides effective ways of working to avoid blaming, inter-agency scapegoating and placing further stress on families. The short-term nature of family therapy combined with its systems perspective offers considerable advantages in this context, particularly if welded to a feminist perspective.

Organising services across the spectrum of multi-agency provision in partnership between family welfare professionals and *all* parents, offers the opportunity to bring out dormant protective factors to interrupt the causal chain of events so often set in train under retrenched child protection work (Little & Mount, 1999). Work with parents which creates a positive environment where strengths are amplified and children's emotional well-being is promoted, is preferable to reacting negatively to the consequences of neglect or abuse. Efforts are being made to design family support services to enable men to access support as single parents or child care partners, but such services are the exception. Research has shown that the absence of men from these opportunities is a factor in raising perceptions of risk except where a history of domestic violence is indicated (Holt, 1998).

Family Support and Family Therapy

Family support is used extensively in public policy documents, yet is rarely closely defined. It is a general term used to describe a variety of interventions practiced by voluntary sector staff, charitable organisations and non-statutory agencies. Family support can be perceived as an overall aspiration within which particular models and techniques of practice are employed. These models and methods can be rooted in behavioural, psychodynamic or task-centered theories and focus on individuals, couples or the whole family (Hardiker, 1995; Gardner, 1998; Walker, 2003c). Family therapists using systems theory might also characterize their work in terms of a range of methods including, for example, structural, psychoanalytic, systemic, cognitive-behavioural, solution-focused or constructionist. Equally, the focus can be on the individual, couple or whole family. Thus Feminist-informed family therapy practice has the capacity within these methodologies to utilise an overarching perspective to link family problems to deeper societal structures.

Within a family support or family therapy mode of working there are a wide variety of techniques and approaches. The difference is that family therapists have usually trained to a high level and generally work in statutory health and social care agencies. Family support is undertaken by less qualified staff in the voluntary sector. Family support is used by public policy makers to make women feel such work is common sense, part of their inherent nature and–especially–their responsibility. For example, research into Home Start family support initiatives demonstrated how publicity and resources were targeted at women receiving welfare benefits (McCauley et al., 2004). So when terms such as family support and family therapy are used in multidisciplinary professional contexts such as inter-agency meetings or case conferences, there are a number of different possible assumptions about what was actually being proposed or had already been tried in practice. Implicitly decisions about how to intervene signal that therapy or support is women's work. The terms can become morphed cognitively and verbally whereby family support is discussed as both a policy aspiration and therapeutic intervention and vice versa. Without clarification about what these terms mean the potential for confusion is high with the increased possibility that families receive mixed messages and fathers feel excluded (Walker, 2003b).

Thus, while the government seeks solutions to problems affecting the integrity of the family and children's welfare, it simultaneously is sending out an ambivalent message about how it expects services to respond. On the one hand statutory family welfare provision is reduced to a minimum level of support targeted on high-risk, poor families with a largely supervisory function for agency staff. On the other hand non-statutory charities and voluntary organisations are being encouraged to offer a diverse mosaic of family support services to a more general client group. This consists of women doing unpaid caring work inside or outside their own family network. Authoritative data consistently demonstrates the scale of unpaid caring work undertaken by women (Dominelli, 2002). Family therapy practiced in each sector is consequently very different.

Many continental European models of family welfare imply a residual role for the state and have a history of church, charitable and non-governmental provision. Almost the reverse can be observed in the development of the British welfare state–until recently. Recent social policy initiatives and government statements confirm a redefinition of the welfare state whereby a larger role for the voluntary and independent social care sector is prescribed. In effect this relegates women to traditional homemaker and unpaid caring roles. Thus therapeutic and preventive work is being excluded from the responsibility of professional staff whose family welfare role is being more narrowly defined in assessment, surveillance and child protection terms (Hellinckx et al., 1997).

A combination of economic circumstances and sociological changes in people's behaviour has nevertheless prompted British social policy-makers to consider how to meet the needs of contemporary families in addition to shifting the locus of support away from the state. Recent evidence provides a developing picture of changing family characteristics in Britain generally similar to other older developed countries. These family characteristics include increasing stress levels in families that are associated with increased child and adolescent mental health problems (Home Office, 1997; General Household Survey, 1997; NCH Action for Children, 2000). Examples of changes in family characteristics include:

- Rising trend in divorce
- Increase in single parent households and cohabitation
- Disruption in patterns of family relationships
- Increased rates of teenage pregnancy
- Widening gap between rich and poor

- Ageing of the population
- Increased reporting of child abuse and domestic violence
- Increasing child and adolescent mental health problems
- Increased alcohol and substance misuse

PART TWO: THE PRACTICE CONTEXT

Child and Adolescent Mental Health

All the above trends have been cited in the literature as risk factors for the genesis of, or symptoms consistent with, child and adolescent mental health problems (Rutter et al., 1994; Vostanis & Cumella, 1999; ONS, 2001; Dogra et al., 2002; Walker, 2003d). In recent years the volume and complexity of child and adolescent mental health problems in Britain as elsewhere in industrially developed societies has increased rapidly, prompting demands for help from parents, carers, and professionals. Public health enquiries and other research have highlighted the need for a collaborative response between all social care and welfare agencies as existing specialist provision has stretched beyond its capacity to cope adequately (Rutter et al., 1994; Rutter & Smith, 1995; Health Advisory Service, 1995; Harrington, 1997; Mental Health Foundation, 1999; Rawlinson & Williams, 2000). Government policy directives encourage multidisciplinary and interprofessional working methods as part of the strategic response (House of Commons, 1997; Audit Commission, 1999; Walker, 1999). Public policy pronouncements are punctuated with the term "family support," while practitioners in both the statutory and voluntary agencies are increasingly interested in training to enable them to use systemic and family therapy methods and skills.

The Mental Health Foundation's latest inquiry into child and adolescent mental health (1999) concluded that a cultural shift was required which prioritised family support with a universally acceptable service of non-stigmatising provision. This should be available in schools, family doctor clinics, and other accessible venues in order to address the increased trend of mental health problems in children and young people. Service-driven models of assessment for children and families are the product of a reactive system geared to responding to concerns relating to child protection, developmental harm, or disturbed symptoms within a negative and deficit framework. This leads to a focus on risk analysis which can be experienced by parents as undermining, or psychiatric treatment which constructs the child as suffering an individual disease requiring individual treatment.

The literature on child and adolescent assessment, and current public policy guidance are improving to emphasize multifaceted assessment but nevertheless they are still influenced by adapted adult psychiatric classifications located in a medico-biological model constructed by white middle-class males (Dept of Health, 1999; Baradon et al., 1999). There is less emphasis on psycho-social factors, including the effects of poverty, racism, unemployment, social exclusion and poor housing and little mention of the use and abuse of male power. The Framework for Assessment of Children in Need, which is the preferred operational tool (DOH, 2000), has been criticised for failing to properly distinguish family support from child protection with many agencies organising their child welfare service as child protection (Calder, 2004). This again places women in a double-bind of being blamed as inadequate mothers and expected to raise children without much state support.

A number of themes emerge from the research literature that can help staff to consider the social context of family and children's difficulties. These include the importance of multifactorial causal explanations and the contribution of structural variables to childhood problems articulated by several authors (Rutter et al., 1994; Colton et al., 1995; Sutton, 1999; Carr, 2000). These demonstrate the value of taking a wider systems view of the situation being assessed. The importance of variation in perception of children's behaviour depending on the theoretical model used, and the evidence on assessment methodology, is crucial in determining the course and type of support offered. The interplay of these factors and the beneficial effects of developing a synthesis of models of intervention suggest precise targeted responses to particular children's difficulties combined with an expansive approach addressing social issues affecting children and families (Hill, 1999).

Differing views of children's behaviour (as understood by the child, the parent or carer and the professionals who encounter the child) are important to acknowledge and incorporate in any care plan or supportive intervention. A feminist informed systems framework has the capacity to hold these divergent concepts and practices, valuing the contribution each makes (Rutter, 1985). Differences in perception can therefore be seen as explanatory potential rather than as implicitly conflictual. Family therapists can help all the different players to see the wider picture and find common ground from which solutions can spring.

Racism and xenophobia have increased as wealthier European countries struggle to manage economic constraints and humanitarian aid to refugee and asylum-seeking families who have been shattered and scattered often in traumatic and extremely distressing circumstances. Changes in the socio-geographic texture of Europe have produced moral panics and hasty policy changes to tackle the symptoms and consequences without much evidence of planning or thought put into understanding the different needs of immigrant families. The emphasis seems to be on dealing with large population movements as a political and economic problem rather than about the welfare of vulnerable children and families (Walker, 2002; Walker, 2003d).

Family therapists know only too well the value and cost-effectiveness of early intervention and preventive work with families in trouble. Family support in Britain has tended to attract much less attention in terms of government policy emphasis or research and development than the more clearly defined systems for children in need of statutory protection and/or those looked after by public authorities. Yet it is covered by the same legal requirement of the Children Act (1989), and underpinned by the 1989 UN Convention on the Rights of the Child, and expressed in recent policy initiatives such as The Department of Health refocusing children's services initiative (1995), the Quality Protects programme (1999), new Assessment guidance (2000), Every Child Matters (2003) and The Children Act (2004). These are all evidence of a policy shift designed to influence practice prompted by research into family support services and the limitations of the child protection system (Department of Health, 1995).

Detailed studies have detected intra-familial changes in traditional patterns of kinship relationships, contact and support, where significant numbers of families have lost touch or were unable to rely on help when it was needed (Thoburn et al., 1998). These findings are of enormous interest to practitioners seeking to intervene therapeutically while harnessing the natural network of support often preferable to many people (Speak et al., 1995; Coleman et al., 1997; McGlone et al., 1998). Further complexity is revealed by research into subgroups of the population which, although sparse, offers evidence of the nature and variety of contemporary family life.

For example, Modood and Berthoud (1997) found that while all ethnic groups had high levels of contact with non-resident parents, Asian and African-Caribbean people had higher levels of contact with aunts and uncles. The potential of other family members and grandparents as helpful resources is indicative of a need for the widening of the focus for practitioners expected to assess strengths within the existing family constellation and work preventively. Elevated rates of mental health problems have also been detected in children and young people from refugee and asylum-seeking families consistent with post-traumatic stress disorder (Hodes, 2000). Family therapy offers the appropriate combination of psycho-social knowledge and skills that can help make sense of all these variables affecting the relationships within families.

It has been established that a confluence of several risk factors in childhood can create the conditions for later psycho-social difficulty, including socioeconomic disadvantage, child abuse, and parental mental illness. But there are protective mechanisms that can mitigate the chance of some children going on to develop anti-social behaviour or serious mental health problems. These can be obscured by the imperative for medical diagnosis or the overreactions of inexperienced child protection professionals or untrained volunteer family support workers. Feminist-informed practice can help women challenge these notions which in child protection cases carry the double-bind of making them feel at fault whilst insisting they are the only parent who can do the job (Walker, 2003a).

The consequent lack of support and eventual mother-blaming highlight the importance of assessment methods in child and adolescent mental health contexts informed by systems theory that take account of not just individual characteristics within the child but equally within the family and broader social environment. It is unlikely this holistic level of assessment is available to unqualified family support workers however well-intentioned. These tend to be the lowest paid, least supervised, and lowest qualified employees or volunteers. Family therapists, on the other hand, are usually graduates with a professional qualification who undergo several years advanced training before becoming accredited family therapists.

A social model of Europe incorporating the continental European heritage of social action could enlarge the panorama of assessment activity. In combination, a sophisticated assessment process using systems theory identifying strengths and protective factors, together with a more explicit social mandate, could create a chain of indirect links that foster improved family functioning in a context of social inclusion (Walker, 2001a).

Early Intervention and Prevention

In the government policy consultation paper "Supporting Families" (1999), the focus of attention emphasised better support and education for current and future parents as a preventive strategy. Key themes included the intention to improve advice and information to parents, and achieving a reduction in child poverty, while offering financial help for working parents. The policy argues that by strengthening adult relationships and targeting serious family problems, an impact could be made on priority areas such as children's learning, youth offending, teenage pregnancy, and domestic violence. These are all areas that could be enhanced by a family therapy approach that can appraise the interrelationship between and within them.

Various initiatives aimed at children and their families living in disadvantaged areas such as the Sure Start programme are evidence of the practical implementation of the implicit preventive aspects of this policy which are based on evidence of success from the USA Head Start scheme (Gross et al., 1995; Newman, 2004). This scheme demonstrated long-term reductions in anti-social activity, marital problems, child abuse, adult mental health difficulties, and unemployment in later life, in a group of children who received the intervention, with a comparison of children who did not receive the intervention.

Quantifying the impact of preventive family support work is complex and to achieve systematic results is expensive, therefore there is little in the way of evidence of long-term effectiveness in Britain or the rest of Europe (Eayrs & Jones, 1992). However, there are signs that while outcome measures from various projects are intangible, small-scale social action projects can evidence changes in relationships between parents and professionals, how to work in partnership, and how to engage positively with parents (Robbins, 1998). All of these contributed to supporting families better and were more user-focused.

The lessons for family therapy practice are for emphasising empowering strategies, searching hard for creative solutions beyond narrow service-led resources, and refining relationship-building skills. This challenges the service management orthodoxy for short-term focused assessments aimed at identifying risk and need according to a limited range of resources provided by other non-statutory agencies. It offers the opportunity to provide professionally-qualified staff with more satisfying work over longer time periods, and provides service users the chance to feel respected, valued, contained, and supported in a consistent and reliable way. The prospect is for combining the best features of welfare practice grounded in a solid psycho-social systems theoretical base.

Parent education or training programmes have expanded in the face of exponential demand for help from parents, to deal with a range of child and adolescent difficulties from toddler tantrums to suicide and drug and alcohol addiction (Webster-Stratton, 1997). This form of intervention is popular and is now expected to be offered as part of a repertoire of contemporary family support measures. Studies of parent education programmes, while they are limited in number, show they can be an effective way of supporting families by improving behaviour in pre-adolescent children (Miller & Prinz, 1990; Bourne, 1993; Lloyd, 1999). They highlight the impact group-based behaviourally oriented programmes have in producing the biggest subsequent changes in children's behaviour and are perceived by parents as non-stigmatising. Programmes where both parents are involved and which include individual work with children are more likely to effect long-term changes.

However, parent education/training programmes, whilst enjoying a growth in popularity in Britain and other European countries, are generally not subject to rigorous evaluation (Pugh & Smith, 1996). Research shows that in a number of studies 50 percent of parents continue to experience difficulties, and it is not clear to what extent changes are due to the format, the method of intervention, the group support or the practitioner's skills. High attrition rates from some programmes are attributed to practitioner variables such as their level of qualification and experience, and qualities such as warmth, enthusiasm, or flexibility (Barlow, 1998). There is also some evidence that by operating a "gender-neutral" format–meaning the service is offered without restrictions or eligibility, men find it difficult to attend and engage in groups where discussion of feelings and partner relationships is a focus. Equally, women with abusive partners present can feel further disempowered in such contexts where they cannot open up to explain their domestic circumstances for fear of retribution. It may also be the case that some programmes are inappropriate for parents lacking motivation or feeling compelled to attend under the pressure of child protection concerns.

Few British studies have used randomized controlled trials which inhibit identification of the most beneficial elements of a programme; and because most provision is geared to rectifying problems in socially disadvantaged groups, the available research evidence reflects that bias. Those that have been conducted are nevertheless yielding important qualitative data from stakeholders' perspectives (Ghate & Daniels, 1997; Morrow, 1998). It is argued that the tendency for the masculine managerialist preference for evaluating work on the basis of the three E's (efficiency, effectiveness, economy) reflects a limited agenda for quantitative outcome measures. These data need to be supplemented with the three P's (partnership, pluralism, process) which better reflect feminist-informed principles seeking to incorporate service users' perspectives (Dominelli, 2002). Further studies which pay attention to realistic models of parenting in the community would counter this bias by identifying skills that lead to successful parenting–focusing on what went right, rather than what went wrong.

Anti-racist practice demands attention to the family life cycle of black and other ethnic minority families focussing on transitional points, strengths and acceptable support (Kemps, 1997; Bhui & Olajide, eds., 1999). The term "black" is used here to mean all ethnic minority communities who are systematically subjected to personal and institutional discrimination and prejudice. It is also noteworthy that the views of parents and children are largely absent from the research, particularly in families with lone parents, gay and lesbian parents, and stepparents. There is also very little systematic incorporation of culture and ethnicity as factors influencing parenting styles, or on disability and the particular issues facing parents with disabled children who may have emotional and behavioural problems, and on gender influences within families and within professional groups. A feminist-informed systems approach offers a perspective that can incorporate and address every possible social, political, economic, psychological and relational influence on family experience.

Families for whom parent education is unlikely to be a sufficient response to child management difficulties are those which feature maternal depression, socioeconomic disadvantage and the social isolation of the mother (Quinton, 2004). Extra-familial conflict combined with relationship problems, contribute to the problem severity and chronicity and therefore influence the ability of family therapists to introduce change. While parental misperception of the deviance of their children's behaviour is a significant impediment to engaging in constructive family support, the prospects for unqualified staff attempting to help without professional supervision are further diminished (Macdonald & Roberts, 1995).

Parenting education or training programmes seem to be a response to a demand for a variety of support, including information, child development knowledge, and skills development in managing children of all ages. This reflects the continuation of the fragmentation of families in the industrialised European economies where social and economic mobility are a feature of everyday life. This results in unstable communities where friends, relatives, female and male networks become transient while the traditional grandparent figures are often missing or live long distances apart. This leaves little in the way of a secure emotional and social base for vulnerable parents to use as a resource.

The renaissance of the concept of family support in Britain is currently perceived as an alternative to child protection, rather than part of a connected architecture of resources to be activated as different needs emerge. Therefore the public policy to develop indirect voluntary provision of family support services in Britain can be better seen as a symptom of, rather than a solution to, retrenchment in family support offered by professional workers using family therapy approaches. The concern is that economic and political pressure to promote a renaissance of voluntary, non-statutory family support, will produce the greatest stress on those women least equipped to cope, and therefore precipitate child protection crises leading to further retrenchment of family welfare services away from planned support towards reactive, repressive state surveillance (Cannan et al., 1992; Shardlow & Payne, 1998; Adams et al., 2000).

Developing Feminist-Informed Practice

One way that children's services can tilt the balance away from repressive child protection procedures and illustrate the pragmatic use of feminst-informed systems theory is reflected in the example of family group conferences (FGC). Introduced some years ago and borrowing from New Zealand Maori traditional practices, they have challenged the orthodoxy in British social services planning which places primacy on the professional social worker's power, values and perceptions. The key idea in these conferences is that family meetings are convened where there are concerns about the welfare of a child or children. The family in these circumstances is defined widely and extended family members are encouraged to participate. Their task is to create their own plan for the child of concern by assuming responsibility in deciding how to meet the needs of the child (Morris & Tunnard, 1996).

Thus the social workers' role changes dramatically from an inspectorial/adversarial role largely prescribed by procedures and a restricted definition of their task, to one more consistent with the skills and knowledge of family therapy. In the context of family group conferences social workers can emphasise communication, negotiation, mediation and facilitation skills that are better informed by a systems approach seeking to emphasise problem-solving and highlight the strengths within a family system. Clearly, a therapeutic stance is required that means social workers have to embrace the concept of partnership practice and resist the seductive simplicity of deciding what is best for children and their families.

At the heart of the family group conference is a redefinition of social work practice with children and families. It puts into sharp focus a tangible example of the elusive and often ill-defined notion of empowering practice. It is a challenge to social work that is driven by a defensive culture and to social workers comforted by the ability to retreat into procedural safety when faced with complexity, uncertainty, and the normal swings and roundabouts of family life. On the other hand, this approach fits with social workers using a family therapy approach to their work. The FGC model proposes limits to the intrusion of the professional planning model. It suggests the model should form the frame within which family decision-making should take place, and that decision-making should be carried out in whatever way is appropriate for each particular family (Morris & Tunnard, 1996).

Feminist critics of family therapy refer to domestic violence and the abuse of children by men as examples of the way many families are organised by male abuse of power, which is not sufficiently addressed by systems theory. The hidden nature of the abuse together with the impossible dilemmas faced by women attempting to protect themselves and their children mean that it is likely to be a factor affecting the interactions between family members. Social workers have equally been criticised for doubly oppressing women who, whilst attempting to manage their dilemmas and contradictory feelings, find themselves accused of failing to protect their children. Various studies have over the years confirmed that there is an underreporting of this crime, and that in Britain domestic violence occurs in 30-50 percent of male-female relationships (Kelly, 1996; Walker, 2001b).

Critics argue that family therapy therefore colludes with male abuse of power because in seeking, for example, to foster parental control over difficult children the method is actually reinforcing patriarchal authority. Statutory child care workers are themselves in a bind having a primary duty to prioritise the safety of children whilst recognising the risks posed to women who are frightened to report domestic violence and face having their children removed. The child protection system and the criminal justice system reflect public policies that implicitly collude with actual and threatened violence against women and children and deter both from testifying and providing evidence against male perpetrators.

Recent research has highlighted the serious physical, psychological and emotional consequences for children who witness or are unwittingly involved in domestic violence. In 90 percent of recorded incidents the child/ren were in the next room and in 30 percent children tried to intervene to protect their mother from assault (Hester et al., 2000).

Students of systems theory thus face having to make sense of concepts of interactivity and circular process, while simultaneously recognising the inequality and structural privileges provided to men. A thorough understanding of this crucial variable in contemporary relationship dynamics is required, therefore, for family support staff seeking to incorporate family therapy into their work with families where domestic violence is likely to be a major, yet unacknowledged factor.

Fortunately there is a growing body of literature that offers reliable evidence to employ in seeking to intervene in a thoughtful, ethical and empowering way for the victims as well as *the perpetrators* of domestic violence (Home Office, 2000; Hague, 2000; Walker, 2001; Vetere & Cooper, 2001). Apart from direct work with a family where there is a suspicion but no open acknowledgement of domestic violence, systems theory can be put into practice within an inter-agency context. Well-coordinated multi-agency collaboration has the potential to improve services to women and children experiencing domestic violence and to maximise their continual safety and well-being (Hester et al., 2000; Rivett & Rees, 2004). Using a feminist framework permits an understanding of the inter-agency relationships, rivalries, and different power positions that are played out in attempts at partnership practice.

CONCLUSION

British public policy has in recent years gradually diminished the role of the State and reduced welfare provision leading to a widening of the gap between the richest and poorest citizens. Child poverty is among the highest in the developed European nations while women consistently earn less than men in equivalent jobs. Family therapy in Britain has developed over the past 50 years from a narrow theoretical base, and a first-order change perspective aimed at pressuring families to change; to a more recent engagement with multiple post-modernist ideas, second-order cognitive change and feminist theory. This paper has tried to illustrate how these two themes are interacting in contemporary British family support activity and to discuss where feminist-informed family therapy has an opportunity to influence social policy and the consequent process and practice of those striving to help families in need. There is indeed a detectable morphing between family support work and family therapy as more opportunities for practitioners are created in voluntary and private sector services. Thus family support can be seen to take on the characteristics and techniques of family therapy and vice versa. This reflexive process is mirrored in the way social policy is influencing family therapy and vice versa. Feminist-informed family therapy has the advantage of bringing an understanding of the social, economic and political context of family relationships into this complex equation in order to promote an empowering and liberating experience for all the family.

REFERENCES

Adams, A., Erath, P., & Shardlow, S. (2000). *Fundamentals of social work in selected European countries*. Lyme Regis, UK: Russell House Publishing.

Baradon, T., Sinason, V., & Yabsley, S. (1999). Assessment of parents and young children–a child psychotherapy point of view. *Child Care Health and Development*, 25(1), 37-53.

Barlow, J. (1998). Parent training programmes and behaviour problems–Findings from a systematic review. In A. Buchanan & B. Hudson (Eds.), *Parenting, schooling, and children's behaviour: Interdisciplinary approaches*. Alton, UK: Ashgate Publishers.

Barnes, M., & Warren, L. (1999). *Paths to empowerment*. Bristol: The Policy Press.

Bayley R. (1999). *Transforming children's lives: The importance of early intervention*. London: Family Policy Studies Centre.

Bhui, K., & Olajide, D. (Eds.) (1999). *Mental health service provision for a multi-cultural society*. London: Saunders.

Bourne, D. (1993). Over-chastisement, child non-compliance and parenting skills: A behavioural intervention by a family centre social worker. *British Journal of Social Work. 5*, 481-500.

Calder, M. (2004). The assessment framework: A critique and reformulation. In *Assessments in Child Care: A comprehensive guide to frameworks and their use* (pp. 88-114). Lyme Regis, UK: Russell House Publishers.

Cannan, C., Berry, L., & Lyons, K. (1992). *Social work and Europe*. London: Macmillan/BASW.

Carr, A. (2000). *What works with children and adolescents?* London: Routledge.

Coleman, M., Ganong, L., & Cable, S. (1997). Beliefs about women's intergenerational family obligations to provide support before and after divorce and remarriage. *Journal of Marriage and the Family, 59*(1), 165-176.

Crisp, S. (1994). *Counting on families: Social audit report on the provision of family support services*. London: Exploring Parenthood.

Dallos, R., & Draper, R. (2000). *An introduction to family therapy*. Buckingham: Open University Press.

Department of Health (1995). *Child protection: Messages from research*. London: HMSO.

Department of Health (1997). *General household survey*. London: HMSO.

Department of Health (1999). Lac circular (99) 33. *Quality protects programme: Transforming children's services 2000-01*. London: HMSO.

Department of Health (2000). *Framework for the assessment of children in need.* London: HMSO.

Dominelli, L. (2002). *Feminist social work theory and practice.* Basingstoke, UK: Palgrave.

Dominelli, L. (Ed.) (1999). *Community approaches to child welfare.* Aldershot, UK: Ashgate.

Eayrs, C., & Jones, R. (1992). Methodological issues and future directions in the evaluation of early intervention programmes. *Child Care, Health and Development, 18,* 15-28.

Eliason, M. (1996). Lesbian and gay family issues. *Journal of Family Nursing, 2*(1), 10-29.

Gardner, R. (1998). *Family support: Practitioners guide. BASW.* Birmingham: Venture Press.

Ghate, D., & Daniels, A. (1997). *Talking about my generation.* London: NSPCC.

Goldner, V. (1991). Sex, power and gender: A feminist analysis of the politics of passion. *Journal of Feminist Family Therapy, 3,* 63-83.

Gordon, G., & Grant, R. (1997). *How we feel: An insight into the emotional world of teenagers.* London: Jessica Kingsley.

Gorrell Barnes, G. (1998). *Family therapy in changing times.* Basingstoke, UK: Palgrave.

Gross, D., Fogg, L., & Tucker, S. (1995). The efficacy of parent training for promoting positive parent-toddler relationships. *Research in Nursing and Health. 18,* 489-499.

Hague, G. (2000). *Reducing domestic violence: What works? PRCU Briefing Note.* London: HMSO.

Hardiker, P. (1995). *The social policy contexts of services to prevent unstable family life.* York: Joseph Rowntree Foundation.

Hare-Mustin, R. T. (1991). Sex, lies & headaches: The problem is power. *Journal of Feminist Family Therapy, 3,* 39-61.

Hellinckx, W., Colton, M., & Williams, M. (1997). *International perspectives on family support.* Aldershot, UK: Ashgate Publishing.

Hester, M., Pearson, C., & Harwin, N. (2000). *Making an impact–children and domestic violence.* London: Jessica Kingsley.

Hill, M. (1999). *Effective ways of working with children and their families.* London: Jessica Kingsley.

Holt, C. (1998). Working with fathers of children in need. In R. Bayley (ed.), *Transforming children's lives: The importance of early intervention.* London: Family Policy Studies Centre.

Holterman, S. (1995). *All our futures: The impact of public expenditure and fiscal policies on Britain's children and young people.* Barkingside, UK: Barnardos.

Home Office (1997). *Social trends.* London: HMSO.

Home Office (2000). *Living without fear: Multi-agency guidance for addressing domestic violence.* London: HMSO.

House of Commons (1997). *Child and adolescent mental health services.* London: HMSO.

Kelly, L. (1996). When woman protection is the best kind of child protection: Children, domestic violence and child abuse. *Administration, 44*(2), 118-135.

Kemps, C. (1997). Approaches to working with ethnicity and cultural issues. In K. Dwivedi (Ed.), *Enhancing parenting skills* (pp. 59-77). London: Wiley.
Kiddle, C. (1999). *Traveller children: A voice for themselves*. London: Jessica Kingsley.
Little, M., & Mount, K. (1999). *Prevention and early intervention with children in need*. Aldershot, UK: Ashgate.
Lloyd, E. (Ed.) (1999). *Parenting matters: What works in parenting education?* London: Barnardos.
Macdonald, G., & Roberts, H. (1995). *What works in the early years? Effective interventions for children and their families*. Barkingside, UK: Barnardos.
McCauley, C., Knapp, M., Beecham, J., McCurry, N., & Sleed, M. (2004). *The outcomes and costs of Home-Start support for young families under stress*. York: Joseph Rowntree Foundation.
McGlone, F., Park, A., & Smith, K. (1998). *Families and kinship*. London: Family Policy Studies Centre.
Mental Health Foundation (1999). *The big picture: Promoting children and young people's mental health*. London: Mental Health Foundation.
Middleton, L. (1997). *The art of assessment*. Birmingham: Venture Press.
Miller, G., & Prinz, R. (1990). Enhancement of social learning family interventions for childhood conduct disorders. *Psychological Bulletin, 108*, 291-307.
Modood, T., & Berthoud, R. (1997). *Ethnic minorities in Britain*. London: Policy Studies Institute.
Morris, K., & Tunnard, J. (1996). *Family group conferences: Messages from UK practice and research*. London: FRG.
Morrow, V. (1998). *Understanding families: Children's perspectives*. London: National Children's Bureau.
NCH Action for Children (2000). *Fact file*. London: NCH.
Newman, T. (2004). *What works in building resilience?* Barkingside, UK: Barnardos.
Office for National Statistics (2001). *Child and adolescent mental health statistics*. London: HMSO.
Perelberg, J., & Miller, A. (Eds.) (1990). *Gender and power in families*. London: Routledge.
Pilatis, J., & Anderton, J. (1986). Feminism and family therapy–A possible meeting point. *Journal of Family Therapy, 8*, 99-114.
Pugh, G., & Smith, C. (1996). *Learning to be a parent*. London: Family Policy Studies Centre.
Quinton, D. (2004). *Supporting parents: Messages from research*. London: DFES/Department of Health.
Rivett, M., & Rees, A. (2004). Dancing on a razor's edge: Systemic group work with batterers. *Journal of Family Therapy, 26*(2), 142-163.
Robbins, D. (1998). The refocusing children's initiative: An overview of practice. In R. Bayley (Ed.), *Transforming children's lives: The importance of early intervention*. London: Family Policy Studies Centre.
Rutter, M. (1985). Resilience in the face of adversity. *British Journal of Psychiatry, 147*, 598-611.
Rutter, M., Hersov, L., & Taylor, E. (1994). *Child and adolescent psychiatry*. Oxford: Blackwell Scientific.

Rutter, M., & Smith, D. (1995). *Psychosocial disorders in young people: Time trends and their causes.* London: Wiley.

Rutter, M. (1995). *Psychosocial disturbances in young people: Challenges for prevention.* Cambridge: Cambridge University Press.

Salmon, D., & Hall, C. (1999). Working with lesbian mothers: Their healthcare experiences. *Community Practitioner, 72*(12), 396-397.

Shardlow, S., & Payne, M. (1998). *Contemporary issues in social work: Western Europe.* Aldershot, UK: Arena.

Speak, S., Cameron, S., Woods, R., & Gilroy, R. (1995). *Young single mothers: Barriers to independent living.* London: Family Policy Studies Centre.

Statham, J. (2000). *Outcomes and effectiveness of family support services: A research review.* London: Institute for Education, University of London.

Sutton, C. (1999). *Helping families with troubled children.* Chichester: Wiley.

Thoburn, J., Wilding, J., & Watson, J. (1998). *Children in need: A review of family support work in three local authorities.* Norwich: University of East Anglia/Department of Health.

Tunstill, J. (1996). Family support: Past present and future challenges. *Child and Family Social Work, 1,* 151-158.

Utting, D. (1995). *Family and parenthood: Supporting families, preventing breakdown.* York: Joseph Rowntree Foundation.

Vetere, A., & Cooper, J. (2001). Working systemically with family violence: Risk, responsibility and collaboration. *Journal of Family Therapy, 23*(4), 378-397.

Vostanis, P., & Cumella, S. (1999). *Homeless children: Problems and needs.* London: Jessica Kingsley.

Walker, S. (2001a). Consulting with children and young people. *International Journal of Children's Rights, 12,* 1-12.

Walker, S. (2001b). Domestic violence: Analysis of a community safety alarm system. *Child Abuse Review, 10,* 170-182.

Walker, S. (2002). Culturally competent protection of children's mental health. *Child Abuse Review, 11,* 380-393.

Walker, S. (2003a). Multidisciplinary family support in child and adolescent mental health services. *Clinical Child Psychology and Psychiatry, 8*(2), 215-226.

Walker, S. (2003b). Inter-professional work in child and adolescent mental health services. *Emotional and Behavioural Difficulties, 8*(3), 189-204.

Walker, S. (2003c). Family support and family therapy–Same difference? *International Journal of Social Welfare, 12*(4), 307-314.

Walker, S. (2003d). *Working together for healthy young minds.* Lyme Regis, UK: Russell House Publishers.

Walker, S. (2003e). *Social work and child and adolescent mental health.* Lyme Regis, UK: Russell House Publishers.

Walker, S., & Akister, J. (2004). *Applying family therapy–A guide for caring professionals in the community.* Lyme Regis, UK: Russell House Publishers.

Walker, S. (2005). *Culturally competent therapy–Working with children and young people.* Basingstoke, UK: Palgrave.

Walters, M., Carter, B., Papp, P., & Silverstein, O. (1988). *The invisible web: Gender patterns in family relationships.* New York: Guilford Press.

Webster-Stratton, C. (1997). Treating children with early-onset conduct problems: A comparison of child and parent training interventions. *Journal of Consulting and Clinical Psychology, 65*(1), 93-109.

The Notion of Interdependence and Its Implications for Child and Family Policy

Susan L. Brooks
Ya'ir Ronen

SUMMARY. The authors claim that the recognition of interdependence as a guiding principle of child and family policy has the potential to transform legal systems to make them less punitive and more constructive, less judgmental towards individuals and more empathic to the protection of relationships and self-constructed identities. By embracing the notion of interdependence, our societies can be moved toward greater recognition of our common humanity to the great benefit of children and their families, particularly those who are most vulnerable.

Four lenses are articulated in this paper: Therapeutic jurisprudence, preventive law, family systems theory, and culture. The paper shows how these lenses point toward more supportive rather than punitive types of interventions in the lives of children and their families. The paper demonstrates that, despite the fact that questionable parental behavior may initially engender feelings of anger and aversion, an empathic public response–one that recognizes the reality of the interdependence between parents and children–not only comports with current enlightened interdisciplinary approaches, but also promotes child and family

---

Address correspondence to: Susan L. Brooks, JD, Vanderbilt University Law School, 131 21st Avenue South, Nashville, TN 37203-1181.

[Haworth co-indexing entry note]: "The Notion of Interdependence and Its Implications for Child and Family Policy." Brooks, Susan L., and Ya'ir Ronen. Co-published simultaneously in *Journal of Feminist Family Therapy* (The Haworth Press, Inc.) Vol. 17, No. 3/4, 2005, pp. 23-46; and: *The Politics of the Personal in Feminist Family Therapy: International Examinations of Family Policy* (ed: Anne M. Prouty Lyness) The Haworth Press, Inc., 2005, pp. 23-46. Single or multiple copies of this article are available for a fee from The Haworth Document Delivery Service [1-800-HAWORTH, 9:00 a.m. - 5:00 p.m. (EST). E-mail address: docdelivery@haworthpress.com].

© 2005 by The Haworth Press, Inc. All rights reserved.
doi:10.1300/J086v17n03_02

well-being. The authors suggest that such a response not only be contemplated and understood, but that it should also reframe child and family policies and practices. The family group conference model represents a tool for such reframing. *[Article copies available for a fee from The Haworth Document Delivery Service: 1-800-HAWORTH. E-mail address: <docdelivery@haworthpress.com> Website: <http://www.HaworthPress.com> © 2005 by The Haworth Press, Inc. All rights reserved.]*

KEYWORDS. Children's rights, domestic violence, family group conference, family systems theory, identity, interdependence, mediation, preventive law, therapeutic jurisprudence

INTRODUCTION

A neighbor hears the cries of young children from the apartment next door. She calls the police, who arrive to find two young children locked in a tiny room no bigger than a storage closet. The children are wet and hungry, but otherwise unharmed. A little while later, their mother, an African-American woman struggling on her own to make a living at a low paying job, arrives home. She states that she had to run to the grocery store to pick up some milk and other necessities and had no one available to look after the children. She thought the safest thing would be to lock them in a small space where they couldn't get into anything dangerous, given that she would be returning soon.

The police are appalled and charge the mother with criminal neglect. The media jumps on the story and uncovers the fact that the mother has a history of involvement with the child welfare authorities, and only recently regained custody of the children. She also has a history of drug addiction. The media and the public are ready to condemn the mother and want to see her severely punished for leaving the two children in such a condition. There is palpable disappointment when she is placed on probation instead of receiving jail time, despite this being her first criminal charge, and despite the fact that the child welfare agency still removes her children from her care.

This is a story taken from today's local headlines. It demonstrates the "*othering*" that takes place in our societies. For every "we" there is "them," the excluded *others*, who might include, for instance, poor, Black, single mothers with a history of drug addiction. We are habituated to construct barriers between friends and strangers. Although the barriers do not have to be static, they are often perceived as such. We may, as individuals and as societies, see these barriers as an invitation to expand our awareness of injustice toward those who are perceived as the *other* and to overcome a sense of threat when encountering difference, but often we fail to do so. If we see *otherness* as an invitation to care for the *other* and thus respect that person's basic human rights, for example through the universally recognized Golden Rule, we become less alienated from him or her. Identity–"mine" and "hers," "ours" and "theirs"–can be dynamic and can then become more inclusive.

Inspired by Levinas and others (Connolly, 1996; Kleinman, 1996; Levinas, 1988; Minow, 1990; Minow, 1996), we suggest that fully seeing a person is antithetical to his *othering*. Following Levinas, we see the genuine face-to-face encounter with the *other* as an ethical experience with normative implications. In the process of fully recognizing the *other* as a human being, we create the potential for responding to human suffering. When one is open to the humanness of the *other*, a responsibility which is not reciprocal in nature is born (Levinas, 1988; Minow, 1990; Rosalyn, 2000; Smith, 1997). An acceptance of this notion of responsibility is a necessary underpinning of the type of reform this paper advocates.

When considered in this light, it is perhaps unsurprising that the mother in this story is an economically disadvantaged woman of color. Treating her as the *other* excuses us from having to apply the same understandings to her and her children as we would want to have applied if our own children were at stake.

Now let us suppose the mother in this story has also been affected by domestic violence. Suppose she has been a victim of physical or verbal or emotional abuse. Suppose the perpetrator is the father of her children, and she has returned to the relationship with him numerous times after he has demonstrated violent tendencies toward her. The mother in this scenario will then be further vilified by the public for returning to this relationship and for failing to prosecute the father, as well as for potentially placing her children at greater risk. This same indigent woman of color will be subject to further *othering* based on the domestic violence in her life and it may be used as an additional piece of ammunition to remove her children from her care, temporarily or permanently.

Our public policies that condemn this unfortunate mother ignore the interdependence of all of the members of this family system. Such policies fail to recognize the reality that in our haste to punish this mother, we are also punishing her young children by depriving them of their critical need to maintain the continuity of their relationship with her. Further, the policy that demands the universal prosecution of perpetrators of domestic violence fails to account for the roles of a husband and a father in a family system. Perhaps the hypothetical father here should be prosecuted, but perhaps he is willing to acknowledge his responsibility for harm he has caused, receive services and try to mend this harm, and the mother of his children supports his effort to be rehabilitated so that the family unit can be maintained.

This paper proposes that the recognition of human interdependence should be a driving force of child and family policy. This notion of interdependence rests squarely upon principles articulated in the United Nations Convention on the Rights of the Child (CRC), and is also consistent with the child's right to a self-constructed identity. Interdependence is further informed by considerations of therapeutic jurisprudence, preventive law, family systems, and culture. To illustrate how recognition of interdependence can and should drive child and family policy, we will offer examples using the child welfare and domestic violence contexts. Further, the paper demonstrates that this significant reform can best be accomplished by corresponding changes in procedural justice in the form of alternatives to traditional adversarial legal mechanisms.

INTERDEPENDENCE VERSUS INDIVIDUALIST APPROACHES

The liberal individualist ethos traditionally underlying human rights jurisprudence emphasizes individual rights and remedies. It also provides the conceptual basis for individualistic adversarial representation typical in present day western legal systems (Cover, 1998). This individual or atomistic approach also fits with the traditional medical model, which courts historically have relied upon in legal proceedings (Mulvey, 1982). Further, courts have often interpreted the "best interests of the child" standard, which governs much of the legal decision-making related to children and families, using a psychodynamic approach–one which also focuses on individuals (Brooks, 1996). Courts and advocates thus cling to an individual orientation toward children and families despite the fact that this approach does not reflect the larger scope of current professional knowledge.

Michael Grossberg, an American historian, traces the beginnings of this atomistic approach to the nineteenth century. He states that the legacy of American domestic relations law from this era is the concept of the family as a collection of separate individuals rather than an organic legal entity (Grossberg, 1985). This atomistic approach has also contributed significantly to creating an adversarial individualistic framework for decision-making processes in family law, which has persisted until today in traditional legal systems.

Mary Ann Glendon echoes this concern by observing that our present legal system recognizes only the entities of the state and the individual, with nothing in between (Glendon, 1991; Grossberg, 1985). According to Glendon, the legal image of the family emphasizes the separate personalities of family members rather than its unitary aspect, including the treatment of children as fully independent individuals. Glendon points out that the absoluteness of individualistic "rights talk" heightens social conflict and inhibits dialogue that might lead toward consensus, or at least the discovery of common ground. Moreover, she claims it contributes to the *othering* of vulnerable populations: "[i]n its relentless individualism, it fosters a climate that is inhospitable to society's losers, and that systematically disadvantages caretakers, young and old" (Glendon, 1991, 14). We suggest such individualism, originating in highly competitive western culture and permeating child law and policy in different jurisdictions all over the globe, is fostering the development of alienated men and women. These men and women are liable to be in denial of their own vulnerability and their dependency needs and thus particularly prone to engage in *othering*.

This discussion points out the pitfalls of *misusing* the terminology of individual rights to frame child and family policy. However, international law, primarily in the form of the United Nations Convention on the Rights of the Child, represents an articulation of children's rights that demonstrates the potential for a rights-based framework to reflect an ethos of interdependence rather than rigid individualism. The Convention also reflects a strong international consensus, and therefore, provides a solid foundation upon which to construct a regime based on interdependence. Specifically, the children's rights principles laid out in the CRC affirm the reciprocal attachments of the child and his/her family and community.

An important construct that stems directly from these principles is the notion that our societies should ideally be responsive to the complementing needs "to be" and the need "to become." This is what we refer to as the child's right to a self-constructed identity. The notion of a self-constructed identity draws upon the child's need for both autonomy and connectedness. The granting of a right to autonomy, responding to the child's need "to become," is often perceived as the most advanced and most problematic stage in the evolution of child law (e.g., Franklin, 1986, 27-38; Van Bueren, 1995, 15). Of equal importance, though, is the child's need to be interconnected to significant others, which is often neglected by child advocates (Ronen, 2004).

In addition to the constructs described above, the complementary lenses of therapeutic jurisprudence, preventive law, family systems theory, and culture, support our contention that we need to re-conceive human rights to include an understanding of interdependence–an understanding that recognizes that the "rights" as well as the needs and interests of children and parents generally are intertwined. It thus makes no sense to speak of them as always dichotomous, or worse, as always opposed to each other.

The writings of other feminist scholars, such as Carol Gilligan and Martha Minow, reflect similar perspectives. In her seminal essay, Gilligan (1982) demonstrates how mainstream discourse reflecting an atomistic model of human behavior offends both males and females by denying or ignoring the basic insight that human beings naturally mature to interdependence rather than independence (Cohn, 1991; Freeman, 1997; Gilligan, 1982). Martha Minow (1996) uses a similar approach in writing about children's rights, by emphasizing the centrality of the protection of the child's relationships with significant others founded on an ethos of interdependence.

THE UNITED NATIONS CONVENTION ON THE RIGHTS OF THE CHILD ("CRC")

The CRC is clearly founded on an ethos of interdependence. Article 5 of the Convention, perhaps the most important article for the purposes of this paper, reads as follows:

> State parties shall respect the responsibilities, and duties of parents or, where applicable, the members of the extended family or community as provided for by local custom, legal guardians or other persons legally responsible for the child, to provide, in a manner consistent with the evolving capacities of the child, appropriate direction and guidance in the exercise by the child of the rights recognized in the present convention.

The article thus clarifies that the state's primary responsibility towards the child is to respect the role of the nuclear and extended family and of the community in the child's life, rather than to intervene in order to protect the child from them.

A possible tension exists between Article 5 and Articles 12 and 13, which grant the child a right to be heard, a right to participate in decisions relating to him and a right to free expression–rights that theoretically could conflict with parental direction and guidance. Parents entrusted to guide the child in the exercise of his rights might be tempted to obstruct the child from exercising his rights because of their own interests (Fortin, 1998, 42; Freeman, 1997, 68) or because they perceive the exercise of a specific right or the concept of children's rights as detrimental to the child. Nevertheless, Article 5, when understood in combination with Articles 12 and 13, can contribute to a conception of children's rights reflecting an evolutionary process that ultimately advances the child's legal status at the same time as it reinforces the significance of the child's important connections.

In short, the Convention encourages adults with whom the child maintains meaningful ties to find culturally appropriate ways to respect the rights of the child including his right to participation in decisions relating to him. Essentially, through this tension or better yet, balancing, the CRC overcomes the temptation to entertain a crude atomistic vision of the child's interests. The CRC is not a children's liberation manifesto–it does not purport to liberate children from subjugation of adults through abandoning them to adult liberties. Children who are granted the CRC's participation rights and civil rights, and who also enjoy protected adult guidance, enjoy an opportunity to develop into well-rounded, interdependent adults. Such adults not only exercise autonomy, but also function within relationships of commitment and responsibility (Freeman, 1997, 37-40; Smith, 1997, 103).

THE CHILD'S RIGHT TO A SELF-CONSTRUCTED IDENTITY

Having established a foundation for interdependence using the CRC's definition of children's rights, it is critical to highlight a specific set of considerations stemming from this same framework. These considerations relate to a child's right to a self-constructed identity. This concept of a right to a self-constructed identity reaches beyond the CRC's explicit guarantees related to identity.

Here we are talking about a nuanced definition of identity. A child's right to identity is an entitlement to the protection of ties meaningful to him. These are primarily ties to the human world, but they can also be ties to an animal or to an inanimate object, such as a book or a tree, or to a geographic place such as a village or a physical home. Moreover, the child does not exist in a universe separate and apart from the child's familial relationships, as may sometimes seem to be the case when reading children's rights texts based on a liberal individualistic ethos. Recognition of a right to a self-constructed identity allows us to see the individual child as struggling to achieve autonomy, not independence.

As explained earlier, children who exercise the CRC's participation rights and civil rights can also enjoy protected adult guidance. The right to a self-constructed identity, which is only partially protected through the UN Convention, enhances the child's opportunities to develop into an interdependent adult by responding to the guidance he receives in consolidating his identity.

At the same time, this "uniqueness" has a universal quality because all human beings develop their own cultural identities as they grow. Thus, we need to appreciate the uniqueness of the culture of all adults as well as children. It is important that this appreciation of difference does not become a license to exclude or marginalize. Rather, the commonality of the experience of identity formation in all of us calls for an empathic understanding of the child's or adult's experience, an understanding that is admittedly difficult to achieve within a traditional adversarial legal setting.

For example, from the child's perspective, it typically makes no sense to prosecute a mother victimized by domestic violence or to punish her for failure to protect her child in any other way. Such an approach often leads to separating the child from her or making it more difficult for her to fulfill her parental role. This separation in turn deprives the child of his right to a self-constructed identity, because often a child's tie to his mother is a most (if not THE most) meaningful tie in the child's life. On the other hand, the child's right to a self-constructed identity would potentially support responding to child abuse by offering some form of protection to the mother that would allow her continued maternal functioning in relation to the child, inasmuch as the child's tie with her is meaningful, given the evidence that mothers who are themselves protected from spousal violence tend to more effectively protect their children from violence (Davidson, 1995).

We have established a solid foundation for the recognition of interdependence based upon principles articulated in the CRC, which have been extended and further developed using the concept of the child's right to a self-constructed identity. Our discussion now turns to several lenses that lend strength to the position that recognition of interdependence should inform child and family policy, and also may contribute to a broader understanding of the implications of the recognition of interdependence.

The Lens of Therapeutic Jurisprudence

The first of these lenses is the growing movement known as therapeutic jurisprudence (TJ)–the study of the role of law as a therapeutic agent (Wexler, 1997). This movement, co-founded well over a decade ago by two legal scholars, David Wexler and Bruce Winick (Wexler, 1990; Wexler & Winick, 1996), now has an international following among judges, lawyers, and mental health professionals (Wexler, 1999). Therapeutic jurisprudence promotes exploration of the effects of laws and the legal system on the well-being of the persons they are supposed to serve. A TJ inquiry asks: is this particular law or aspect of the legal system "therapeutic" or "anti-therapeutic" for the persons affected by it? Identifying and understanding what is anti-therapeutic ideally will lead to positive law reform.

Therapeutic jurisprudence provides a lens through which to critique the rules, policies, and practices around children and families to see whether or not they are truly therapeutic. Specifically, TJ would inquire whether the current system serves a therapeutic purpose for children and their families. Even without further analysis, it is readily apparent that this one-size-fits-all approach is likely not to be therapeutic for all children and families, whether we are discussing child welfare, domestic violence, or some other issue.

The assessment of whether child and family policy is therapeutic also requires reference to current mental health knowledge about child and family functioning, as well as important social and cultural realities about the systems affecting children and families. Once these dimensions are fully considered, it will become even more evident that not only is fundamental policy reform necessary, but the recognition of interdependence is a key to moving policy in a therapeutic direction for children and families.

In the child welfare arena, one glaring example is that of traditional closed adoption, which often does not serve a therapeutic purpose for children, especially children in the foster care system. A broader menu of permanency options, including open adoption, must be fully supported in order to be responsive to the needs of these children. In the domestic violence arena, the notion of a categorical approach is just as problematic. Instead, there need to be "flexible packages of responses" (Paradine, 2000). This requires focusing on the unique facts and circumstances of each case, and allowing the survivors to direct the process, based upon their own definition of their family system.

The Lens of Preventive Law

Therapeutic jurisprudence provides strong support for arguments favoring reforms in child and family policy that reflect the recognition of interdependence, such as alternatives to traditional adoption and more open-ended domestic violence processes. A second movement, known as "preventive law," lends additional support. The preventive law movement has developed parallel to the TJ movement, and shares a somewhat similar approach (Stolle & Wexler, 1997). The proponents of preventive law believe that legal practitioners need to be proactive in their work, and to engage clients in the avoidance of adversarial litigation (Hardaway, 1997). The preventive law approach is to a great extent modeled after preventive medicine, including the idea of "legal check-ups" (Stolle, Wexler, Winick, & Dauer, 1997). Preventive lawyering requires practitioners to view their clients in a holistic manner, and to try to anticipate the kinds of legal issues they might confront. By having legal check-ups, the lawyer engages in an assessment process together with the client. Through that process, he or she can help the client to take steps to resolve impending legal issues in a peaceful manner that is conducive to the client's well-being. This process has also been referred to as identifying "legal soft spots" (Hardaway, 1997).

These two approaches, TJ and preventive law are highly compatible. In synthesizing the two movements, TJ and preventive law scholars have described their work as that of identifying "psycho-legal soft spots" (Stolle, 1997). Accordingly, in the process of regularly checking in with clients, lawyers can be sensitive not only to the potential legal pitfalls of the client's situation, but also to the client's vulnerabilities from a mental health perspective.

The child welfare and domestic violence schemes that are currently in place do not adhere to a preventive law approach. In child welfare, this inadequacy is evidenced by the overemphasis on traditional adoption within the system (Brooks, 1999; Ronen, 2004). Adoption is often the result of inadequate or non-existent preventive efforts. Very little support of any kind, let alone legal support, is available to vulnerable families in the U.S., Israel, and other Western democracies to help prevent the need for the families' involvement with the legal system, or to remedy concerns once they are so involved. Moreover, the failure to provide such preventive and supportive services often leads to the termination of the parent/child relationship and adoption. The lack of preventive services is exacerbated by the adversarial court processes that prevail around traditional adoption. In order for a closed adoption to take place, it is necessary first to sever the parents' legal ties to the child. The court proceedings through which this severance occurs tend to be highly adversarial because in order to terminate the parents' legal ties to the child, the opposing party, usually the state, must present evidence of parental unfitness (Beyer & Mlyniec, 1986). The present system therefore does not comport with notions of preventive law.

In contrast, alternatives such as open adoption fully embrace TJ and preventive law principles. Open adoption preserves a child's important attachments, including the child's relationship with his or her birth parents. A considerable body of theoretical and empirical literature indicates that children generally benefit from maintaining important family attachments in their lives, even if those attachments are faulty or if the family members have significant deficits (e.g., Brooks, 1996; Davis, 1996; Garrison, 1996). Focusing on maintaining the continuity of those attachments will naturally lead to more therapeutic and preventive efforts aimed at family preservation or, at a minimum, at avoidance of adversarial litigation.

With respect to domestic violence, we need to promote processes that offer acceptance and support for survivors and their feelings, regardless of whether they choose to stay or leave their relationships. While working to ensure survivors' safety, we need to embrace the complexities involved in domestic violence situations. We need to be mindful that "universally applied, inflexible application of criminal sanctions risks disempowering and alienating some survivors, and may ignore their own assessment of their lives" (Paradine, 2000, 45).

Few would argue that generally the law and policies related to children and families should serve a therapeutic purpose. It would also seem that most would agree that optimally the system should minimize children's and families' exposure to adversarial litigation. What is antitherapeutic about our traditional ways of responding to vulnerable families, both in the fields of child welfare and domestic violence, is primarily the failure to recognize the interdependence of the members of the family. These examples illustrate that the lenses of TJ and preventive law not only lend support, but also shed more light on the case for such recognition. At this point, we will turn to a further explanation of the importance of family attachments, which is a fundamental underpinning of the concept of interdependence.

The Lens of Family Systems Theory

The reigning approach within the mental health fields focused on the importance of family attachments is known as family systems theory (Babb, 1997; Brooks, 1996). The unifying principle of family systems approaches is the idea that the family is a dynamic system with interacting parts (Brooks, 1996). One statement that captures this way of thinking is that the whole is greater than the sum of the parts–a family is not simply a collection of individuals, but has qualities that belong to the whole family as an entity. For this purpose, family must be defined in a broad manner, using bonds of intimacy rather than blood ties (Brooks, 1996; Ronen, 2004). Members of a family system may include relatives as well as friends and neighbors and foster parents (Brooks, 1996; Ronen, 2004).

Family systems have two other unique overlapping principles: mutual interaction and shared responsibility. Mutual interaction means that any conduct by one family member will affect the other members of the family, and the family as a whole. Shared responsibility means that every family member plays a role in what occurs within a family. It is critical to understand these two important principles in the context of two other aspects of family systems theory. First, family systems approaches are descriptive and not evaluative, and focus more on present situations than past conduct. Second, family systems approaches focus on family strengths rather than pathology. These last two characteristics mean that family systems theory approaches families from a non-judgmental posture (Brooks, 1996).

A family systems approach is completely foreign to the way most legal systems operate, including in the area of child and family law (Brooks, 1996). Legal systems generally are not set up to take account of family systems, but rather focus on individuals' rights and responsibilities (Brooks, 1996). They also do not accept mutual interaction or shared responsibility. A fundamental principle of most legal systems is the fact that in every proceeding, responsibility or liability is attached to one individual (Brooks, 1996).

On the other hand, it cannot be emphasized enough that "mutual responsibility," when used in the family systems context, is simply descriptive of the family dynamic. It by no means implies mutual "blame" or liability in the legal sense–it is simply a characterization of how a family should function in psychological terms. Although mutual responsibility is difficult to appreciate in the legal context, it is an essential component of the understanding of children and families and how they operate. Moreover, we would argue that the failure to appreciate this dynamic often undermines the success of efforts to promote the well-being of children and families, whether in the child welfare or domestic violence contexts.

Understanding family systems approaches thus helps to explain why our traditional legal systems are anti-therapeutic, both in the areas of child welfare and domestic violence (Brooks, 1999). Both of these legal arenas reflect failure to embrace the importance of the child's attachments to members of his or her family system, as well as interconnectedness of all members of the family system, which is exactly what we mean by interdependence.

In child welfare, an example of this inadequacy is the priority given to traditional adoption in the current system, in which a child's family ties must be severed prior to the adoption. This means that not only is the child cut off from the birth parents, but also from siblings, grandparents, and other extended family members. The child will likely also be cut off from other important parts of the family system, such as friends or neighbors, as well as larger intersecting systems, like the child's school, religious institution, and neighborhood. Traditional adoption practices tend to be inconsistent with family systems approaches and, accordingly, may be anti-therapeutic for children.

In contrast, adoption alternatives such as open adoption fully embrace family systems principles. When combined with procedural justice, as is reflected in alternative dispute resolution mechanisms such as family group conferencing and mediation, a picture begins to emerge of how policies informed by interdependence would transform child and family policy consistent with TJ and preventive law principles.

In the domestic violence context, it is crucial that legal actors not only understand the experience of fear and real danger, but also understand "the feelings of connection and commitment" experienced by women living through domestic violence (Paradine, 2000, 41). Kate Paradine (1998, 2000), who approaches domestic violence through a TJ lens and also seems to contemplate family systems principles, states that the legal system fails to take account of the complexities involved in the dynamics of domestic violence, and in doing so, plays an anti-therapeutic role in the lives of those affected by violence. "The challenge for legal actors is to condemn domestic violence while understanding the complex journeys of survival, so that women are not judged or blamed for their situation. . . . Blaming a woman for the violence or reprimanding her for her attempts to make the relationship work can only add to her sense of shame and isolation" (Paradine, 2000, 42).

Paradine goes on to state that "[w]hen emotional factors like love and attachment are ignored, legal products are not usually flexible enough to meet individual needs" (Paradine, 2000, 45). Legal actors are generally seeking success in the form of a conviction or injunction. However, any identifiable legal process or product is rarely an unqualified success for the survivor, according to Paradine. Most traditional legal processes cause survivors trauma and pain, and most legal products are not really responsive to survivors' actual needs (Ronen, 1994).

It is important to emphasize that, like TJ and preventive law, family systems theory offers a framework and a thought process. It does not preference a particular outcome. There is no doubt that family members do not always act in ways that are consistent with the family's best interests. Once a family systems analysis is applied to a particular set of facts, it may lead to a conclusion that a family should remain intact, or it may lead to a different conclusion, depending on the circumstances. This is particularly important to bear in mind when approaching domestic violence situations. Engaging in a family systems analysis does not mean that in every situation the victim should leave, or that in every situation an effort should be made to rehabilitate the perpetrator. Nevertheless, while women should never be encouraged to remain in violent relationships, Paradine encourages us to develop ways of understanding the attachment described by women and supporting those who choose to remain with their partners. A family systems approach offers such a framework.

In sum, family systems theory offers a normative framework that can guide child and family policy toward the recognition of interdependence, especially if we view the law through the lenses of TJ and preventive law. One final important lens, which is linked to the earlier discussion of identity, is that of culture. Further exploration of cultural considerations demonstrates that interdependence does not only take account of familial ties, but also broader connections to one's community and other "macro-systems" (Babb, 1997).

The Lens of Culture

Culture can be viewed as a subset of identity, as it has been described above. Accordingly, the cultural identity that the child should be allowed to enjoy, whether mainstream or minority, is not an abstract derivative of the decision maker's theoretical knowledge. The child is entitled to a culture that is part of his personal world; thus, culture is defined by a set of related meanings by which the child interprets the reality of life and its unique circumstances (Ronen, 2004).

This particular vision of culture needs to figure prominently in the effort to reform child and family policy. In the United States, for example, this urgent need is reflected by the disproportionate representation of African-American children and families in the foster care system (Roberts, 1999). The effect of the American child welfare system on African-American children has been likened to a funnel–easier to remain in than to escape.

The American child welfare system, however, has not been structured to support the culture traditions of African-American children and families. American scholars have well documented the informal, communal nature of the African-American extended family, and its cooperative, child-centered focus on child-rearing. Gilbert Holmes (1995) has described how, throughout history, African-American children have benefited from the love, training, and child rearing given by fictive and real kin in their extended families, as well as ongoing contact with and knowledge about their birth kin provided to those children. These informal cooperative parenting and child-rearing arrangements became solidified during the era of slavery, when innumerable children were separated from their birth families.

Holmes (1995) and others have applied this cultural understanding to the support of greater use of open adoption for children in the foster care system. Based upon her extensive research, Carol Stack (1984) advocated over two decades ago that informal adoptive parents in the United States should not be forced to pursue legal adoption and terminate the legal rights of biological parents, in violation of cultural traditions. She pointed out that termination of a biological parent's rights may also violate the rights of her kin group. The focus on protecting individual legal rights may thus be needlessly in conflict with the cooperative and communal values of the African-American community to the extent that the child's right to a self-constructed cultural identity and to guidance of significant others in his family and community are neglected.

A key component of moving child welfare policy in the U.S. and elsewhere toward a more appropriate appreciation of culture, therefore, would be to support alternatives to traditional adoption that allow children to maintain relationships with their birth families and their extended family systems. Instead, in the U.S., there has been a heavy emphasis on "transracial adoption," which has misleadingly been presented as an effort to remove barriers for children awaiting permanency. In reality, however, this effort only serves the interests of white families interested in adopting African-American children. It also reinforces a "deficit view" of the African-American family and community, rather than addressing the systemic barriers that make it difficult for African-American families to care for their own children within their own communities (Howe, 1997).

Culture includes the intersection of class issues and race issues. Again, using the U.S. as an example, not only are a disproportionate number of foster care children from minority cultures, they are also overwhelmingly poor (Cahn, 1999; Roberts, 1999). These demographics hold true for many other societies, including Israeli society. In practice, our societies generally respect the privacy and autonomy of middle-class families, but we accede to coercive intervention and intrusion in low-income or otherwise excluded disempowered families, by convincing ourselves that such interventions are unavoidable from a child-centered perspective (Ronen, 2005; Ronen & Ben Harush, 2005).

Meanwhile, we discount and devalue the cultural backgrounds and the solid parenting skills of many such parents. In trying to protect children, we are often liable to disregard their parents' needs and interests, and their communities' cooperative values (Stack, 1984), and thus evade the responsibility of mainstream society for the flawed development of children. It is less painful psychologically to point an accusing finger at dysfunctional parents than to face our responsibility to address systemic factors which contribute to such dysfunction (Ronen, 2003).

Leroy Pelton (1999) has castigated the American child welfare system as a coercive system that thrives on punishment and blame of the poor. As he and others describe it, the *othering* of poor families, in the U.S. context, particularly when they are of color, makes it easy for the dominant culture to devalue them: to view them as dysfunctional and not families at all (Appell, 1997; Pelton, 1999). Annette Appell, a proponent of openness in adoption, criticizes the "growth industry" that has arisen from the state's "protective" involvement with poor families and families of color and the state's punitive treatment, particularly of the mothers of these families. Appell describes these mothers as evading white, middle-class mother norms, or myths in a number of ways, including the simple fact that they are poor, but also because they depend upon informal kinship and community networks for child care. Similar observations have been made concerning the Israeli context (Ronen, 2003; Ronen & Ben Harush, 2005).

As stated earlier, many of the same families whose "cultures" are marginalized and misunderstood by the child welfare system are also affected by domestic violence. The preceding discussion thus applies with equal force to the domestic violence context. The *othering* of victims/survivors makes it easier for us to condemn them for their choices, and to fail to appreciate the complexities of their situations.

Procedural Justice

The approaches described previously, particularly TJ and preventive law, also emphasize the need for appropriate procedural justice mechanisms, meaning mechanisms that give the parties a greater voice in determining the solutions to their own legal dilemmas. We believe that increased use of these mechanisms needs to be part and parcel of child and family policy reform, and will facilitate the recognition of interdependence in this effort. Examples of processes that tend to offer greater procedural justice include non-adversarial dispute resolution and planning processes, such as family group conferencing (Lowry, 1997) and mediation (Wilhelmus, 1998). These alternative processes are being successfully implemented in many jurisdictions, and are being used in many different types of child and family law proceedings. The use of these non-adversarial processes offers great promise for reform of child and family policy.

Family Group Conferencing. The general idea behind the family group conference (FGC) is to empower the family, including as much as possible of a child's extended family system, to develop a plan to keep the child safe, and promote the child's and family's well-being (Brooks, 2004; Lowry, 1997; Ronen, 2003). A basic premise of the FGC is that the family has unique strengths and often has the best information about how to use those strengths to address existing concerns about the child and family. Through the FGC process, professionals are initially given the opportunity to present their concerns to the family members with the help of a professional facilitator. After the concerns are presented, all of the professionals leave the room and allow the family to work on a plan to address those concerns. The family is also given the opportunity to access appropriate services and community resources to assist them in carrying out the plan. Assuming the plan developed by the family is acceptable to the professionals and to the court, it can become the official resolution of the matter (Brooks, 2004; Lowry, 1997).

FGC is a relatively new process, but its popularity has increased dramatically in the past several years. Many states have tried to implement the use of FGCs at the earliest possible point in time, such as when the child or family first comes to the attention of their child protective services agencies. FGCs are a primary tool for identifying and increasing involvement of capable members of the family system, as well as for preventing more drastic state intervention. Early evaluations of the effectiveness of FGCs have been very positive. Studies have found that families often develop more creative plans and also have a better rate of following through and sticking with the plans they themselves develop (Brooks, 2004; Lowry, 1997). In Israel, it has been extensively and successfully utilized with adolescent offenders and their families, but unfortunately has not been well-supported or funded in the child protection arena (Ronen, 2003; Ronen, 2005).

Mediation. Mediation is an alternative dispute mechanism that has become a well-established component of many court systems in the U.S., particularly in the area of domestic relations (Brooks, 2004; Duquette & Hardin, 1999). Often, mediation is an appropriate alternative once a court proceeding has already been filed. It allows the parties to assume greater control over the process, with the assistance of a trained, independent mediator. The parties then have the opportunity to resolve the case in a way that serves both their interests and the child's best interests. Through the mediation process, members of the family system may better identify common interests and be able to work collaboratively to meet the needs of the child (Brooks, 2004; Duquette & Hardin, 1999).

The use of these alternative processes has increasingly become accepted in the child welfare arena. With respect to domestic violence, it has been more controversial; however, courts are beginning to experiment with more problem-solving approaches and other alternative processes in domestic violence matters as well (Eaton & Kaufman, 2005). Paradine (1998) suggests that family group decision-making may be constructive in domestic violence situations in a number of ways. By widening the circle of support around the family, the process may help the family face up to the violence. Further, by empowering the victim, the conference may help her overcome the shame that she often experiences, and also reduce the tendency of the criminal justice system to "re-abuse" the victim. "Researchers have seen families develop in a conference from feeling ashamed of their failure to protect relatives to a strong sense of pride in their capacity as a family to act responsibly" (Paradine, 1998, 639). In general, a recognized strength of alternative dispute mechanisms, which Paradine (1998) also acknowledges in the domestic violence context, is the ability of families to discover unique solutions which could only be known, and, therefore, offered by the families themselves.

CONCLUSION

This paper has articulated a vision for child and family policy reflecting not only current thinking in the mental health fields, but also an emerging perspective of scholars, judges, and advocates in the field of law. It is hoped that this convergence, exemplified by the therapeutic jurisprudence and preventive law movements, signals the evolution of traditional ways of approaching law and policy.

We firmly believe the recognition of interdependence as a guiding principle of child and family policy has the potential to transform legal systems, to make them less punitive and more constructive, less judgmental towards individuals and more empathic to the protection of relationships. By embracing the notion of interdependence, we can move our societies toward greater recognition of our common humanity, to the great benefit of our most vulnerable children and families.

We opened the paper with a story that suggested children were placed at risk by the actions of their mother. To demonstrate how the proposed lenses would affect child and family policy, let us revisit this scenario as it might have unfolded in a legal system incorporating the notion of interdependence. Recall that the mother in the scenario, who was young, single, poor, and also happened to be African-American, locked her two young children in a closet as a way of trying to ensure their safety while she ran to the store to buy some necessities. The authorities who discovered the children were quick to file criminal charges against the mother and to remove the children, despite the fact that the children appeared to be unharmed.

Had the notion of interdependence prevailed, in the first instance, the authorities would have paused and given greater thought to the situation before pressing charges. Under the general principles articulated in the CRC, and Article 5 in particular, the authorities would have recognized that because their primary responsibility towards the child is to respect the role of the child's family and community, they needed to work with the mother to identify supportive services for her and her children rather than responding punitively.

This same supportive response would be consistent with the children's right to a self-constructed identity. The rights of the children in the scenario, assuming they were not only unharmed, but otherwise were generally receiving good care, were essentially violated by the state authorities who removed them from their mother on that day. By punishing the mother, the authorities also punished her children who, as stated earlier, were then deprived of their most meaningful relationship–their relationship with their mother.

We may now turn to the four lenses articulated earlier in this paper. Therapeutic jurisprudence and preventive law both would have encouraged responses that would enhance the well-being of the children by providing additional resources and supports to their mother, rather than removing them from her care. Therapeutic jurisprudence and also preventive law would have embraced offering preventive services to this family to attempt to avoid more drastic interventions, such as removal and criminal prosecution. As stated earlier, focusing on maintaining the continuity of important attachments, such as the attachments between these children and their mother, is consistent with both therapeutic jurisprudence and preventive law approaches.

Family systems theory and cultural competence, taken together, would also have urged more supportive rather than punitive types of intervention in this instance. There was every reason to believe that this mother and her children were inextricably connected as part of the same family system. Given that this was an African-American family, there may well have been extended family members or even "fictive kin" who were also part of the family system.

With respect to procedural justice, an approach consistent with these lenses would have been to convene a family group conference. The facilitator or convenor of the conference would have located as many members of the family system as possible, and would have invited them to attend. He or she would also have asked the mother to invite anyone the mother wished to have present at the session. At that conference, the authorities who investigated and discovered the children would have stated their concerns, as well as anyone else who was present. The participants would also focus on the family's strengths–in particular, the mother's strengths–and any resources available to the family.

Next, the convener would have given the family the opportunity to discuss privately possible solutions and to develop a plan to address whatever concerns were raised. For instance, perhaps someone in the extended family would have been able to provide child care assistance to the mother so that she could have the necessary time to do her grocery shopping. Perhaps the family could have created a phone tree or some other system so that in an emergency, the mother would have known that there were family members who were willing to step in and care for the children. Assuming the family was able to develop a plan that the authorities believed addressed their concerns, undoubtedly the children would have been better off and the family as a whole would have been strengthened and probably follow through more effectively as a result of being given the opportunity to develop its own solutions.

This discussion demonstrates that, despite the fact that this mother's behavior may initially engender feelings of anger and aversion, an empathic public response–one that recognizes the reality of the interdependence between this mother and her children–not only comports with all of the approaches that have been presented in this paper, but also promotes children's well-being. We suggest that such a response not only be contemplated and understood, but that it should also frame child and family policies and practices.

REFERENCES

Appell, A. R. (1997). Protecting children or punishing mothers: Gender, race, and class in the child protection system. *South Carolina Law Review, 48*(3), 577-613.

Babb, B. A. (1997). An interdisciplinary approach to family law jurisprudence: Application of an ecological and therapeutic perspective. *Indiana Law Journal, 72*(3), 775-808.

Beyer, M., & Mlyniec, W. J. (1986). Lifelines to biological parents: The effect on termination of parental rights and performance. *Family Law Quarterly, 20*(2), 233-254.

Brooks, S. L. (1996). A family systems paradigm for legal decision making affecting child custody. *Cornell Journal of Law & Public Policy, 6*(1), 1-22.

Brooks, S. L. (1999). Therapeutic jurisprudence and preventive law in child welfare proceedings: A family systems approach. *Journal of Psychology, Public Policy & Law, 5*(4), 951-965.

Brooks, S. L. (2000). Therapeutic and preventive approaches to school safety: Applications of a family systems model. *New England Law Review, 34*(3), 615-622.

Brooks, S. L. (2004). Kinship care as a preventive child welfare movement in the United States: One state's efforts (181-182). In *Creative Child Advocacy: Global Perspectives,* 181-182. New Delhi: Sage Publications India.

Cahn, N. R. (1999). Children's interests in a familial context: Poverty, foster care, and adoption. *Ohio State Law Journal, 60,* 1189-1223.

Cohn, H. H. (1991). A human rights theory of law: Prolegomena to a methodology of instruction. In A. Barak & R. Gabizon (Eds.), *Haim H. Cohn–Selected Essays* (pp. 17-43). Tel Aviv: Bursi Publishing House.

Connelly, W. (1996). Suffering justice and the politics of becoming. *Culture, Medicine and Psychiatry, 20,* 251-277.

Cover, R. (1987). A Jewish jurisprudence of the social order. (Originally published as Obligations: A Jewish Jurisprudence of the Social Order.) *Journal of Law & Religion, 5*(1), 65-74.

Davidson, H. A. (1995). Child abuse and domestic violence: Legal connections and controversies. *Family Law Quarterly, 29,* 359-73.

Davis, P. C. (1996). The good mother: A new look at psychological parent theory. *New York University Review of Law & Social Change, 22,* 347-370.

Duquette, D., & Hardin, M. (1999). *Adoption 2002: Guidelines for public policy and State legislation governing permanence for children,* V-5. Department of Health and Human Services, Administration for Children and Families, Administration on Children, Youth and Families, Children's Bureau.

Eaton, L., & Kaufman, L. (2005). Judges turn therapist in problem-solving court. *New York Times* (April 26, 2005), A1.

Fineman, M. L. (1989). The politics of custody and the transformation of American custody decision making. *U.C. Davis Law Review, 22*(3), 829-864.

Fortin, J. (1998). *Children's rights and the developing law.* London: Butterworths.

Franklin, B. (1986). Children's political rights. In B. Franklin (Ed.), *The Rights of Children* (pp. 24-53). Oxford: Basil Blackwell.

Freeman, M. (1997). *The moral status of children–Essays on the rights of the child.* Hague: Kluwer Law International.

Garrison, M. (1996). Parent's rights vs. children's interests: The case of the foster child. *New York University Review of Law & Social Change, 22*(2), 371-396.

Gilligan, C. (1982). *In a different voice.* Cambridge, MA: Harvard University Press.

Glendon, M. A. (1989). *The transformation of family law: State, law, and family in the United States and western Europe.* Chicago: University of Chicago Press.

Glendon, M. A. (1991). *Rights talk: The impoverishment of political discourse.* New York: Free Press.

Glendon, M. A. (1993). General report, symposium: Individualism and communitarianism in contemporary legal systems: Tensions and accommodation. *Brigham Young University Law Review, 2,* 385-419.

Grossberg, M. (1985). *Governing the hearth: Law and family in nineteenth century America.* Chapel Hill, NC: The University of North Carolina Press.

Hardaway, R. M. (1997). *Preventive law: Materials on nonadversarial legal process.* Cincinnati, OH: Anderson Publishing.

Hawkins-Leon, C. G. (1997-98). The Indian Child Welfare Act and the African-American Tribe: Facing the adoption crisis. *Brandeis Journal of Family Law, 36,* 201-218.

Holmes, G. A. (1995). The extended family system in the Black community: A child-centered model for adoption policy. *Temple Law Review, 68*(4), 1649-1685.

Howe, R. W. (1997). Transracial adoption (TRA): Old prejudices and discrimination float under a new halo. *Boston University Public Interest Law Journal, 6,* 409-472.

Kleinman, A. (1996). Suffering, ethics and the politics of moral life. Comments on "Suffering, justice and the politics of becoming" by William Connolly. *Culture, Medicine and Psychiatry, 20,* 287-290.

Levinas, E. (1988). Useless suffering. In R. Bernasconi & D. Wood (Eds.), *The Provocation of Levinas: Rethinking the Other* (pp. 156-167). London: Routledge.

Levinas, E. (1990). *Nine Talmudic readings.* Bloomington, IN: Indiana University Press.

Lowry, J. M. (1997). Family group conferences as a form of court-approved alternative dispute resolution in child abuse and neglect cases. *University of Michigan Journal of Law Reform, 31,* 57-92.

Minow, M. (1990). Words and the door to the land of change: Law, language and family violence. *Vanderbilt Law Review, 43*, 1665.
Minow, M. (1996). Comments on "Suffering, justice and the politics of becoming" by William E. Connolly. *Culture, Medicine & Psychiatry, 20*, 279-286.
Minow, M., Ryan, M., & Sarat, A. (Eds.) (1998). *Narrative, violence and the law–The essays of Robert Cover*. Ann Arbor, MI: The University of Michigan Press.
Mulvey, E. P. (1982). Family courts: The issue of reasonable goals. *Law and Human Behavior, 6*, 50.
Paradine, K. (1998). Community, shame and anger: Family group conferences and domestic violence. *Revista Juridica de Puerto Rico, 67*, 635-640.
Paradine, K. (2000). The importance of understanding love and other feelings in survivors' experiences of domestic violence. *Court Review, 37*, 40-47.
Pelton, L. H. (1999). Welfare discrimination and child welfare. *Ohio State Law Journal, 60*, 1479-1492.
Roberts, D. E. (1999). Is there justice in children's rights? The critique of federal family preservation policy. *University of Pennsylvania Journal of Constitutional Law, 2*, 112-140.
Ronen, Y. (1994). Victimization in the family and penal policy. *Israel Journal of Penal Law, Criminology and Military Law, 4*, 283.
Ronen, Y. (2003). The child's right to identity as a right to belong. *Tel Aviv University Law Review, 26*, 935-984 (Hebrew).
Ronen, Y. (2004). Redefining the child's right to an identity. *International Journal of Law, Policy and the Family, 18(2)*, 147-77.
Ronen, Y. (2005). On the strengths of the child and his family in a legal context. In B. Cohen & B. Buchbinder (Eds.), *The Strengths Perspective in Social Work–from Potential to Reality* (pp. 133-156). Tel Aviv: Tel Aviv University Press (Hebrew).
Ronen, Y., & Ben Harush, Y. (2005). The legal treatment of youth: Between reality and prevalent conceptions. In Y. Wozner & G. Rahav (Eds.), *Youth in Israel* (pp. 207-246*)*. Tel Aviv: Interdisciplinary Center for the Study of Child and Youth Policy and Treatment, Tel Aviv University (Hebrew).
Rosalyn, D. (2000). What is (feminist) philosophy? [Part 3 of 3]. *Hypatia–A Journal of Feminist Philosophy, 15(2)*, 115-132.
Smith, C. (1997). Children's rights: Judicial ambivalence and social resistance. *International Journal of Law, Policy and the Family, 11*, 103-139.
Smith, N. (1997). Comment: Incommensurability and alterity in contemporary jurisprudence. *Buffalo Law Review, 45*, 503-553.
Stack, C. B. (1984). Cultural perspectives on child welfare. *New York University Review of Law & Social Change, 12*, 539-547.
Stolle, D. P., & Wexler, D. B. (1997). Preventive law and therapeutic jurisprudence: A symbiotic relationship. *Preventive Law Reporter, 16*, 4-5.
Stolle, D. P., Wexler, D. B., Winick, B. J., & Dauer, E. A. (1997). Integrating preventive law and therapeutic jurisprudence: A law and psychology based approach to lawyering. *California Western Law Review, 34*, 15-51.
Wexler, D. B. (1990). *Therapeutic jurisprudence: Law as a therapeutic agent*. Durham, NC: Carolina Academic Press.

Wexler, D. B. (1997). Therapeutic jurisprudence in a comparative law context. *Behavioral Science & the Law, 15*, 233-246.
Wexler, D. B. (1998). Practicing therapeutic jurisprudence: Psycholegal soft spots and strategies. *Revista Juridica Universidad de Puerto Rico, 67*(2), 317-342.
Wexler, D. B. (1999). Therapeutic jurisprudence and the culture of critique. *The Journal of Contemporary Legal Issues, 10*, 263-277.
Wexler, D. B., & Winick, B. J. (Eds.) (1996). *Law in a therapeutic key: Developments in therapeutic jurisprudence.* Durham, NC: Carolina Academic Press.
Wilhelmus, M. (1998). Mediation in kinship care: Another step in the provision of culturally relevant child welfare services. *Social Work, 43*(2), 117-125.

Babies and Bosses:
Family Policy Directions in the OECD

Celia Briar

SUMMARY. Mothers' increased entry to paid work has not been equally matched by fathers' extra unpaid work. Managing multiple and conflicting roles is a source of stress for mothers, which can impact negatively on their health and family relationships. Direct assistance provided by some governments (such as subsidised childcare and long paid parental leave) has been found effective in reducing gender inequalities in domestic labour and so also easing mothers' overwork and stress.

The current policy context is a projected labour shortage for the coming half century, caused by low birthrates and an aging population. The Organisation for Economic Cooperation and Development (OECD) Babies and Bosses series (2002-2005) makes recommendations to the governments of its member states on how to obtain still more increases in women's labour force participation without further falls in the birthrate. Will this be liberating for mothers or add to their burdens and stress? Much depends on the generosity or otherwise of government policies.

The Babies and Bosses reports recommend that the least generous welfare states provide more assistance for working mothers. However, the reports also suggest cutbacks in the most generous states, even though these are the most successful in helping parents combine childcare and paid employment. The OECD is concerned to use more of women's labour power, but, is also committed to streamlining welfare states. Of concern to many feminists will be that these OECD reports ap-

---

[Haworth co-indexing entry note]: "Babies and Bosses: Family Policy Directions in the OECD." Briar, Celia. Co-published simultaneously in *Journal of Feminist Family Therapy* (The Haworth Press, Inc.) Vol. 17, No. 3/4, 2005, pp. 47-65; and: *The Politics of the Personal in Feminist Family Therapy: International Examinations of Family Policy* (ed: Anne M. Prouty Lyness) The Haworth Press, Inc., 2005, pp. 47-65. Single or multiple copies of this article are available for a fee from The Haworth Document Delivery Service [1-800-HAWORTH, 9:00 a.m. - 5:00 p.m. (EST). E-mail address: docdelivery@haworthpress.com].

© 2005 by The Haworth Press, Inc. All rights reserved.
doi:10.1300/J086v17n03_03

pear to want women to "work more" but without generous government assistance, and also recommend further reductions in welfare benefits to lone mothers, as these are seen as reducing incentives to paid work. *[Article copies available for a fee from The Haworth Document Delivery Service: 1-800-HAWORTH. E-mail address: <docdelivery@haworthpress.com> Website: <http://www.HaworthPress.com> © 2005 by The Haworth Press, Inc. All rights reserved.]*

KEYWORDS. Women, mothers, employment, welfare, OECD, social policies, parental leave, childcare, family public policy

INTRODUCTION

Social policies impact strongly upon women's personal relationships with partners, children and extended family. Gender power relations in the home are affected by policies on pay and employment equity, as these affect women's earning power and status. Parents' relationships with their children and each other are mediated by policies determining the availability of paid parental leave, benefits, affordable good quality childcare, whether the length of the working day allows for sufficient time to be spent together. Women's most intimate choices about who is a suitable sexual partner, about starting and ending relationships, and about whether and when to have children are conditioned by policy decisions made at national and international levels. Policy is personal.

The Organisation for Economic Cooperation and Development (OECD) exerts significant influence on government policies in the countries that are members of this international agency. In a series of publications entitled *Babies and Bosses* (OECD, 2002, 2003, 2004, 2005), the OECD describes a range of work-family reconciliation policies in thirteen of its member states and makes recommendations for future directions. The central concern of the *Babies and Bosses* series is how to increase women's labour force participation whilst at the same time avoiding further falls in birthrates.

For the most part, the recommendations on how to reconcile work and family life in the *Babies and Bosses* reports are presented in gender-neutral terms, such as "parents" and "families." The title of the series highlights the rich nations' economic need for more babies, and also employers' need for more people in the paid work force. The cover picture depicts a baby in a suit working in an office at a computer. There is no specific mention of women or mothers in the title. Yet these policies have a crucial impact upon mothers. Only women have babies, and it is mainly mothers who are being expected to "harmonise" paid work and family life.

Some of the emerging policies that are recommended in *Babies and Bosses* may appear to be a cause for optimism: more state funding for childcare, gender equity at work, policies to encourage greater sharing of unpaid work at home and reductions in child poverty. However, the series suggests that mothers who choose to stay at home with their children for long periods of time should receive less help than at present. *Babies and Bosses* also recommends that the most generous and family-friendly welfare states cut back their levels of spending. There is clearly a need for greater feminist involvement in monitoring these emerging policies. This article outlines some of the opportunities and dangers for women contained within the policy recommendations in this OECD series.

THE CONTEXT OF BABIES AND BOSSES

Family policies occur in the context of demographic trends and the anticipated demand for working people. Currently these include smaller family sizes, a shrinking working-age population and an ageing work force. Birthrates have been declining worldwide. Since the economic changes of the 1990s fertility has fallen to very low levels in Eastern Europe. It is also now low in many parts of Asia including Thailand, Taiwan, Korea, Singapore, Iran and China. Within the OECD in particular, fertility rates have been falling and are currently very low in most of Western Europe, even in Catholic nations such as Italy and Ireland. It is now projected that by 2050, of all European nations only Sweden (and tiny Luxembourg) will have a higher working-age population than in 1995, and in some nations the numbers of working-age people will be substantially lower (Rubery et al., 2001: 35). Fertility is also very low in Australia, New Zealand, Canada and Japan.

Family policies in OECD nations put a strong emphasis on women's freedom to choose whether, when, and how many children to have. Nevertheless, policy frameworks since the late 1980s have inadvertently led to women having fewer babies. The increasing long hours culture in full-time jobs, based on the assumption that the typical employee has a wife and no care-giving responsibilities, has led many women to have fewer children or none at all. A growth in insecure, casualised employment and cutbacks in state supports to families in the 1980s and 90s increased the risk of poverty and so also acted as a deterrent to motherhood. Thus in almost all OECD nations women have been delaying having children, and having fewer births than previous generations (OECD, 2002: 13). For example, around 20 percent of Australian women are reaching the end of their fertile years with no children even though most had previously intended to become mothers (Franklin and Tueno, 2004: 38). Educated women are particularly likely to wait, as studying and becoming established in a career, plus in many nations paying back a student debt, takes a large part of women's fertile years. One significant exception to this general trend is Sweden, where the relatively high fertility rates seem to be the result of generous social policies that reduce the costs to parents of having children.

In addition, the aging population means that until around 2050 there will be a shortage of people of working age. Mothers who are currently not in paid work are seen as the largest source of potential labour power. The *Babies and Bosses* series recommends a range of policies to encourage or propel mothers into the paid work force in greater numbers.

In recognition of the effects of policy upon personal choices, the *Babies and Bosses* series looks for examples of effective policies that meet its economic goals. In doing so, a series of reports examines work-family policies in three main types of policy regimes under welfare capitalism: "liberal" welfare states (Australia, Canada, New Zealand, Japan and the UK), social-democratic countries (Denmark, Finland and Sweden) and "conservative" regimes (Ireland, Switzerland, The Netherlands, Austria and Portugal). Broadly speaking, the liberal nations appear to offer women freedom of choice about whether they prioritise paid work or family, or manage to combine the two: however, their governments provide very limited amounts of support to families raising children. This frequently leads to stress and overload among working mothers. Conservative regimes are more overt in their support of traditional family types with a breadwinner male head of family and a dependent wife; and these policy regimes tend to discourage mothers' paid employment through the tax/benefits systems and shortages of childcare. The social-democratic nations provide generous supports for working parents of both sexes and have an active commitment to gender equity in paid and unpaid work. Sweden, Denmark and Finland have high rates of labour force participation by mothers (Rubery et al., 2001: 41).

Policies that come under scrutiny in all thirteen nations include childcare provision, taxes/benefit systems (including paid parental leave) and policies to make paid work appear more "family-friendly." The work/family policy directions of the thirteen nations, together with the OECD recommendations for the future in these three areas, as outlined in *Babies and Bosses*, will now be examined.

CHILDCARE

Throughout the 1990s, cuts in state spending became the norm, particularly in the liberal nations. However, many governments have increased spending on direct provision and state subsidies for childcare in recent years. In the liberal nations since the late 1990s, state spending on childcare has increased in the UK, Canada, New Zealand and the USA to assist mothers moving into paid employment, although these nations are starting from a lower position than the more generous social-democratic states. In the European Union since 1997, and particularly since the Lisbon summit in 2000, there has been an explicit drive to increase women's participation in paid employment and a linked commitment to providing more and better childcare (Rubery et al., 2002: 32). The *Babies and Bosses* reports add to the call for increased numbers of childcare places across the OECD.

At present, however, there is still a shortfall in the numbers of quality affordable child care places in both the liberal and conservative nations covered in these OECD reports, and this makes it difficult for mothers of preschool children to return to full-time paid employment. As a result of the shortage of affordable substitute care for children in these nations, women have moved mainly into low paid insecure part-time employment and retained their domestic responsibilities (OECD, 2002; Murphy-Lawless, 2000: 90).

The *Babies and Bosses* series recommends that governments provide a larger number of affordable childcare places. However, the OECD recommendations are not radical. They suggest building upon the systems that already exist, and which currently create barriers for mothers who want to return to paid employment. For example, the OECD (2005) suggests that the Canadian government provide funding for childcare centres in deprived areas to increase labour force participation by mothers in low-income families: the addition of targeted and selective additional provision. In the UK, which has long had a patchwork childcare system, it is recommended that nursery school places be extended to three hours per day and better integrated with day care and playschools (OECD, 2005). Out-of-school care for older children, using existing school buildings where necessary, is also recommended (OECD, 2004: 12-13).

The social-democratic nations already have generous provision of quality childcare that is affordable to parents. In Denmark such childcare is available to most children over the age of two, and is regarded as an investment in the future of the nation (OECD, 2002: 19). Finland guarantees subsidised childcare places to all families raising children (OECD, 2005). In Sweden high quality child-care and extensive out-of-school care is heavily subsidised by government, so that parents pay only 11 percent of the cost and around 85 percent of two-year-olds attend formal childcare (OECD, 2005).

However, despite the high level and quality of childcare in the social-democratic nations, as exemplified by Sweden, the 2005 *Babies and Bosses* report comments disapprovingly on the high cost of this and recommends "family day-care services" as a cheaper alternative (OECD, 2005). Low-cost informal childcare is also recommended for some other nations, including The Netherlands, to increase supply (OECD, 2002: 21).

There are several problems with this recommendation. Childcare services cannot be provided cheaply without exploiting childcare workers, most of whom are women. In many OECD nations, better-off parents are increasingly employing nannies from poorer countries (Isaksen, 2004). The professionalisation of early childhood teaching is hampered by cuts in the costs of preschool care. A further difficulty is that unsubsidised childcare that is affordable to parents may not be of high enough quality. This may cause stress, guilt and anxiety in employed mothers and behaviour problems in children, thus putting a strain on family relationships. In addition, mothers have generally preferred childcare centres rather than informal family day care arrangements (Briar, 1997). This is because formal facilities are generally more reliable and the quality of care provided is more easily monitored. Good quality childcare that is affordable to parents is not a cheap option for governments; and it is of concern that the *Babies and Bosses* series recommends a scaling back of the Swedish system, which at present provides excellent services.

TAX/BENEFITS SYSTEMS

Tax/benefits systems can facilitate or discourage mothers' involvement in the paid work force. Until the 1990s tax/benefits systems in the liberal and conservative nations often discouraged mothers from reentering paid work. In the context of the projected demand for mothers as paid workers, many nations have already begun to modify their tax/benefits mix. Nations are providing additional resources for types of social assistance believed to increase women's work incentives, and are reducing spending on measures which encourage women to stay at home with their children for long periods of time. The *Babies and Bosses* reports recommend a continuation and intensification of these policy directions.

Paid Parental Leave

Paid Parental Leave is seen as one means of increasing women's attachment to the paid work force. So the general trend in OECD nations in recent years has been towards increasing the amount of paid leave given to mothers, and sometimes also to fathers, upon the birth of a child. Paid Parental Leave certainly has advantages for families. The leave eases the financial strain upon families when a child is born. It also treats women as an integral part of the paid work force, thus improving gender equity in paid employment. This also has implications for the empowerment of women as mothers.

The duration of paid parental leave (PPL) varies enormously between OECD countries. Some, such as New Zealand, provide only the minimum amount of paid leave recommended by the International Labour Organisation (ILO): 14 weeks. The *Babies and Bosses* reports are critical of PPL that is regarded as too short, as in the case of Ireland (OECD, 2003: 21). At the other end of the scale, the social-democratic nations provide long periods of PPL. Sweden introduced PPL many decades ago and now provides paid leave of up to 16 months. Finland and Denmark also have substantial periods of paid parental leave, at the end of which children are generally eligible for high quality childcare (see above). The level of payment during PPL is also substantially higher in the social-democratic nations than in the liberal ones.

Children who are able to be well cared for early in life are likely to experience less troubled lives later on. The *Babies and Bosses* series regards long periods of paid parental leave as undesirable, however, claiming that "it only postpones the point where parents have to confront the difficulties of balancing work and family commitments" (OECD, 2002: 140). This overlooks the fact that in the social-democratic nations, where long paid parental leave is followed by high quality childcare, parents do not encounter these difficulties in reconciling paid work and family life. Their relatively high birth rates and levels of labour force participation by mothers reflect this.

Generally in OECD nations PPL is taken either exclusively or mainly by mothers. Even where some of the PPL can be transferred to fathers only a minority of families do this. Encouraging fathers to share the existing amount of PPL with their partners allows governments to appear progressive and family-friendly without adding to public spending. However, in countries where the PPL is short, mothers, who are likely to be establishing breastfeeding, are unlikely to want to share the leave with a partner. For example, in New Zealand which has only 14 weeks PPL, very few couples share their entitlement to PPL.

To enable fathers to become more involved as parents it is generally more effective to provide an additional specific non-transferrable period of "daddy leave." In Sweden in 2002, the month of designated "daddy leave" was increased to two months. In 2001, 75 percent of fathers in Sweden had taken some parental leave, but the government's aim was to improve upon this. In Portugal, which allows fathers to take 15 days leave upon the birth of a child, 30-40 percent of fathers do so. The *Babies and Bosses* series notes approvingly that "daddy leave" and sharing parental leave helps to increase fathers' longer-term involvement with their children, with implications for greater sharing of care within families. However, there is a tendency for these reports to conflate PPL and designated "daddy leave." This is liable to give cost conscious governments the opportunity of choosing the cheaper and less effective option of simply allowing couples to choose to share PPL.

Tax Systems

The *Babies and Bosses* reports recognise that the structure of tax systems has a major effect on whether mothers will consider it worthwhile putting their children in care and going out to work. Indeed, tax structures and childcare are cited as the two major deciding factors in mothers' decision-making about returning to paid work (OECD, 2002: 19). High marginal effective tax rates (METRs) create poverty traps for women entering paid work and are cited as a key factor in many women's decisions to delay returning to employment in countries such as Australia and New Zealand (OECD, 2002: 19). This is because of the ways that benefits are abated, low tax thresholds, and the lack of tax-free allowance for families on low incomes. Some nations are already raising tax thresholds to reduce this disincentive effect. If this policy becomes more widespread, the effect will be to improve the position of low-income families as well as making paid work worthwhile for more mothers.

However, high levels of personal taxation do not reduce mothers' incentives to engage in paid work, provided that the tax system is progressive and is used to finance good levels of support to families. On the contrary, the nations that have high and progressive income taxes also have much higher levels of labour force participation by mothers than most nations with low rates of income tax. Nevertheless, the *Babies and Bosses* reports are critical of the high rates of tax levelled in social-democratic nations.

State Welfare Benefits for Solo Mothers

The *Babies and Bosses* reports state that they recognise that for mothers without a partner, combining paid work and a family life is a particular challenge, and that adequacy of state supports is therefore crucial. Despite this, the reports recommend strongly that policies encouraging solo mothers to stay at home with their children should be cut back and that alternative measures which increase solo mothers' attachment to the paid work force should be expanded. This is the policy direction already being followed by OECD member states to greater or lesser extents, but the OECD is clearly calling for an intensification of these policies.

The *Babies and Bosses* reports are critical of welfare policy in the Irish Republic, where lone mothers can receive benefits until their youngest child reaches 18 (or in some cases 22), without being work-tested. They recommend that the government provides training, childcare and out-of-school care to assist solo mothers back into employment (OECD, 2003: 13). In addition, however, the OECD is recommending further cutbacks in nations that have already pared down benefits to lone mothers. The *Babies and Bosses* series recommends that the UK develop a comprehensive system of work-focussed interviews to be brought in as soon as possible, and that later on some form of compulsory work-related activity be introduced for lone parents as a condition of benefit receipt (OECD, 2005). The OECD recommends that in New Zealand policies to "make work pay" could also include a lower rate of the Domestic Purposes Benefit (DPB) paid to lone mothers (OECD, 2004: 12-13). This would have serious implications for lone mothers in New Zealand, where welfare benefits were cut severely in 1991 and have never been restored to their previous level. In addition, the DPB is stringently administered (McIvor, 2004: 98-103); 61 percent of the children of lone mothers are being raised in poverty (Else, 2005: 9). Low wages and long hours in full-time employment also create barriers to lone mothers in New Zealand.

The *Babies and Bosses* series notes with approval that in Denmark the vast majority of lone mothers return to paid work full-time once the period of parental leave is over, and that very few rely on state benefits from then on (OECD, 2002: 165-6). Overall, 75 percent of Danish lone mothers and a similar proportion of partnered mothers are in the paid work force (OECD, 2002: 64). As noted above, this is facilitated by the relative ease of transition between long periods of paid parental leave and high quality, heavily subsidised childcare. In the less generous welfare states, mothers have lower rates of labour force participation. For example, in Australia, only 47 percent of lone mothers have jobs (OECD, 2003: 17) and in New Zealand, 50 percent of mothers raising children alone are in paid work (OECD, 2004: 12-13). The reason is the lower levels of support in these nations to mothers wishing to combine paid and unpaid work.

International evidence of the kind provided above shows that when provided with enough support for combining paid work and family life, the majority of lone mothers do choose to return to the labour force. The minority of mothers who, even when well-supported, choose not to return to paid employment, often have good reasons, such as wanting to take time to settle their children after a difficult relationship breakdown.

The OECD is correct in its view that social policy regimes in liberal nations create barriers to lone mothers' participation in paid work. Short PPL, long hours in full-time jobs, a shortage of reliable affordable quality childcare and benefit abatement rates which create poverty traps all act as disincentives for many lone mothers who would otherwise want to return to paid employment. Unfortunately, because of its concerns about the costs of family-friendly policies, the OECD is recommending reductions in spending in those nations that are most successful in assisting mothers returning to paid work. Instead, the OECD's suggestions echo the welfare polices of the USA (not covered in the *Babies and Bosses* series), where reliable state benefits for lone mothers were discontinued in the 1990s. These types of punitive policies are likely to succeed only in forcing one-parent families off benefits and into working poverty.

FAMILY-FRIENDLY WORK

The first *Babies and Bosses* report notes that "people should not have to choose between work and a family life" (OECD, 2002: 13). The series states that family-friendly policies should not only facilitate child development and parental choice, but should promote gender equity. However, there seems to be an implicit expectation that the necessary changes should be brought about mainly by employers rather than governments. However, this is unlikely to occur. At previous times in history where there have been severe labour shortages, the large-scale recruitment of women into the work force occurs only when governments have decisively intervened (Briar, 1997).

Gender Equity in Paid Employment

The *Babies and Bosses* series recognises that lack of gender equity is associated with low rates of labour force participation by women, and in the reports the promotion of gender equity is regarded as advisable although not put forward as a strong recommendation. In places, the reports conflate women's rates of employment with gender equity (OECD, 2003: 17); whereas other parts of the reports exhibit greater recognition of the importance of the terms and conditions of women's work.

The series acknowledges a need to avoid child poverty, but tends to regard mothers' employment as the key to avoiding poverty. However, because women are the majority of low paid workers, paid work is not always sufficient to keep families out of poverty. This is especially the case for women-headed families. Combined with other policies, paid work can help raise mothers out of poverty. For example, effective minimum wage legislation has the potential to keep families out of poverty without subsidising low pay (Hyman, 2004). However, this was absent from the recommendations in *Babies and Bosses*. The report acknowledges that Sweden child poverty levels are extremely low–just four percent. However, the report also suggests that Sweden's government should find ways of meeting its goals at the same standard but at a lower cost (OECD, 2005).

The *Babies and Bosses* series does provide comment on differences between men's and women's pay in the thirteen OECD nations. At present the gender pay gap is still an enduring feature of OECD nations, even those that have the best record of pay equity (Silvera, 2000). Despite women's greatly increased educational attainments, women with the same qualifications as men still earn less on average. Mothers earn less than women without children (Ang and Briar, 2005). The *Babies and Bosses* series shows large differences in the size of the gender pay gap between nations, with the social-democratic nations having greater equality overall than the liberal or conservative nations.

There has been a world-wide reduction in the gender pay gap amongst lower paid workers, mainly because of a relative fall in the earned incomes of low paid men. This puts additional stress on mothers in poor families to earn enough to make up this shortfall. By contrast, amongst employees with the highest incomes, the gender pay gap is increasing in many countries. This is because as pay inequalities between richer and poorer working people have grown, men have obtained most of the very highly paid jobs. The OECD (2005) notes that this has occurred even in Sweden, and takes the opportunity in its recommendations to criticise the country's government for the lack of pay equity in the top jobs. This is despite the fact that Sweden has an excellent record in terms of pay and employment equity compared with other OECD nations.

Although, no nation has complete pay and employment equity, some have been more successful than others. Amongst the social-democratic OECD nations in the *Babies and Bosses* reports, such as Sweden and Denmark, working women's average pay relative to men's is higher than in most of the liberal and conservative nations. States that have the most effective pay equity laws have a smaller gender pay gap than other countries. However, the *Babies and Bosses* recommendations do not comment on the need for pay and employment equity legislation.

Flexible Working Hours

"Flexible working hours" can mean working arrangements such as flexitime or glide time arrangements for full-time staff, or they can mean part-time employment. There is a great deal of difference between the two, although often they are conflated. Full-time career jobs are often very "family-unfriendly," especially in nations that have a long hours culture (see below). Flexitime can ease the problems faced by families where two parents are in full-time employment, for example, allowing one parent to take children to school and the other to collect them. This is less of an option for one-parent families, however, even though they have the greatest need for a good income.

Work-life balance policies that reduce working hours are often offered to parents of young children on the assumption that this is a useful way to help them manage their dual role. However, parents need the higher incomes that can only be obtained by longer hours of paid work. This may explain a lack of correlation between parenthood and a desire for shorter hours of paid work (MacInnes, 2005: 273). In nations lacking a generous level of support to families with young children, mothers with partners are in many cases already accepting shorter hours of paid work. In the UK approximately half of women are employed part-time (OECD, 2005). Mothers employed part-time are frequently cast as marginal, "atypical" workers. For example, in many of the European nations part-timers do not qualify for unemployment benefits. In the 1990s part-time working increased markedly in Europe, mainly amongst women (Meulders, 2000).

The *Babies and Bosses* series acknowledges that part-time employment of mothers can reinforce women's role as main providers of domestic labour and childcare (OECD, 2002: 17). In other parts of the series, it recommends an expansion in part-time employment opportunities in nations where mothers might otherwise have no paid employment. The OECD recognises that part-time employment can provide a point of entry to paid work for mothers, but that it also frequently creates low paid female-dominated ghettos in the labour force (OECD, 2002: 18). In addition, it acknowledges that much part-time employment is casual and low paid (OECD, 2002; OECD, 2005).

In the UK there are regulations obliging employers to agree to discuss flexible hours with parents. In the first year of operation, around a million employees made such requests, and these were granted in nine-tenths of cases. Flexible start and finish times are very popular (Work Family Life Balance Centre, 2004). However, of still more value to parents would be a lower ceiling on working hours, as a long and expanding hours culture is particularly difficult and stressful for people who have family responsibilities.

Work/Life Balance Issues

Hours of work in the thirteen nations are commented upon in the OECD *Babies and Bosses* series but are not the subject of specific recommendations. In nations such as Japan, Austria and Ireland and the English-speaking nations, hours of work in full-time jobs are long compared with social-democratic nations such as Denmark (OECD, 2002). In Australia, 70 percent of men work over 40 hours per week, and 25 percent work over 50 hours (OECD, 2002: 47). In a large scale survey in Australia, 47 hours was the average number (McPherson, 2004) and a recent New Zealand study found university teachers working an average of 49 hours per week (Doyle et al., 2005). By contrast, the nations of the EU are covered by a directive that forbids working more than 48 hours per week in member states.

For women in full-time career jobs who also have families, the long hours culture in employment poses problems. In addition to the growth in formal hours, there is also a culture of unpaid overtime which employees are expected to do. Teachers and lecturers have the longest hours of unpaid overtime (TUC). Women balancing a university academic career and motherhood have been found to experience more stress and less institutional support for balancing their dual roles than male counterparts (O'Laughlin, 2005: 1).

Workers not complying with the requirements of the long hours culture may be seen as uncooperative or unpopular workmates; they may lose opportunities for promotion or not be able to keep their job. These pressures and the poverty they engender have implications for the quality of family life. A large UK study in 2004 found that most respondents work longer than they are contracted to do, and a majority do not take a lunch break every day, in order to keep up with the workload. Many respondents reported that work stress made them irritable with family members. A third of women felt that working so hard had affected their relationships with their children and that they did not see their children as much as they would like to (Work Life Balance Centre, 2004: 3-5).

Although long hours directly affect more men, women are expected to compete on these terms if they want a career, or indeed a living wage. The effects upon partners of men's (and some women's) overwork include a reduction in companionship, shared leisure activities, communication, emotional closeness and sexual intimacy (McPherson, 2004: 7; New Zealand Council of Trade Unions, 2002). Commonly, when a man is overworked in his job the domestic burden falls onto a female partner (Work Life Balance Centre, 2004: 20), which frequently leads to resentment, and sometimes to relationship breakdown. It also restricts the female partner's career potential and earning power (McPherson, 2004).

DISCUSSION

The policy direction being promoted in the *Babies and Bosses* series sounds superficially attractive, even progressive. The series talks approvingly of policies promoting gender equity in paid work, and of supporting families in a variety of ways. However, closer examination reveals a glaring contradiction: the OECD expects additional supports to be provided in an overall cost-cutting environment. The first report of the series states an aim to promote:

... families with more secure incomes, better able to stand the strains of modern life, and if relationships do break down, better able to move on in their lives; better child development outcomes; less public expenditures (sic); higher fertility (or at least the chance to have their desired number of children) and gender equity. (OECD, 2002: 13)

How can more supports to working families be provided at less expense? The OECD's own evidence shows clearly that the countries which have the best record of meeting the goals of enabling women to combine paid work and parenting are those with comprehensive and generous welfare states. Yet the series recommends that the most successful nations cut back their taxation and levels of spending on key supports to families such as long PPL and high quality childcare, and adopt elements of the policies of the less successful nations. The key to understanding the apparent contradictions is as follows.

From the late 1980s and throughout the 1990s the OECD recommended reductions in state spending in its member nations. This was in line with the structural adjustment policies being applied in both richer and poorer nations in line with recommendations from the International Monetary Fund and World Bank. It is clear from the recommendations in the *Babies and Bosses* series that pressures to reduce overall welfare state spending have not disappeared from the OECD policy agenda. It has simply become overlaid with a new concern about labour shortages and low fertility rates. The policy mix being recommended in *Babies and Bosses* does provide for some additional spending in the nations with leaner welfare states, mainly on childcare. However, this is to be clawed back through further cuts in benefits for lone mothers. This is of deep concern. Welfare benefits are already at poverty levels, but they exist as a lifeline to mothers in violent or unhappy family relationships. To reduce welfare benefits still further will make it unviable for women to exit miserable and/or dangerous family situations, and cause untold misery and even deaths of women and children.

The overall aim of the policies recommended in this series is to expect both single and partnered women to "work more." The *Babies and Bosses* series uses the word "work" when they are referring to paid employment, as though caregiving and domestic labour were not work, and as if women had spare capacity. In most countries, women's total hours of work (paid and unpaid) already exceed men's (United Nations, 1995). The OECD series underestimates the amount of other domestic work and caregiving done unpaid by the "sandwich generation." Many women whose children have been born later in life are already trying to combine paid employment, the care of teenage children and providing assistance to elderly parents. The aging population will further increase the need for care of elderly parents, and the likelihood is that most of this support will be provided by women. The amount of extra paid work that can be performed by women without serious implications for their mental and physical health and the quality of their family lives may have been seriously overestimated by the OECD.

Will there be benefits to women from increased participation in paid work? Much depends on the kind of work provided. At present mothers in two-parent families are usually the second earners. Consequently, partners' careers are prioritised and mothers frequently accept lower paid part-time jobs with fewer prospects. Effective pay and employment equity legislation and an increase in minimum wages would help overcome women's economic dependency in the home and help equalise gender relations at home. Although the OECD regards pay equity as improving women's work incentives, it makes no specific recommendations as to how to achieve this.

In some liberal nations, mothers' entry to paid work has been accompanied by a growth in working poverty. Where money is short, it is frequently the woman of the house whose needs go unmet. Child development is also harmed by poverty. Social-democratic nations, which provide generous support for parents as workers, have very low rates of poverty amongst families. The *Babies and Bosses* series recommends increased assistance (such as tax credits) to working parents in liberal nations, but it is important that these should be adequate and supplemented by a wider range of supports.

In general, women's mental health is improved by entry to paid work. Being paid and having the company of coworkers are preferable to the isolation and low status women frequently experience when performing unpaid work at home. However, these gains are offset by poor conditions of employment, low wages, high demands and the dual burden of paid employment and unpaid caregiving work. This is a particular problem for women in nations with minimalist welfare systems. Work-related stress can negatively affect women's family relationships, especially when other family members are not sharing the load.

The *Babies and Bosses* reports talk favourably about greater sharing of domestic labour between partners, but are their recommendations likely to make this more of a reality? In social-democratic nations housework and caregiving are more equally shared between men and women than in other OECD nations. Individual renegotiation of housework and childcare between couples, favoured in the liberal nations, has been found to be the least effective. Market options such as paying poorer women to do the cleaning and employing nannies to care for the children are increasingly used by women in career jobs. This is less attractive for the women who become low paid cleaners and nannies. Furthermore, this does not encourage men to share domestic responsibilities. The option that has been found to work the best in helping promote gender equity at home is state provision of key services such as childcare, greater pay equity and generous paid parental leave for either parent (Bittman, 1999: 27-39). However, long PPL and high quality childcare are the very policies that the OECD wants to see scaled back. Overall it seems unlikely that the *Babies and Bosses* recommendations will improve women's family lives.

CONCLUSIONS

The recommendations in the recently completed OECD *Babies and Bosses* series advise member states to meet the coming labour shortage mainly by increasing mothers' participation in paid work, and in ways to achieve this without further reductions in birthrates. However, they strongly suggest that this should be done without reversing existing policies of cutting state welfare spending in OECD member states.

Effective gender equity measures cannot be provided in a cost-cutting environment. Already women are subsidising the economy through unpaid and underpaid work. The OECD recommendations in the *Babies and Bosses* series will add to the exploitation and overwork of women. This is likely to lead to increasing stress and conflict within families.

It is possible to find ways of addressing the crisis in the shortage of labour, and at the same time promote gender equity, but this cannot be done cheaply. The nations that have the most success in promoting mothers' employment, and maintaining low rates of family poverty, are also those with the highest rates of taxation and public spending.

It is essential that feminists recognise and use the bargaining power that is currently available to women to press for family policies which fully value the work done by women as mothers and paid workers. One way will be to organise in trade unions for fairer pay. Another may be to press for stronger enforcement of international treaties and conventions of the United Nations (UN) and its subsidiary, the International Labour Organisation (ILO), whose aims are to reduce gender discrimination at work.

The projected labour shortage for the next half-century potentially offers a unique opportunity to women. We may be able to bargain for more generous and supportive family policies, and if so, women could finally gain a permanent position as core workers with equal pay, opportunities and more family-friendly terms and conditions in paid employment. If we are successful, more women may at last be able to negotiate more equal personal relationships, and have greater security when raising their children. However, this is not what women will obtain from the recommendations in the *Babies and Bosses* series.

REFERENCES

Ang, E. K., & Briar, C. (2005). Valuing motherhood? Experience of mothers returning to paid employment. *Women's Studies Journal, 19*(1), 11-25.
Bittman, M. (1999). Parenthood without penalty: Time use and public policy in Australia and Finland. *Feminist Economics, 5*(3), 27-42.
Briar, C. (1997). *Working for women? Gendered work and welfare policies in twentieth century Britain.* London: UCL Press.
Doyle, S., Wylie, C., Hodgen, E., & Else, A. (2005). *Gender and academic promotions.* Wellington: NZCER.
Else, A. (2005). 'What is it about the DPB?' *Women's Studies Association (NZ). Newsletter, 25*(3), 9-10.
Franklin, J., & Tueno, S. C. (2004). Low fertility amongst women graduates. *People and Place 12*, 1, 37-45.
Hyman, P. (2004). Significant increases in the minimum wage: A strategy for gender pay equity? *Women's Studies Journal, 18*(2), 11-24.
Isaksen, L. W. (2004). Gender and globalisation: Care across borders–the case of Norway. Paper presented at the annual Conference for Feminist Economics, Oxford, UK, August 5.
MacInnes, J. (2005). Work-life balance and the demand for reduction in working hours: Evidence from the British social attitude survey 2002. *British Journal of Industrial Relations, 43*(2), 273-295.
McIvor, T. (2004). The feminisation of poverty: From the frontline. *Red and Green, 3*, 98-103.
McPherson, M. (2004). *Paid work and personal relationships.* Auckland: EEO Trust.
Meulders, D. (2000). European policies promoting more flexible labour forces. In J. Jenson, J. Laufer, & M. Maruani (Eds.), *The gendering of inequalities: Women, men and work.* Aldershot: Ashgate.
Murphy-Lawless, J. (2000). Changing women's lives: Child care policy in Ireland. *Feminist Economics, 6*(1), 89-94.
O'Laughlin, E. M. (2005). Balancing parenthood and academic work: Work/family stress as influenced by gender and tenure status. *Journal of Family Issues, 26*, 1-79.

Organisation for Economic Cooperation and Development (2002). *Babies and bosses: Reconciling work and family life, Vol 1. Australia, Denmark and The Netherlands.* Paris: OECD.

Organisation for Economic Cooperation and Development (2003). *Babies and bosses: Reconciling work and family life, Vol 2, Austria, Ireland and Japan.* Paris: OECD.

Organisation for Economic Cooperation and Development (2004). *Babies and bosses: Reconciling work and family life, Vol 3, New Zealand, Portugal and Switzerland.* Paris: OECD.

Organisation for Economic Cooperation and Development, (2005). *Babies and bosses: Reconciling work and family life, Vol 4, Canada, Finland, Sweden and the United Kingdom.* Paris: OECD.

Rubery, J., Smith, M., Anxo, D., & Flood, L. (2001). The future European labour supply: The critical role of the family. *Feminist Economics, 7*(3), 33-70.

Silvera, R. (2000). The enduring wage gap: A Europe-wide comparison. In J. Jenson, J. Laufer, & M. Maruani (Eds.), *The gendering of inequalities: Women, men and work.* Aldershot: Ashgate.

United Nations (1995). *Human development report, 1995.* New York: Oxford University Press.

Work Life Balance Centre (2004). *The twenty four/seven survey.* Keele, UK: Keele University.

A Response to the Babies and Bosses Report: The Effects of Policies on Therapy and the Influence of Therapists on Politics

Markie Twist

INTRODUCTION

The recommendations put forth by the Organisation for Economic Cooperation and Development (OECD) in the *Babies and Bosses* series will clearly maintain and in some instances contribute to the ongoing exploitation and overworking of women worldwide (Briar, 2005). A myriad of problems seem inevitable not only for women, but for diverse couple and family forms, through the adoption and implementation of such policies. Put simply, there is bound to be an increase in stress and conflict within families (Briar). As feminist-based practitioners, the potential problems for families and women presented in relation to the development and practices recommended in the *Babies and Bosses* report are of great concern.

It is clear that feminist-based practitioners need increased awareness of this report and the possible problems that it poses for our clientele. By increasing one's awareness, we as practitioners can become better prepared to meet the needs of the people that this policy most directly affects. Not only can we address these needs inside the therapy room, but

---

[Haworth co-indexing entry note]: "A Response to the Babies and Bosses Report: The Effects of Policies on Therapy and the Influence of Therapists on Politics." Twist, Markie. Co-published simultaneously in *Journal of Feminist Family Therapy* (The Haworth Press, Inc.) Vol. 17, No. 3/4, 2005, pp. 67-77; and: *The Politics of the Personal in Feminist Family Therapy: International Examinations of Family Policy* (ed: Anne M. Prouty Lyness) The Haworth Press, Inc., 2005, pp. 67-77. Single or multiple copies of this article are available for a fee from The Haworth Document Delivery Service [1-800-HAWORTH, 9:00 a.m. - 5:00 p.m. (EST). E-mail address: docdelivery@haworthpress.com].

© 2005 by The Haworth Press, Inc. All rights reserved.
doi:10.1300/J086v17n03_04

it may be possible for us to address the problems posed in the report outside of therapy, as well.

SYSTEMIC PROBLEMS

At first glance, a clinician might wonder what effect the *Babies and Bosses* report might have on them, their work and their clients. However, when we consider the report from a systems perspective, the effect becomes clear and so do the potential problems for our clientele. Through a systems perspective, we see that a change in policy does not happen in isolation: one change leads to other changes at all levels within a society. Thus, the policies recommended in *Babies and Bosses* are not just policies, they are vehicles for change at all levels in a system–even an international system. The effect of such recommendations must be considered in terms of the influence not only on women, but on couples and families. The central goal of the *Babies and Bosses* series is to address the need for increasing women's labour force participation while simultaneously increasing birthrates (Briar, 2005). However, as was pointed out by Briar, there are many areas for concern for women centred on issues of childcare, tax benefits and systems, and family-friendly work. Each of these problems has a systemic effect.

In exploring some of these problem areas, we see this systems level effect and may be able to envision the clients who will come to us as they experience these problems. For instance, in relation to tax benefits and systems the *Babies and Bosses* series calls for nations to provide additional resources in the form of more social assistance aimed at encouraging women to work and reducing the amount of time women spend staying home with their children for long periods of time (Briar, 2005). The report extends support for paid parental leave, but not for long periods of time (Briar, 2005). This can be problematic in that when infants and children are not provided with adequate time to form attachment bonds with their caregiver, this can evoke feelings of anxiety in children (Cassidy, 1999). However, when there is ample time to form an attachment relationship it promotes psychological health and well-being throughout the lifetime (Thompson, 1999).

The *Babies and Bosses* recommendations can attend to some of this concern in that it is noted that more parental leave for fathers needs to be increased to help increase fathers' longer-term involvement with their children (Briar, 2005). It is true that infants can form a solid attachment relationship with their primary caregiver whether they be the mother or the father. However, this supposed recommendation does not consider single mothers. In this instance, the attachment bonds would take place with someone other than a parent; typically, this is a less permanent and stable person in the infant's life. Therefore, there could be detrimental effects in this practice for the development of not only the child, but also the family.

In such circumstances, as a clinician we might see any member of the system present to us for therapy vocalizing problems related to this policy. For instance, there may be reports of individual guilt over not being able to be both a breadwinner and a primary care provider for a child. Alternatively, perhaps the problems would be between the couple, who might report intimacy issues, which could be related to not having any time to spend with each other. It could also be that the presenting complaint is centred on the child and his or her problem behaviours, which might be connected to not having developed attachment bonds with his or her parent/s.

Another problem area is that of the policies around family-friendly work. In relation to attempting to create family-friendly work, the *Babies and Bosses* series calls for more recognition and promotion of gender equity, in that it is associated with low rates of labour force participation by women, but it does not directly discuss recommendations on how to go about improving gender equity (Briar, 2005). An example of gender inequity is that men are still paid more than women for equal work (Briar, 2005). The problems with gender inequity are evident to feminist-based practitioners and are so great that they are almost incomprehensible.

For instance, in countries where male-breadwinner marriages are encouraged, rather than gender equity partnerships, the relationships are more unstable and more likely to end in divorce (Cooke, 2005). The problems also include an increased risk of poverty for women and children, as many of these relationships that end in divorce leave women to be the primary caregivers of children–women who do not typically earn as much as their male counterparts; so they have fewer economic resources to sustain their family (Cooke, 2005). With more single mother families lacking sufficient economic resources to raise their children, there is in turn an increase in the likelihood that the state will ultimately need to offer support for such families (Cooke, 2005). However, the *Babies and Bosses* series calls for a reduction in welfare benefits even though these benefits are already at poverty levels (Briar, 2005).

The ability for women to exit gender inequity-based relationships by divorce or other means is a necessity, particularly in the case where the difference in power differentials within the couple has lead to violence for women (Gottman, Driver, Yoshimoto, & Rushe, 2002). A policy that decreases or discourages welfare benefits makes the exiting of such relationships difficult and potentially dangerous (Briar, 2005). As clinicians, single parent families and mothers often present to us, as do women deciding whether or not to leave a couple relationship. Our ability to explore options and choices with such clientele is, at the very least, affected by and, at the most, directly hampered by family policies like those posed in the *Babies and Bosses* report.

It is also important to give attention to another systemic problem–the problem of the inherent heterosexist bias throughout the *Babies and Bosses* report as a whole. Heterosexual bias can be defined as the conceptualization of the human experience in nothing but strictly heterosexual terms; often at the cost of ignoring, invalidating, and/or denigrating gay, lesbian and bisexual people, and their related behaviours, lifestyles and relationships (Herek, Kimmel, Amaro, & Melton, 1991; Long, 2002). Furthermore, bias such as this leads to misinformation, ignorance, prejudicial practices, and ongoing negative stereotyping of gay, lesbian, and bisexual people (Bepko & Johnson, 2000; Dines & Humez, 1995; Long, 2002).

One example of the heterosexist nature of the *Babies and Bosses* report is that it makes the claim of being family-friendly, however, in the report only male/female couples and the children of such pairings are considered family. This narrow conceptualization of what constitutes family excludes family types like gay- and lesbian-headed families. In so doing, this report and the policies associated with it fail to acknowledge and respond to the needs of a fairly large and ever-growing part of our worldwide population. For instance, in just the United States alone, there are reportedly up to 2 million lesbian mothers and gay fathers of 14 million children (Galvin, Bylund, & Brommel, 2004; West & Turner, 1995).

The exclusion of gay- and lesbian-headed families in the *Babies and Bosses* report through this heterosexist bias has a profound effect. For instance, a significant contributor to distress and trauma in same sex couples and gay/lesbian-headed families are experiences of heterosexist bias (Green & Twist, 2005). Problems that arise through such biased practices and policies are centred around issues of denial or lack of recognition of tax benefits and health insurance for such family configurations (Green & Twist, 2005). Additionally, gay and lesbian family forms have to endure the hardships of dealing with stigma, discrimination, and prejudice from those who do not see their families as "real" or "legitimate" (Green & Twist, 2005).

For lesbian-headed families in particular there is the potential for additional economic hardships. These hardships are related to the inequity of pay between men and women, with men typically making economically more than women. What this means for a family headed by two women is that there is the potential for them to make significantly less and experience more of a scarcity of resources than ones that are headed by either male/female or male/male dyads. As clinicians we see these problems related to heterosexist bias bring gay- and lesbian-headed families into our offices. The *Babies and Bosses* report does not consider these complex economic and social issues, specifically those associated with lesbian-headed families, and therefore, it continues the perpetuation of global inequity for diverse family forms. This means that we must consider and struggle with such ongoing social justice issues with our clientele and in our work with them.

While the overall aim of the *Babies and Bosses* series is to increase both women's work force participation and the birthrates of the state, in the course of doing so, the policies recommended may lead to the myriad of problems pointed out above, and many others, for clients and practitioners working with them (Briar, 2005).

CLINICAL IMPLICATIONS

Through the above overview, there seems to be clear reason for feminist-based practitioners to be concerned about the policies posed in the OECD report and the potential problems associated with such policies for our clients. While we may have concern about such policies and the effect they have on women, couples, and families, we might not have any idea what to do about such systemic problems. Therefore, the question we must ask ourselves as feminist practitioners is: How will we assist women and families facing the potential problems presented by the *Babies and Bosses* report?

Awareness

Practitioners can start by being aware of the problems with which women will enter into therapy and how these problems go beyond the therapeutic room. Indeed, many of the presenting problems are connected to the dominant patriarchal society in which we all exist, and in which the *Babies and Bosses* report is a product. Connecting the problems of female clients as rooted in the dominant discourse of the society can be a first step towards empowering women in working through their problems. Therefore, it is of the utmost importance in offering assistance, to first increase our awareness of the problems associated with this policy as clinicians, while simultaneously increasing the awareness of our clients.

Techniques aimed at self-awareness and empowerment for female clientele may help counteract some of the problems women may experience related to the *Babies and Bosses* policy. One therapeutic technique that can be helpful in terms of empowerment, is that of listening to a woman's fears and helping her by asking clarifying questions around what she is and is not directly responsible for in her network of systemic relationships (Avis, 1991). This can have the effect of beginning to help a woman feel more self-empowered rather than overpowered.

The focus on empowerment in therapy can also come from a shared understanding of a woman's social context. This context is responsible in shaping all aspects of her life–including the political, economic, biological, and social forces (Avis, 1991). Some key questions that feminist therapists can introduce to help elucidate this context include the following: Are there problems in your life that you feel most responsible for and ones you do not? What is the difference? Who is responsible, if you are not? Does being a woman play a part in these problems? If so, how? Would men experience these problems differently? What part does society play in these problems? What part does policy play in these problems?

Systemic Thinking

Additionally, practitioners will need to recognize the need to change things systemically. Through interventions with one part of the system, they can have the effect of changing the system as a whole. This means that if the clinician works with one woman around the problems that can arise through this policy, this working relationship presents an opportunity for change and coping for this female and all the people with which she is connected.

Furthermore, this network of interconnectedness is even more evident when viewed through a gendered perspective of which women are often unaware. In many instances, women may enter therapy with problems related to these economic policies and not even be aware that their problems are connected to these policies. This is because women are often so caught up in their network of systemic entanglements, including the dominant patriarchal society, that they come into therapy believing that they alone are to blame for their problems (Avis, 1991). Besides the problems noted in the previous section, women entering therapy might also report problematic feelings in relation to this network of entanglements–feelings of negation, over-responsibility, and invisibility to those with whom they are in significant relationships (Avis, 1991). When these issues are framed in therapy as a symptom of systemic connectedness to such policies, women are provided an opportunity to share the burden of such emotional hardships, which can be a source for positive change in their lives.

Acknowledgement of Gender Inequity and Power Differentials

Furthermore, practitioners need to be aware of the power differentials and gender inequity reinforced in the *Babies and Bosses* report. The problems related to gender inequity and power differentials between men and women are many. However, female clients and their partners who enter therapy may not see their problems as connected to these overarching themes. Feminist therapists need to be aware of these themes and recognize the benefits for their clients and society by raising consciousness in these areas and practicing therapeutic techniques that do so.

The benefits of more equitable partnerships are numerous. For instance, when couple relationships are of a more equitable power pattern or configuration, there tends to be higher levels of marital satisfaction, more sustained intimacy, increases in positive regard, empathy, and affirmation, as well as higher levels of marital adjustment (Gray-Little, Baucom, & Hamby, 1996; Zimmerman, Haddock, & McGeorge, 2001). Furthermore, couples who share power are typically better able to reach mutual decisions based on compromise than those couples who do not (Gray-Little et al., 1996). Feminist-based practitioners can use gender and power-sensitive therapeutic approaches and techniques to help attend to these issues of power and gender in couple therapy.

Attention to Diverse Family Forms

In terms of attending to the issues associated with the exclusion of diverse family forms through the *Babies and Bosses* report, therapists first need to be aware of their own constructions of what constitutes family. This means that as practitioners, we need to challenge ourselves and our colleagues to think outside of our familiar heterosexist constructions of family life (Green & Twist, 2005). When we are able to recognize these constructions we can then take steps towards seeing our own biases and in turn raise our awareness to include and accept other family forms. By offering a legitimizing view of diverse family forms in therapy this leads to a validating effect for the families and their problems.

Therapists can recognize their dominant heterosexist constructions by becoming more aware of themselves as persons of culture and paying attention to the biases and prejudices that they bring with them into their practice (Green & Twist, 2005). Self-awareness is a step towards becoming more capable of negotiating multicultural worlds when working with diverse populations, and broadening one's meaning of family (Green & Twist, 2005). The ability to successfully negotiate multicultural worlds has the effect of leading to feelings of increased comfort when working with someone from a different culture (Green & Twist, 2005). This is of particular importance in the case of the therapeutic setting where the cultures of the client and the practitioner have reciprocal influence, but ultimately the mental health practitioner is in a position of power (Plummer, 1995). Because of this position of power, the therapist has a professional obligation to be particularly aware and attentive to his or her own culture and how this influences the therapeutic relationship and outcomes.

When practitioners have taken these critical steps, they can better assess the influence of dominant heterosexist bias, discourses, and privileges on the problems of gay and lesbian clientele. From this position, clinicians can more successfully contextualize such issues with clients and collaboratively work with them to co-create change in the family system and the larger system as well. However, it is recommended that practitioners who do not support gay and lesbian families and their rights, or who are not comfortable in working with them, refrain from doing so (Twist, Murphy, Green, & Palmanteer, 2005). Indeed, it may be considered unethical to engage in clinical work with any population of which a therapist is unsupportive.

BEYOND THERAPY

As feminist practitioners, recognition of the problematic issues related to *Babies and Bosses*, and attending to these problems in therapy through one's thinking and practical applications, is a good start, but it is not sufficient. It is also important that feminist practitioners become involved on a personal and political level to help curb the practices of social injustices that the dominant discourse has imposed through policies like the *Babies and Bosses* report. As such, we need to attend to issues related to such policies both inside and outside the therapy room. Indeed, it seems we have a professional responsibility to combat social injustices with our positions of power as professionals and as part of a predominately female profession.

We need to do this by incorporating a social justice perspective into our professional and personal practices. Indeed, definitions of social justice seem to be consistent with feminist perspectives of social change (Worell & Johnson, 1997; Twist et al., 2005). Social change can take place through changes in the network of systemic connectedness. It can start with us as therapists, who do hold some power and therefore have some ability to affect change with our clientele in hopes of bringing about empowerment for them and all levels within our society (Twist et al.).

Inside the therapy room, we can practice social justice. There are certain approaches that lend themselves to encouragement of social and personal well-being for clientele and people as a whole. For instance, the role of the therapist as being one of sociopolitical activist is possible through some narrative approaches (Monk & Gehart, 2003). From this position, the clinician has an opportunity to focus on the political nature of therapy and take a stand with clients against oppressive practices they face from the dominant society (Payne, 2000; White & Epston, 1990). Moreover, therapists can advocate for social justice outcomes for their clients (Monk & Gehart, 2003).

In the case of working with gay and lesbian clientele, recent research has shown that therapists who have a concern for social equality and justice for gays and lesbians are reportedly more comfortable working with such populations (Twist et al., 2005). Such concern for social justice on a personal and professional level starts with self-awareness and in turn attention to the realities of those of varied and shared cultures. After one establishes such awareness, it is important to become invested in social justice topics and how they affect members of a particular community. For instance, for gays and lesbians some of the topics that are of particular concern include equal rights, civil liberties, health insurance, tax benefits, domestic partnerships, and marital agreements.

Outside of the therapy room, we can practice social justice, as well. We can do this by being involved in the politics in our communities through being active in the supporting of causes we believe in and combating those that we do not. We can contact our government representatives and give our opinions on family policy issues before they become policies or laws. We can then encourage others to do the same. If we as feminist practitioners engage in social justice practices inside and outside of therapy, we then have a chance to be a part of changing the professional, personal and political forces that shape all of us (Twist et al., 2005).

REFERENCES

Avis, J. M. (1991). Power politics in therapy with women. In T. J. Goodrich (Ed.), *Women and power: Perspectives for family therapy* (pp. 183-200). New York: W.W. Norton.

Bepko, C., & Johnson, T. (2000). Gay and lesbian couples in therapy: Perspectives for the contemporary family therapist. *Journal of Marriage and Family Therapy, 26*, 409-419.

Briar, C. (2005). Babies and bosses: Family policy directions in the OECD. *Journal of Feminist Family Therapy, 17*(3/4), 47-65.

Cassidy, J. (1999). The nature of the child's ties. In J. Cassidy & P. R. Shaver (Eds.), *Handbook of attachment: Theory, research, and clinical applications* (pp. 3-20). New York: Guilford Press.

Cooke, L. P. (2005). Policy, gender, power and family outcomes. *National Council on Family Relations Report, 50*, F2-F3.

Dines, G., & Humez, J. M. (Eds.) (1995). *Gender, race and class in media: A text-reader*. Newbury Park, CA: Sage.

Galvin, K. M., Bylund, C. L., & Brommel, B. J. (2004). *Family communication: Cohesion and change*. Boston, MA: Pearson.

Gottman, J.H., Driver, J., Yoshimoto, D., & Rushe, R. (2002). Approaches to the study of power in violent and nonviolent marriages, and in gay male and lesbian cohabitating relationships. In P. Noller & J. A. Feeney (Eds.), *Understanding marriage: Developments in the study of couple interaction* (pp. 323-345). New York, NY: Cambridge University.

Gray-Little, B., Baucom, D. H., & Hamby, S. L. (1996). Marital power, marital adjustment, and therapy outcome. *Journal of Family Psychology, 10*, 292-303.

Green, M. S., & Twist, M. (2005). The importance of self-awareness for practitioners working with gay and lesbian headed families. *National Council on Family Relations Report, 50*, F19-F20.

Herek, G. M., Kimmel, D. C., Amaro, H., & Melton, G. B. (1991). Avoiding heterosexist bias in psychological research. *American Psychologist, 46*, 957-963.

Long, J. K. (2002). Sexual orientation: Implications for the supervisory process. In T. C. Todd & C. L. Storm (Eds.), *The complete systemic supervisor* (pp. 59-71). New York: Authors Choice Press.

Monk, G., & Gehart, D. R. (2003). Sociopolitical activist or conversational partner? Distinguishing the position of the therapist in narrative and collaborative therapies. *Family Process, 42*, 19-30.

Payne, M. (2000). *Narrative therapy: An introduction for counsellors*. London: Sage.

Plummer, D. L. (1995). The therapist as gatekeeper in multicultural counseling: Understanding ourselves as persons of culture. *Journal of Psychological Practice, 1,* 30-35.

Thompson, R. A. (1999). Early attachment and later development. In J. Cassidy & P. R. Shaver (Eds.), *Handbook of attachment: Theory, research, and clinical applications* (pp. 265-286). New York: Guilford.

Twist, M., Murphy, M. J., Green, M. S., & Palmanteer, D. (2005). *Therapists' support of gay and lesbian human rights.* Manuscript submitted for publication.

West, R., & Turner, L. H. (1995). Communication in lesbian and gay families: Developing a descriptive base. In T. Socha & G. Stamp (Eds.), *Parents, children and communication* (pp. 147-170). Mahwah, NJ: Lawrence Erlbaum.

White, M., & Epston, D. (1990). *Narrative means to therapeutic ends.* New York: W. W. Norton.

Worell, J., & Johnson, N. G. (1997). Introduction: Creating the future: Process and promise in feminist practice. In J. Worell & N. G. Johnson (Eds.), *Shaping the future of feminist psychology: Education, research, and practice* (pp. 1-14). Washington, DC: American Psychological Association.

Zimmerman, T. S., Haddock, S. A., and McGeorge, C. R. (2001). Mars and Venus: Unequal planets. *Journal of Marital and Family Therapy, 27,* 55-68.

Aging Societies and Intergenerational Equity Issues: Beyond Paying for the Elderly, Who Should Care for Them?

Steven K. Wisensale

SUMMARY. As members of a global society that is the oldest in the history of the world, we recognize that much of the financial burden of supporting the old will be shouldered by younger workers. However, with fertility on a steady decline among industrialized societies and longevity on the rise, the challenge of the future may extend well beyond the question of who will pay for the elderly and how much. Often overlooked is the question of who will care for the elderly and for how long. As more women enter the job market in the midst of growing aging populations, the problem of balancing caregiving responsibilities between the family and the state will be exacerbated, as will the debate over the allocation of resources across generations. Discussed here is how the intergenerational equity debate has emerged in the United States and three European countries: France, Italy, and Germany. Also discussed is the future role of caregiving in

---

Address correspondence to: Steven K. Wisensale, PhD, Professor, Public Policy, School of Family Studies, U-2058, 348 Mansfield Road; University of Connecticut, Storrs, CT 06269-2058 (E-mail: steven.wisensale@uconn.edu).

[Haworth co-indexing entry note]: "Aging Societies and Intergenerational Equity Issues: Beyond Paying for the Elderly, Who Should Care for Them?." Wisensale, Steven K. Co-published simultaneously in *Journal of Feminist Family Therapy* (The Haworth Press, Inc.) Vol. 17, No. 3/4, 2005, pp. 79-103; and: *The Politics of the Personal in Feminist Family Therapy: International Examinations of Family Policy* (ed: Anne M. Prouty Lyness) The Haworth Press, Inc., 2005, pp. 79-103. Single or multiple copies of this article are available for a fee from The Haworth Document Delivery Service [1-800-HAWORTH, 9:00 a.m. - 5:00 p.m. (EST). E-mail address: docdelivery@haworthpress.com].

© 2005 by The Haworth Press, Inc. All rights reserved.
doi:10.1300/J086v17n03_05

general and the role of women in particular in light of ongoing major demographic changes. *[Article copies available for a fee from The Haworth Document Delivery Service: 1-800-HAWORTH. E-mail address: <docdelivery@haworthpress.com> Website: <http://www.HaworthPress.com> © 2005 by The Haworth Press, Inc. All rights reserved.]*

KEYWORDS. Global aging, intergenerational equity, family caregivers, family policy, social policy, feminist family

INTRODUCTION

While our demographic concerns in the previous century focused primarily on the "population explosion" and various problems associated with migration from rural to urban areas, the twenty-first century is providing us with an entirely new challenge: world population aging. Longer life expectancies, combined with lower fertility rates, have produced a demographic profile in which developed nations have about the same number of children under age 15 as they have adults over 55. Consequently, we are members of a global society that is the oldest in the history of the world and we are getting older. In 2000, for example, the world's elderly population (aged 65 and over) grew by more than 795,000 a month. By 2010 the projected net gain will be 847,000 older people per month (U.S. Bureau of the Census, 2000). Put another way, the world population of those 65 and over was around 435 million in 2002, an increase of 15 million elderly since 2000.

But there is much more to say. According to Bengston and Lowenstein (2003), there are at least three facts associated with world population aging that we need to bear in mind as we study this emerging challenge and address its potential ramification. First, population aging is occurring in both developed and developing nations. Today, more than half the world's elderly (those 65+) reside in developing nations (59 percent, or 249 million people). By 2030 it is expected that this will increase to 71 percent, or 689 million people (United Nations, 1999; U.S. Bureau of the Census, 2000).

Second, Western European nations and Japan have the oldest populations in the world. It is expected that by 2030 most European nations will have elderly populations that constitute about 25 percent of the total. In Japan the elderly are expected to make up nearly 30 percent of the nation's population by 2030 and one-third of the population by 2050 (Kojima, 2000).

And third, the aged are aging. That is, in most industrialized countries the fastest growing group of elderly residents are 80 years old or older. In 1996-97 the growth rate of the world's "oldest old" was a relatively small 1.3 percent. However, by 1999-2000 it had increased to 3.5 percent (Bengston and Lowenstein, 2003). By 2030 in Europe, almost 12 percent of all Europeans are projected to be over 75 and seven percent are expected to be over 80 (U.S. Bureau of the Census, 2002). In Japan the percentages will be 17 percent and 12 percent respectively for those over 70 and 80 years of age.

However, the problem does not end there. Individual nations are experiencing shifts in their particular age structures that, ultimately, will affect their respective dependency/support ratios. This ratio represents the number of people under age 15 and over age 64 who are dependent on those who are usually participating in the work force (ages 15-64) and paying taxes to support the "too young" and the "too old." It is precisely at this intersection where questions concerning intergenerational equity are spawned. That is, how should resources be allocated across different age groups? And, who should pay how much, for what programs, to serve which populations within a given society? Or, put another way, will older people be perceived not only as obstacles to economic development, but also as societal burdens who divert needed resources away from other age groups? And what about young children in an aging society? Will they be viewed as a scarce national resource to be treasured or as one more minority group to be ignored?

Within the last year-and-a-half major strikes and demonstrations have been organized in France, Italy, and Germany by pensioners or near-pensioners who are concerned about proposed cuts in welfare programs that will affect them directly during their retirement years. Legislatures in all three countries have begun to explore the controversial issue of allocating resources across generations. Clearly, a debate over intergenerational justice that began in the U.S. nearly two decades ago has migrated to Europe.

But another development is lurking just over the horizon that extends beyond the question of who will pay for the elderly. That is, who will care for the elderly? Not only will there be major debates over the dependency ratio from a financial perspective (such as how much to tax the young to support the old), but there is growing concern about the availability of informal caregivers to assist the elderly as their health declines in their later years. Complicating matters further, most informal caregivers tend to be women and many women in industrialized societies have opted to enter the job market in the midst of growing aging populations. What, then, is the future in front of us as we anticipate major debates over the allocation of resources across generations while, simultaneously, advanced societies will also struggle to balance caregiving responsibilities between the family and the state?

The purpose of this paper is fivefold. First, to review the emergence of the intergenerational equity debate in the United States that still persists. How and why did it come about? Second, to explain how the concern over the allocation of resources across generations has surfaced in three European countries in particular: France, Italy, and Germany. Third, to explore the specific policies or strategies proposed by the governments in each of these three nations to address the intergenerational equity issue. Fourth, to discuss the future role of caregiving in general and the role of women in particular in each of these aging societies. And fifth, to create a framework for analyzing equity issues within aging societies.

These countries were chosen for two reasons. One, they were in the news frequently for having extremely low fertility rates, growing aging populations, and for major street demonstrations that protested government cutbacks and/or proposed tax increases to cover pension programs. For example, on April 3, 2004 hundreds of thousands of people in Rome, Berlin, and Paris marched in a coordinated protest against proposed welfare reforms in their respective countries. And two, these three countries spend the greatest percentage of Gross Domestic Product (GDP) on elderly persons in Europe and North America. The United States will serve as a reference point for the ensuing discussion since it has wrestled with many of the questions currently confronting European policymakers.

THE DEBATE IN THE UNITED STATES

Twenty-six years ago, in "The Graying of the Federal Budget," Robert Hudson (1978) identified the tremendous growth pattern in the expenditure of funds on the aged (more than a quarter of the United States' annual budget) and sent forth a warning about the impending backlash that would afflict the aging movement. Interestingly, one of the first indicators of an emerging backlash came in relation to defense spending, not in the form of an intergenerational equity question. In 1982 an economist in the Office of Management and Budget noticed the same "graying of the budget" as reported by Hudson and switched the commonly used metaphor of "guns vs. butter" to "guns vs. canes" (Binstock, 1983).

Reference to the generational equity issue would emerge soon thereafter. In "The Aged as Scapegoat" (Binstock, 1983) and *Age or Need* (Neugarten, 1982), two academically-based gerontologists echoed the alarm sounded by Hudson and, in doing so, identified the potential for intergenerational conflict. Later, others would introduce a new metaphor designed to simplify the problem: "kids vs. canes" (Minkler and Estes, 1984).

Although academics such as Hudson, Binstock, and Neugarten had issued warnings about a potential intergenerational conflict, the backlash had already begun in the private sector by the early 1970s. Following a Social Security tax hike and the adoption of COLAs (cost-of-living adjustments) in 1972, the business community launched a major campaign designed to destroy the public's image of Social Security as an insurance program. "Reconstructing Social Security as an intergenerational tax rather than an insurance program became the goal for program opponents," stated Jill Quadagno, "and under the guise of generational equity a new attack was launched" (1990, p. 637).

When the Federal Reserve Bank issued a special report on Social Security in 1972, the program was described as a "huge Ponzi scheme" (*Fortune*, 1973, p. 53). Writing in *Forbes* in 1980, Jerry Flint noted that the elderly are living well, not in poverty, as most believe, "The trouble is there are too many of them–God bless 'em" (Flint, 1980). Bendix Corporation chairman William Agee predicted that "young and old will be pitted against each other in a fearful battle over the remains of a shrinking economy" (Ehrbar, 1980, p. 118). And by 1982, *Fortune* readers were being informed that "it is part of the sorrowful lot of the baby boom generation that it will have to finance both its parents' retirement and a substantial portion of its own" (Ehrbar, 1980, p. 118). More significant, however, the public debate was looming on the horizon.

In 1984, Richard Lamm, the former Democratic governor of Colorado, stated in a television interview that "older persons have a duty to die and get out of the way" (Slater, 1984, p. 1). In 1993 he made similar statements in the form of two provocative questions: "Is it not only fair, but desirable, to have a different level of care for a 10-year-old than for someone who is 100?" And, "Should not public policy recognize that some people have far more statistical years than others?" (Lamm, 1993, p. 26). The controversy surrounding Lamm's statements spawned a much broader question that demanded greater attention: In an era that is often depicted as one with limited resources, are the aged receiving a disproportional share of those resources in comparison to other groups? Abbreviated, it became the intergenerational equity question, and soon numerous individuals and a variety of interest groups would participate in a very heated debate.

Daniel Callahan (1987), in *Setting Limits,* argued that limited resources should prompt policymakers to consider a health-care rationing program based on age. Philip Longman (1987), in *Born to Pay: The New Politics of Aging in America,* concluded that an unfair burden was placed on the baby boom generation to support a growing aging population through Social Security and Medicare. Laurence Kotlikoff (1992), supported by Peter Peterson (1993), applied "generational accounting" in his analysis of the federal deficit. Created to measure lifetime tax rates (21.5 percent for those born in 1990 compared to 33.5 percent projected for those born in 1990), generational accounting in the United States means that the later people are born, the more they will work for everyone else and less for themselves.

From another perspective, Myles and Quadagno (1993), bolstered by Minkler and Robertson (1991), concluded that the intergenerational equity debate is merely a class war in disguise, designed to undermine the cross-class strengths of the old-age coalition and weaken the power of the elderly lobby. "The rhetoric of young versus old was promulgated by an elite group of policy makers, academicians, and business leaders with a stake in remaking public images of the elderly in ways that would support decreased social spending" (Minkler and Robertson, 1991, p. 19). Put another way by Binney and Estes (1988, p. 104), the intergenerational equity debate "permits abdication of the state from responsibility for human needs" and allows for "massive budgetary reallocations to defense and tax cuts for the wealthy."

Meanwhile, in the popular press the onslaught continued. Two *Newsweek* articles by Robert Samuelson (1988, 1990) concluded that not only are the elderly not needy, but we are pampering them. In the *New Republic,* Henry Fairlie (1988) authored a story on generational equity that referred to the old as "greedy geezers." *Forbes* published an article in 1988 entitled "Consuming Our Children" (Chakravarty and Weisman, 1988), *Fortune* published "The Tyranny of America's Old" (Smith, 1992), and Paul Magnusson (1995) contributed an article to *Business Week* entitled "Victims of the Golden Years: Are Kids Shortchanged as Seniors Reap Vast Federal Benefits?"

Crossing over from academe, Nobel Prize-winning economist Gary Becker (1994) recommended that we "cut the graybeards a smaller slice of the pie" in order to address the federal deficit. He was joined by another academic two years later. In a *New York Times Magazine* article, MIT economist Lester Thurow (1996) strongly suggested that generous entitlements for the elderly at the expense of the young will produce the ultimate backlash: the birth of a revolutionary class. By the fall of 2000, more than 200 articles, books, and reports had been published on the topic of intergenerational equity and the debate continues–often framed as "young vs. old." For example, one day after winning his second term as President, George Bush announced that he would push for Social Security Reform in an effort to ease the burden on our children and grandchildren.

However, often overlooked in the discussions over Social Security, for example, is another dependency ratio: the number of available caregivers compared to the growing number of frail elderly.

The Challenge of Family Care in the U.S.

With the baby-boom population aging, the demand for family care will increase and companies will be pressured by employees for release time to assist aging parents. Signs of this conflict became visible within the last decade. In a 1997 study of 1,509 people conducted for Metropolitan Life by the National Alliance for Caregiving and the American Association for Retired Persons (AARP), surveyors found that one in four families had at least one adult who had provided care for an elderly relative or friend in the previous 12 months. On average, the caregivers surveyed were 45 years of age or older and provided about eight years of care (National Alliance for Caregiving and AARP, 1997).

In a follow-up study two years later, it was learned that 62 percent of 55 individuals surveyed indicated that they had asked supervisors, coworkers, or management for some kind of help or support with their caregiving responsibilities at home (MetLife, 1999). However, only 23 percent of companies with 100 or more employees have programs in place to support elder care (Families and Work Institute, 1997). "Elder care is to the twenty-first century what child care has been for the last few decades," contends Joyce Ruddock, head of the Long-Term Care Group at Metropolitan Life (*New York Times,* 1999d, 1). Indeed, a more recent study funded by MetLife Foundation concluded that 44.4 million Americans serve as caregivers, a service valued at $257 billion a year (National Alliance for Caregiving and AARP, 2005).

Today, nearly 70 percent of women work full-time in the United States and most of them assume a variety of caregiving responsibilities that are in direct conflict with their work schedules. Although the Family and Medical Leave Act of 1993 allows for employees to take time off to care for a child as well as an elderly parent, the law provides no wage replacement, limits leave to 12 weeks per year, applies only to six percent of corporations and covers only 60 percent of the work force. Between 2000 and 2004 about 28 states put forth initiatives to provide paid leave, but only five of those states included elder care; the remaining 23 chose to limit their proposals to "baby care." However, California, the only state to pass paid family leave, did include elder care coverage.

Whether or not working women will be able and willing to provide informal care as they have been expected to do in the past, remains an unknown, as does the role that government will play in addressing both the current and future needs of family caregivers. How the government responds to this challenge may ultimately depend on the particular perspectives of those in power. But regardless of what the private or public sector does in the future to address the challenge of family care, we may still be haunted by two very challenging questions posed by Shirley Burggraf in *The Feminine Economy and Economic Man*. First, "How can society get women's work done when women no longer volunteer for their traditional jobs?" And second, "Now that the opportunity cost of women's productivity in alternative tasks is becoming increasingly and explicitly expensive, who is going to pay the costs?" (Burggraf, 1997, 26).

FRANCE

As a nation, France has been aging steadily for the last 50 years. A declining birthrate from 2.7 in 1950 to 1.7 in 2004, combined with an increase in life expectancy that will increase the average age today of 39 to 44 by 2030, has reshaped the nation's demographic profile, gradually converting it from the classic pyramid to that of a pillar. Or, to put it somewhat differently, the dependency ratio of older people–those aged 65 and over as a proportion of those aged 20-64–is expected to increase from its current rate of 25 percent to 50 percent by 2050. In short, there will be more retired people out of the work force than there will be younger people of working age to support them. By the 1990s this scenario became particularly problematic for France's pension system, which is based on a "pay-as-you-go" (PAYG) model in which those currently working pay for the pensions of those in retirement.

But the problem confronting France and other European countries extends beyond that of demographics. There are also major structural characteristics associated with the French pension system that exacerbate the dependency ratio. In a study of 11 OECD countries, Gruber and Wise (1999) explored the relationship between public pension program structures and the retirement decisions of older workers and reached three major conclusions. First, there is great disparity in the labor force participation rates of older workers across developed nations. Second, there is also much disparity across nations in incentives or disincentives for work at older ages. And third, perhaps most significantly, there is a strong correlation between retirement incentives offered by pensions systems and the actual retirement decisions of older workers.

With respect to France, it has one of the earliest official retirement ages at 60 and an income replacement rate of 91 percent for retirees, equaled only by the Netherlands, also at 91 percent. Also significant, there is an 80 percent tax on work past one's sixtieth birthday. Not surprisingly, the employment rate for France's 55 to 64 year-olds is 36 percent, one of the lowest in the OECD that averages 48 percent. And clearly, the fact that at age 60, nearly 60 percent of France's workers leave the labor force cannot be explained by any means other than a pension policy that encourages and rewards such actions. Over time, and particularly during the 1990s, these two developments, a shifting demographic pyramid and a pension system that encouraged early retirement and burdened younger workers with higher taxes, changed both the content and tone of political debate in France.

Confronted with these realities in early 2003, Prime Minister Jean-Pierre Raffarin declared in an open letter to his fellow countrymen that "if we do nothing today, in 20 years our pensions will be reduced by a half. Our system no longer corresponds to the demographic reality" (British Broadcasting Corporation, 2003). Recognizing that the last attempt by a French government to reform the pension system in 1995 resulted in massive protests and a lost election two years later, France's center-right government moved forward with recommendations designed to force people to pay in more money over the years prior to collecting it in retirement. At the heart of the proposed reforms is a requirement that by 2008 public sector workers will have to pay contributions for 40 years instead of the 37.5 they pay now. Such a measure would bring them into line with the private sector, where the qualifying period was increased from 37.5 to 40 years in 1993. But by extending the qualifying period the government attempted to address two problems simultaneously: more revenues would be collected longer and less money would be distributed to retirees early.

This action in turn prompted a series of strikes and mass protests that crippled transportation, education, health and other public services. On

May 13, 2003 between 1.1 and 1.8 million people participated in 115 demonstrations across France. On May 19th, 700,000 French took to the streets again to protest the reforms. In June, 2003 Christophe Barbier in *L'Express* stated that France is suffering from "social malaria, a chronic disease that won't kill it but will sap all its strength." The reader should also be reminded that the summer of 2003 was extremely devastating for thousands of France's elderly who perished during a severe heat wave. Questions arose concerning the accountability of government and the responsibility of families in caring for the nation's elderly.

It is interesting to note that France's experience was fairly confined in comparison to the experience in the United States. In the U.S. it was framed as old vs. young and our debate has focused on Social Security and health care; France has concentrated on the affordability of pensions and the sharing of the costs. There's little evidence of intergenerational conflict. It has not been framed that way. The French have many universal programs, including health care and child allowances, to name a few. Also, they have a long history of solidarity. So it appears this battle in France was in some ways a battle between the public and private sector. That's where the equity issue was fought, not between age groups. However, after a major heat wave struck France in 2003, causing an estimated 15,000 deaths, most of which were elderly, the issue of intergenerational equity began to be viewed from a much different perspective: the role of family care.

The Challenge of Family Care in France

With respect to family care of the elderly in France, the problem is embedded in a history of gender inequality that is wrapped in two significant events that occurred within the last two years. Today women make up 57 percent of the French work force, compared with 30 percent in the 1960s. However, more than 75 percent of part-time workers are women and they earn on average 25 percent less than men. They are more likely to be concentrated in particular job categories (71% in the service sector), are more likely to be unemployed compared to men, and are far less likely to assume top executive (less than 14%) or managerial (under 35%) positions (Meda, 2004).

But even more pertinent to this discussion is the relatively heavy burden of family and household tasks assumed by women, as they do 80 percent of the hard-core domestic chores. That is, while the husband spends an average of an hour-and-a-quarter on domestic work per day, the wife spends an average of four-and-a-half hours performing such tasks. This division of household labor, which has remained fairly stable over the last two decades, widens upon the arrival of a child, with women investing twice as much time as men (25 hours to 12 hours) on average per week. And clearly, it is even more likely to widen further if the family is required to assume the responsibility of elder care (*Mail & Guardian,* 2005).

Two events within a two-year span have changed the French political landscape with respect to family care, focusing more attention on the well-being of the elderly. In August 2003 nearly 15,000 people, mostly elderly, died during a summer heatwave. Occurring during the nation's traditional vacation month, many bodies remained unclaimed in morgues for weeks. This, coupled with a government study that reported that a third (3,232 of 10,000) of French suicides each year, or 62 a week, are committed by people over 65, produced two policy reforms designed to affect both society at large and, on a micro level, family caregivers as well.

First, to cultivate national solidarity between generations, the French government converted a long-treasured holiday (Pentecostal Monday) to a "free labor" day in an effort to raise 2 billion euros (2.6 billion dollars) for a fund for the elderly and disabled. The primary purpose of the fund is to assure that basic services and care not available during the 2003 heatwave will be guaranteed in the future under similar emergency circumstances. However, in polls prior to the scheduled holiday three out of four Frenchmen opposed the elimination of the holiday and more than two-thirds ultimately refused to go to work on May 16th.

And second, in February 2004 the government announced that it will punish families that do not keep in touch with elderly relatives regularly. Under existing French law, adult offspring are required to provide for aging parents who do not have the means to look after themselves. Article 207 of the Civil Code states that children are obligated to honor and respect their parents, pay them an allowance and provide a fund or a home for them if necessary. But the February 2004 initiative tightens the code further, declaring it a crime for descendants of people living alone to fail to keep themselves regularly informed of their state of heath and not to intervene should they suddenly be taken ill. According to a special government report, relatives' checkbooks had replaced their passion. More was expected from families.

The implications of such a policy for women are quite clear. In light of the fact that most of them work part-time and are available for a variety of caregiving tasks, it is very likely that informal care responsibilities will fall on them. And, with major disparities already existing between men and women in completing housework chores and raising children, one may safely conclude that the future demands on women produced by an ever-growing aging population will only exacerbate the large rift that currently exists between men and women with respect to caregiving responsibilities.

GERMANY

As is the case in France and other OECD countries, Germany is aging and its future is gray. Today, every sixth German is 65 and older; by 2030, every fourth German will be over age 65. A steady increase in longevity, combined with a declining fertility rate, has produced a demographic profile that has spawned major political debates and economic challenges. For several decades, Germany has failed to maintain its reproduction rate. On average, German women of childbearing age have 1.3 children, which is far below the 2.1 fertility rate that is required to maintain the German population at its current level. This continuing development has raised questions about the future viability of Germany's welfare system and focused greater attention on the allocation of resources across generations. Complicating matters further, and despite the nation's unification nearly 15 years ago, significant discrepancies exist between the old East and West Germany. For example, a 10 percent unemployment rate in the former West Germany is doubled at 20 percent in the former East Germany.

Based on current trends, the United Nations predicts that Germany's total population could fall by nearly 14 percent by 2050 (United Nations, 2001). Put another way, the German population would be one-fifth smaller in 2050 than it is today. Among other things, such an outcome would have a massive impact on the economy, with the labor pool shrinking by 11 million or 27 percent, to just 30 million workers by 2040. If correct, the dependency ratio (those in the labor force supporting those who are not) will create a greater tax burden for workers and place more pressure on policymakers to reform a social welfare system that has been particularly generous to retirees. Compounding the problem was a history of early retirement in Germany (only French, Belgian, and Italian workers retire sooner), with a large majority leaving the work force prior to age 60. Consequently, by 2003, a new script was being written and the curtain was about to open for act one.

The major turning point came in March 2003, when Schroeder launched his "Agenda 2010" designed to revamp Germany's health, pension, and welfare system, as well as restructure its rigid labor market laws. Major protests by pensioners, near pensioners, university students, labor unionists, and the unemployed were organized throughout the country. But despite one demonstration in Berlin that attracted more than 100,000 protestors, the Social Democratic Party (SPD)-Green Party coalition government sealed the fate of the German welfare state on December 19, 2003 when it adopted "Agenda 2010."

The reforms included three key components. First, to provide an incentive for people to keep working, taxes will gradually shift from taxing contributions made to the pension funds to taxing payouts that people receive in retirement. However, only half the payouts will be taxed at first, rising slowly to full taxation by 2046. Second, new incentives and disincentives were included to influence workers' retirement decisions. Although Germans can still retire early at age 60, those who do so will lose 3.6 percent of their pension entitlement for each year they retire before age 65. But those who keep working after 65 will be rewarded an extra five percent on their pension for each year they delay taking it. And third, in what may be the most radical reform of all, a "sustainability factor" was introduced. That is, future entitlements will be lowered if the system lacks the funds to pay for them. Actuaries will evaluate the system's financial status annually and calculate the amount individual beneficiaries can receive each year.

Three other components of the reforms include an effort to generate more flexible jobs for elderly workers, a plan to address the problem of a declining population by adopting an Australian-style immigration policy in which particular migrants are targeted and actively recruited, and a pilot scheme of creating all-day schools. Under the current system most children attend school half a day and/or are allowed a one-hour lunch break, which almost forces women to stay home and out of the labor force. This reform, combined with a major increase in the child allowance, are incremental steps that are designed to encourage more women to have children and to leave home for work sooner after giving birth.

Similar to France and unlike the experience in the United States, Germany's "intergenerational war" appears to be on the periphery at this point. However, there is indeed growing concern about the flattening demographic pyramid and there is a legitimate fear that young and old generations may clash in the future. But for now, what Germany needs to do is to venture into areas of social policy where it has had limited success in the past. For example, because of the Nazi legacy, family planning has not been embraced in Germany since the end of World War II. With respect to immigration, there, too, the success rate for integrating immigrants has been quite spotty to say the least. And finally, whereas many other countries have developed comprehensive family policies such as childcare and parental leave that enabled more women to enter the labor market, Germany has been a laggard. So, although Agenda 2010 may do its part to address Germany's current dilemma, other measures such as those discussed immediately above, deserve more attention.

The Challenge of Family Care in Germany

Of all four countries discussed here, Germany perhaps presents the most unique case study, primarily because for 45 years it was actually two countries with each creating its own history. But German reunification in 1990 resulted in two ideologically divergent states being merged into one. With respect to family policy in general and gender equity in particular, it was like oil and water mixing with one another. Women in the former East Germany were not only encouraged to work but were also expected to assume the role of mother and wife, often supported by comprehensive child care and parental leave policies. Consequently, 91 percent of East German women worked before the Berlin wall came down. This is in sharp contrast to women's status in the former West Germany where the male breadwinner model was dominant and women who remained home to keep the house and raise children were viewed as important as the men who were employed in factories. Therefore, only 58 percent of women worked and that figure has not changed much for all German women since 1990 (Adler and Bayfield, 1997).

An equally significant event occurred just five years later when Germany began implementing new provisions in its national health insurance law to provide for long-term care assistance. With the passage of the Social Dependency Insurance Program, payments are available for family caregivers, community-based services and nursing homes and other facilities for the disabled. Funded by eliminating the Pentecostal Monday vacation, the same policy that would throw France into a political tailspin nine years later, the heart and soul of the program is the compensation of family members for caring for their loved ones (Wagner, 2001). Depending on the level of disability, the amount paid to a family caregiver may range from $250 to $450 a month in U.S. dollars. According to a study funded by the Robert Wood Johnson Foundation, "there has been nearly unanimous agreement that Germany's Social Dependency Insurance Program is a public policy success" (Polivka, 2001).

However, while Germany should be applauded for its success in designing effective programs to address the challenges of an aging population, one cannot overlook the fact that in a traditionally patriarchal society in which many women stayed home to care for children, it is highly likely that it will be women who will assume this role in caring for the nation's ill elderly. When the new insurance system was introduced in 1995, only 750,000 people over 65 years utilized it. In 2002, the number of recipients in this age group had practically doubled to 1.43 million. This is occurring when the 65+ population in Germany is expected to rise from 13.4 percent in 2000 to about 23 percent in 2040 and while the number of future contributors to the program and potential caregivers is expected to decline continuously due to lower birthrates (International Labor Organization, 2004).

ITALY

Like France and Germany, Italy is trying to reform its pension system, which consumes about 15 percent of the Gross Domestic Product (GDP)–one of the highest in Europe. Also, as in France and Germany, pensions in Italy are financed through workers' wages. However, with a flattening demographic pyramid, produced by a collapsing fertility rate of 1.2 births, an increasing elderly population, and retirement laws that permit some workers to leave work in their forties, the system has become less and less affordable. On average, Italians are now living 30-40 years beyond retirement, resulting in the shrinkage of the work force simultaneously with an increase in the number of needy pensioners. If current demographic projections hold, 42 percent of Italy's population will be 60 or older by 2050. And, equally significant, Italy's total population is projected to fall from 57 million to 52 million by 2050. Although reforms in the 1990s linked pensions to contributions rather than salaries, the policy adjustments proved insufficient. Today, nearly 14 percent of Italy's national income is spent on pensions and the situation continues to grow worse, as the culture of early retirement persists. For men who have been contributing for at least 35 years, they can retire between the ages of 57 and 65.

More recently, the Italian government has attempted to address its demographic challenge on two fronts: boost the fertility rate and reform the pension system. With respect to the former, in 2003 cash bonuses were given to women who chose to have a second child. A year later the bonus was expanded to include the birth of the first child as well. Despite these efforts, skeptics continue to argue that cash is not the solution simply because many women do not want to assume the burden of working while taking on the responsibility of an additional child. Also, there is greater access to contraception and abortion, and divorce is more common than it was just two decades ago. What is needed, critics argue, is a comprehensive family policy that is more sensitive to the demands of dual-earner couples.

The second strategy employed by the Italian government to address the nation's aging population was to reform the pension system. Prime Minister Silvio Berlusconi contends that Italians have no choice anymore and must be required to work longer. Otherwise, funding for state pensions will evaporate by 2030. Specifically, Berlusconi has proposed that the legal retirement age be raised to 65 for men and 60 for women. He has also called for the work requirement for qualifying for a pension to be raised from 35 years of work to 40 years and, to encourage employees to remain in the work force longer, he offers a 30 percent bonus.

Similar to France and Germany, Italy's workers took to the streets to protest the proposed pension reforms, organizing two general strikes and threatening more. In October, 2003, the country's three largest labor unions orchestrated a national strike that resulted in planes idling on runways, trains not moving, schoolteachers playing hooky, and museum directors and thousands of others refusing to work–all united across generations in protest against the proposed reforms.

Undeterred, on July 28, 2004, Berlusconi won a vote of confidence in parliament for his reform plans with a convincing vote of 333 in favor, 148 opposed, and one abstention. The reforms are to take effect in 2008. The Prime Minister announced to the nation that not only would the reforms address Italy's pension crisis, but, combined with specific spending cuts, the plan would meet EU Stability Pact rules. Woven into the fabric of debate and often overlooked by outside observers was the fact that Italy was in the midst of a sluggish economy that also fueled labor unrest and brought many protesters into the streets.

The Challenge of Family Care in Italy

As Italian women's educational attainment rose beginning in the 1970s, their entry into the job market increased, marriage was delayed, and the national birthrate plummeted. Within two decades, between

1972 and 1993, the fertility rate dropped from 2.4 to 1.2 and has continued downward ever since. But despite these developments, only 38 percent of Italian women work outside the home (University of Southern California, 2004). An equally significant statistic is the fact that more than 50 percent of women are no longer in the work force but 78 percent of women over the age of 75 identify themselves as care providers for relatives (Maroni, 2002).

As is the case with the U.S., France and Germany, Italy not only faces a financial challenge that is produced by a distorted dependency ratio, it must also be concerned about the availability and support of potential caregivers of the elderly. With one-fifth of the population over 65, many Italians are addressing this issue by outsourcing home care for the elderly to immigrants–a recent development that is quite distinct from what has occurred in the other three countries discussed in this article. It is also a far cry from traditional Italian society in which the elderly and disabled lived with their families and were cared for by their female relatives (Screti, 2005). As society has changed, so, too, has the rate of immigration in Italy.

According to statistics provided by the National Social Security Institute (INPS), a total of 51,110 immigrants worked as domestics in Italy in 1994, or nearly 27 percent of all domestic workers, compared with nearly 500,000, domestic workers–or 83 percent–in 2003. Today, foreign caregivers total more than 600,000, with most coming from the Ukraine (21 percent), Romania (16.4 percent), the Philippines (9.5 percent), Poland (7.0 percent), Ecuador (6.4 percent), Moldova (5.7 percent) and Peru (5.0 percent). Not surprisingly, almost all of these immigrant caregivers are women who work at relatively low wages ($900 to $1200 a month), and often leave behind their husbands and children in their home countries (Smith, 2005).

With a government either unable or unwilling to address long-term care of the elderly straight on, families are facing a difficult choice. On the one hand are expensive, private services, and lengthy waiting lists produced by under-funded and inadequate public programs. On the other hand is a cheaper domestic labor pool consisting of cheap labor from abroad. Between the two, Italians have opted for immigrant domestic workers to address their needs. But this approach is not necessarily unsatisfactory for the government. Institutionalizing the elderly would be extremely costly for the government and, therefore, a private system costs much less. And it is even cheaper if foreign labor, rather than Italian labor, is employed.

So, unlike the United States that has tinkered at the margins in supporting caregivers of the elderly, with programs such as the Family and Medical Leave Act, and France and Germany, which have adopted specific policies to address the problem of long-term care, Italy appears content in outsourcing its problem by welcoming more immigrants. Though controversial perhaps, such an approach may solve two problems at once: increase the population while simultaneously addressing the nation's long-term care needs. In fact, to maintain their working age population at 1995 levels, Italy will require approximately 350,000 migrants each year. Germany will require 500,000 per year.

CONCLUSIONS

Discussed here were four countries that are confronted with major demographic challenges, all of which have had to wrestle to some degree with the emerging intergenerational conflict and the issue of gender equity. However, the experience of each of the four countries differs. In the United States, for example, where there is less of a history of national solidarity on social programs as is the case among European nations, the intergenerational equity issue was raised more blatantly. Framed in terms of "kids vs. canes," the debate to some was one more example of the United States being in the vanguard for addressing social problems while other nations, particularly those in Europe, chose to deny the demographic facts staring them in the face. But to others in the U.S. the intergenerational equity debate is little more than a skillfully produced smoke screen designed to gradually chip away at one more government program and ultimately destroy it. Social Security, once viewed as the "third rail of American politics" is now fair game for reform and is listed among the five goals to be achieved during George W. Bush's second term. Medicare reform waits in the wings.

In reviewing the experiences of France, Germany, and Italy, it was learned that the conflicts in each of these countries differ somewhat from that of the United States. For example, in France, rather than seeing an intergenerational conflict, we found instead a conflict between public and private pensioners. On the other hand, in both Germany and Italy, there was not so much a case of intergenerational conflict as there was opposition to the cessation of early retirement and dissatisfaction over sluggish economies. At times it is difficult to distinguish between the challenge of demographics and the malfunctioning of the economy that is both driving the reforms and explaining the reasons for them.

And lastly, it is clear that a major problem that must be overcome in three of the countries (France, Germany, and Italy) is an anemic fertility rate. Not surprising, in two of these countries (Germany and Italy) family policies are lagging in comparison to other European nations, thus offering few, if any, incentives for women who desire to have children and also work. France is much better in this regard, thanks to a fairly generous child allowance policy and a very comprehensive and accessible child-care program. Still, births are low even in countries that can be classified as "family friendly." But again, a dominant tradition in Europe that is lacking in the United States is a deep sense of solidarity. That is, whatever universal programs exist in the U.S., they tend to be geared to the elderly in the form of Social Security and Medicare. Such programs also become lightning rods for the opposition or for those who see major discrepancies between funding for the young versus the old. In Europe, however, where there is national health insurance, universal child allowance programs, and generous child-care and parental leave policies, there is less fertile ground for intergenerational conflict to be cultivated.

We also learned that the intergenerational equity issue is further complicated by the concern over gender equality in each of these countries. While a nation's dependency ratio may serve as an adequate gauge for measuring the financial demands placed on the working population by the dependent population, it is important to remember that the dependency ratio also applies to caregiving. With dwindling birthrates, combined with aging populations, each of these countries has decided to view the role of women as caregivers from several perspectives.

Creating a Framework for Debate and Analysis

The intergenerational equity question, compounded by the gender equity issue, is steadily making its way onto political agendas throughout the world. Because of historical, political and cultural differences, and depending where nations may be on the continuum of economic development, the equity issue, if it emerges at all within a given nation, may take on a variety of forms. Therefore, it is difficult to design and apply a set formula to address it. However, in response to intergenerational conflict in the United States, Generations United (1992), an intergenerational organization formed to diffuse the divisiveness of the equity debate, has put forth seven guidelines and recommendations that other nations may find helpful. Each is presented and discussed below.

1. *Avoid misunderstandings about the implications of population aging.* An aging society can create much anxiety. This anxiety, sometimes referred to as "apocalyptic demographics," often revolves around the "dependency ratio," the number in the labor force compared to those under age 16 and those over 64. However, two points should be emphasized. One, this ratio is questionable because it fails to take into account the constantly changing labor force participation of women, the potential for the elderly to postpone retirement and work longer and the possibility of economic growth. And two, this ratio also tends to ignore the fact that policymakers can make a difference. Adjustments in monetary and fiscal policies, a shift in education policy that can affect worker productivity, and a different focus on research can all help shape a different future than that projected. Demography need not be destiny.
2. *Recognize the diversity of the elderly population.* The elderly population in any nation is heterogeneous. They are rich and poor, strong and weak, "young old" and "old old," conservative and liberal, and at times burdens and contributors. Failure to recognize the heterogeneity among the elderly may lead to how social problems are defined and, therefore, ultimately determine how they are addressed. Stereotyping, particularly that which furthers certain political ends, such as a reduction of social programs, should be challenged.
3. *Be prepared to correct any misunderstanding about relations between generations.* Although examples of conflict between age groups can be found on occasion, even in the United States, which is in its second decade of debating intergenerational equity, such conflict is more the exception than the rule. In short, while there will always be some tension between various groups in society, the bonds between generations remain strong. For in the end, people understand that successive birth cohorts and generations (particularly within families) are interdependent. If the young generation chooses to dismantle social programs for the old, it is also dismantling social programs for itself.
4. *Avoid using narrow and misleading definitions of fairness.* Although it may be desirable to achieve equity between generations, such an outcome would be fairly narrow in that it would not necessarily address other questions of social justice within a given society. For example, the idea that per capita public expenditures on children and the elderly ought to be equal sounds good, but it is probably not realistic. As Norm Daniels (1988) has argued, we all have

different needs at different stages of our lives. Thus, to pit one age group against the other is not only unfair but it diverts attention away from other inequities that may exist. In the words of Robert Binstock (1985), the current preoccupation with equity between generations "binds us to inequities within age groups and throughout our society."

5. *Do not rely on limited measures to draw broad conclusions.* According to Generations United (1992), those who attempt to measure the various flows of resources between generations to determine the fairness to particular cohorts have set an impossible task for themselves (see Kotlikoff, 1992). Since each generation receives transfers from those that precede it and also gives transfers to those that follow it, to reach accurate conclusions about equity between generations would require finding answers to some very difficult questions. For example, how should the economic and social investments made by previous generations be valued? Should part of what is spent on the elderly be counted as a return on their investments in younger generations? Should part of what is spent on children be considered an investment in the future productivity of that society? And, even if one forgets about the elderly, how should investments made in research, conservation, environmental protection and defense be allocated across age groups? Unless adequate answers can be provided for these questions, no major conclusions should be drawn about equity between generations.

6. *Avoid any misunderstanding about the common stake in social policies.* In the United States certain policy issues have been framed in terms of competition and conflict between generations. This way of framing the issue implies that public benefits directed toward the elderly represent only a one-way flow from young to old and that reciprocity between generations does not exist. Such an approach only fuels misunderstandings about the costs and benefits of programs directed towards the older population. An example of a policy that is intergenerational in structure is the Family and Medical Leave Act of 1993. Under the law, an employee may take time off from work to care for a sick child or a frail parent in need. For a nation to ignore the potential social and political benefits gained from carefully crafted intergenerational public policies is risky to say the least (Wisensale, 1988, 1991, 1993).

7. *Avoid participating in a zero sum game.* If the framework that pits young against old in a battle over scarce resources is accepted, it is

assumed then that there exists a "fixed pie" from which only one slice can be cut–for either the elderly or the young. Such a zero sum game assumes wrongly that the limited pie cannot be expanded by economic growth or that slices devoted to military spending cannot be reserved for social needs, whether they be for the young or the old. Today, limited resources are a fundamental reality of all societies. However, it is important to remember that both economic growth and various tradeoffs are still possible. "An approach to public policy that assumes that whatever resources are directed towards one age group diminishes the quality of life for another just does not square with reality." (Generations, 1992)

In 1999, the theme for the United Nations International Year of Older Persons was "Towards a Society for All Ages." Recognizing that the globe is graying rapidly, that this process is not confined to just the wealthier western industrialized societies, and that there is great potential for conflict between generations over limited resources, the United Nations adopted a plan of action designed to initiate and maintain a dialogue on this very important issue.

Meanwhile, the intergenerational equity question is gradually making its way onto the political agendas of nations throughout the world. Whether or not the discussion concerning this issue is always anchored in accurate information is, of course, another question. However, as nations attempt to shape their social welfare policies for the future, there are at least two fundamental questions that should be addressed. First, are intergenerational equity and gender equality morally justified? And second, are intergenerational equity and gender equality the kinds of qualities towards which any society should strive?

It can certainly be argued that both intergenerational equity and gender equality are always morally justified. The real question, however, is whether or not these two goals can be achieved politically at a reasonable price. Obviously, as has been discussed here in some detail, the fair allocation of resources between and among various birth cohorts and age groups is not an easy task. Nevertheless, theoretical models do exist and should be explored further. For example, Norm Daniels (1983) has developed a framework from the work of philosopher John Rawls (1971) that could, in principle, justify age-based allocation or denial of resources according to an equitable distribution procedure over an entire lifespan.

With respect to the second question, intergenerational equity is definitely a goal towards which any society should strive. But equally important, the goal can also serve as a compass throughout the debate. To paraphrase Harry Moody (1982) in his discourse on ethics and long-term care, intergenerational equity should not be viewed as simply a code word for "smart politics" or "sound public policy" or become the latest buzzword of "politically-correct language." Instead, it should become a means to keep the debate going, to keep the dialogue responsible and, whenever possible, to guide us towards a better understanding of our societal principles and toward wiser decisions in our personal lives.

REFERENCES

Adler, M., &, Bayfield, A. (1997). Women's work values in unified Germany: Regional differences as remnants of the past. *Work and Occupations, 24*, 245-266.

Becker, G. (1994). Cut the graybeards a smaller piece of the pie. *Business Week, March 28*, 27-31.

Bengston, V., & Lowenstein, A. (2003). *Global aging and challenges to families.* Hawthorne, NY: Aldine de Gruyter.

Binney, E., & Estes, C. (1988). The retreat of the state and its transfer of responsibility: The intergenerational war. *International Journal of Health Services, 18*, 83-96.

Binstock, R. (1983). The aged as scapegoat. *The Gerontologist, 23*, 136-143.

British Broadcasting Corporation (2003). *Europe's pensioners hit streets, April 3.* London: BBC News.

Burggraph, S. (1997). *The feminine economy and economic man.* Reading, MA: Addison-Wesley.

Callahan, D. (1987). *Setting limits: Medical goals in an aging society.* New York: Simon and Schuster.

Chakravarty, S., & Weisman, K. (1988). Consuming our children. *Forbes, November 14*, 222-232.

Daniels, N. (1983). Justice between age groups: Am I my parents' keeper? *Millbank Memorial Fund Quarterly, Summer*, 489-522.

Ehrbar, A. (1980). The wrong solution. *Fortune, August 17*, 118.

Families and Work Institute (1997). *The 1997 national study of the changing workforce.* New York: Families and Work Institute.

Faoroe, J. (1988). Talkin 'bout my generation. *New Republic, 13*, 19-22.

Flint, J. (1980). The old folks. *Forbes, February 18*, 51-56.

Forbes (1982). The truth about social security. *Forbes, December 6*, 242.

Fortune (1973). Social Security: The real costs of those rising benefits. *Fortune, December 20*, 80-82.

Generations United (1992). *The common stake: The interdependence of generations: A policy framework for an aging society.* Washington: Generations United.

Hudson, R. (1978). The graying of the federal budget and the consequences for old age policy. *The Gerontologist, 18*, 428-440.

International Labour Organization (2004). *Frail older people–the long-term care challenge.* International Labor Organization: Department of Communication.

Kojima, H. (2000). Japan: Hyper-aging and its policy implications. In V. L. Bengston, K. D., Kim, G. C. Myers, & K. S. Eun (Eds.), *Aging in East and West: Families, states and the elderly.* New York: Springer.

Kotlikoff, L. (1992). *Generational accounting: Knowing who pays, and when, and for what we spend.* New York: The Free Press.

Lamm, R. (1993). Intergenerational equity in an age of limits: Confessions of a prodigal parent. In G. Winslow & J. Walters (Eds.), *Facing limits: Ethics and health care for the elderly.* Boulder, CO: Westview.

Longman, P. (1987). *Born to pay: The new politics of aging in America.* Boston: Houghton-Mifflin.

Magnusson, P. (1995). Victims of the golden years: Are kids shortchanged as seniors reap vast federal benefits? *Business Week, May 22,* 16.

Mail & Guardian (2005). *France tries again to give women equal pay.* London: Mail & Guardian.

Maroni, R. (2002). *Statement by the Honorable Roberto Maroni, Italian Minister of Labor and Social Policies.* Madrid, Spain: The Second World Assembly on Aging.

Meda, D. (2004). *Women and work.* Briefing paper. Washington, DC: Embassy of France in the U.S.

Metlife (1999). *MetLife juggling act study.* Westport, CT: MetLife Mature Market Institute.

Minkler, M., & Estes, C. (1984). *Readings in the political economy of aging.* Farmingdale, NY: Baywood.

Minkler, M., & Robertson, A. (1991). The ideology of age/race wars: Deconstructing a social problem. *Aging and Society, 11,* 1-22.

Moody, H. (1982). Ethical dilemmas in long-term care. *Journal of Gerontological Social Work. 5,* 97-111.

Myles, J., & Quadagno, J. (Eds.) (1993). *States, labor markets, and the future of old age policy.* Philadelphia: Temple University Press.

National Alliance for Caregiving and American Association for Retired Persons (AARP) (1997). *Family caregiving in the U.S.* Washington, DC: National Alliance for Caregiving.

Neugarten, B. (1982). *Age or need: Public policies for older people.* Thousand Oaks, CA: Sage.

New York Times (1999). What's the problem? *Week in Review, August 9,* 4.

Peterson, P. (1993). *Facing up: How to rescue the economy from crushing debt and restore the American dream.* New York: Simon and Schuster.

Polivka, L. (2001). *Paying family members to provide care: Policy considerations for the states.* Policy Brief No. 7. Princeton, NJ: The Robert Wood Johnson Foundation.

Quadagno, J. (1990). Generational equity and the politics of the welfare state. *International Journal of Health Services, 20*(4), 632-649.

Rawls, J. (1971). *Theory of justice.* Cambridge, MA: Belknap Press.

Samuelson, R. (1988). The elderly aren't needy. *Newsweek, March 21,* 21.

Screti, F. (2005). *Elderly depend on immigrant women for caregiving.* Briefing paper. New York: Global Action on Aging.

Slater, W. (1984). Latest Lamm remark angers elderly. *Arizona Daily Star, March 29,* 1.

Smith, L. (1992). The tyranny of America's old. *Fortune, January 13,* 68-72.

Smith, T. (2005). *Ageing Italy leans on immigrants*. Briefing paper. New York: Global Action on Aging.
Thurow, L. (1996). The birth of a revolutionary class. *New York Times Magazine, May 19*, 46-47.
United Nations (1999). *The sex and age distribution of the world populations* (1998 revisions). New York: United Nations.
University of Southern California (2001). *Inclusion/exclusion in the workplace*. Briefing paper. Center for the Inclusive Workplace. Los Angeles: University of Southern California School of Social Work.
U.S. Bureau of the Census (2000). *International Data Base*. Washington, DC: U.S. Bureau of the Census.
Wagner, E. (2001). Restructuring care for the elderly in Germany. *Current Sociology, 49*, 3, 175-188.
Wisensale, S. (1985). The oldest old: A fresh perspective on compassionate aging revisited. *Milbank Memorial Fund Quarterly Health and Society, 60*, 420-451.
Wisensale, S. (1988). *Am I my parents' keeper? An essay on justice between the young and old*. New York: Oxford University Press.
Wisensale, S. (1990). Pampering the elderly. *Newsweek, October 29*, 61.
Wisensale, S. (1992). Policies on aging in the post-cold war era. In W. Crotty (Ed.), *Post-cold war policy, vol. 1: Domestic and social*. Chicago: Nelson-Hall.
Wisensale, S. (2001). *World population prospects*. New York: United Nations.
Wisensale, S. (1988). Generational equity and intergenerational policies. *The Gerontologist, 28*, 6.
Wisensale, S. (1991). An intergenerational policy proposal for the 1990s: Applying the Temporary Disability Insurance model to family caregiving. *Journal of Aging & Social Policy, 3*, 124-136.
Wisensale, S. (1993). Generational equity. In R. Kastenbaum (Ed.), *Encyclopedia of adult development*. Phoenix: Oryx Press.

Wisensale's Analysis: Thoughts from a Feminist Family Therapist

Scott Johnson

When the Social Security Act was passed in 1935 average life expectancy for Americans was about 60. Eligibility for Social Security benefits, of course, didn't begin until 65.

While a majority of adults at that time could nonetheless expect to live long enough to collect benefits–most of the deaths accounting for low life expectancy in pre-World War Two America occurred among infants and children–the number of Americans reaching 65 in the last 50 years has increased three-and-a-half times, from about 9 million to 35 million people. Yet, the Social Security Agency reports that, on average, those 35 million seniors live only about five years longer than the seniors of 1940–a welcome improvement, but hardly a sea change.

Such numbers are part of the complex issues surrounding the subject of Steven Wisensale's far reaching and thought provoking discussion of elder care and intergenerational equity. It is particularly interesting for its identification of gender issues in this problem, specifically the conflicting and sometimes contradictory social incentives offered to women to either enter the traditional labor force, or to limit their participation in traditional labor and instead to essentially become unpaid volunteers in an unofficial but critical senior health care industry. Or sometimes, like TV supermoms, to do both.

Address correspondence to: Scott Johnson, PhD, at the Family Therapy Center of Virginia Tech, 840 University City Blvd., Blacksburg, VA 24061-0515.

[Haworth co-indexing entry note]: "Wisensale's Analysis: Thoughts from a Feminist Family Therapist." Johnson, Scott. Co-published simultaneously in *Journal of Feminist Family Therapy* (The Haworth Press, Inc.) Vol. 17, No. 3/4, 2005, pp. 105-107; and: *The Politics of the Personal in Feminist Family Therapy: International Examinations of Family Policy* (ed: Anne M. Prouty Lyness) The Haworth Press, Inc., 2005, pp. 105-107. Single or multiple copies of this article are available for a fee from The Haworth Document Delivery Service [1-800-HAWORTH, 9:00 a.m. - 5:00 p.m. (EST). E-mail address: docdelivery@haworthpress.com].

© 2005 by The Haworth Press, Inc. All rights reserved.
doi:10.1300/J086v17n03_06

Too often the focal length of the American insight into social problems seems constrained by the Atlantic and Pacific Oceans. If it isn't visible between the beaches of New Jersey and California then it probably isn't visible at all. The debates about President George W. Bush's Social Security proposals typically–though not always–have ignored the similar problems debated in other nations. With the exception of a few articles examining what happened when Britain and Chile tried private pension accounts (not great successes), the struggles of other industrialized democracies to provide some kind of guaranteed support for retirees tend to be shoved aside. Perhaps this is because, as Wisensale notes, looking abroad might tend to challenge our habit of seeing Social Security debates as generational struggles rather than in other terms–in terms, perhaps, as he suggests, of gender, or of class, or, as in some countries, struggles between the public and the private labor sectors.

Wisensale rightly quotes former Colorado Governor Roy Lamm's incendiary contribution to the debates about intergenerational equity. But it's worth noting that Lamm's suggestions that we basically let people over a certain age die to preserve health-care resources for those with more years ahead of them was prefigured as early as 1973 in the movie *Soylent Green,* where the elderly of an overpopulated, food starved, futuristic earth were turned into hard tack for the hordes of younger citizens, who themselves would become foodstuffs for the young when they had aged enough.

Ironically, part of the dilemma Wisensale explores has arguably arisen from the success of *Soylent's* and similar ZPG (Zero Population Growth) messages. The societies Wisensale examines–France, Germany, Italy, and the U.S.–all have largely bought into the idea that overpopulation is the chief problem we have faced, which has led to the new difficulty of too few younger workers supporting a growing number of aged.

A further irony Wisensale points out in his discussion, certainly one of the most interesting, is that in some societies, like Italy, the solution to this new challenge is sought not through increased birthrates but through something many Americans of all political stripes have vigorously opposed in recent years–increased immigration. If you don't have enough workers being born to fund your retirement, well, "in source" them from another country. It's hard to imagine all those "Minutemen" doing their Hardy Boys "illegal immigrant" patrols in the Arizona desert lining up behind this concept.

But somewhere in some think tank, we can hear the wheels turning as economic theorists discuss the possibility of levying Social Security taxes on Indian or Bahamian phone bank employees of U.S. credit card companies. After all, if we can outsource the labor that would otherwise be supporting U.S. retirees, why can't we outsource the Social Security revenues too?

Increased immigration to build up the labor force, of course, is hardly a new idea, either in the U.S. or in Europe. Germany and Switzerland in particular were famous in the 1970s for their "Gastarbeiter"–literally, "guest worker"–policies, which invited thousands of immigrant workers to live in those countries to help reduce their chronic labor shortages. Germany, in fact, had a formal treaty with Turkey which brought tens of thousands of Turks to live there. In Switzerland, many of these workers were Italians, a situation made famous by the comic movie *Bread and Chocolate*. In the U.S., our "guest workers" have been called migrant laborers, their struggles memorialized 50 years ago in Woodie Guthrie songs like "Deportee" and "Pastures of Plenty."

But as a long-term solution to the problem of generational inequities, increased immigration has brought obvious social challenges. The clash between dark-skinned immigrants and lighter Germans contributed to a wave of neo-Nazism in the 1990s, while in the U.S. Hispanic immigration in particular, legal and illegal, has produced calls for English only laws, the exclusion of the children of illegal immigrants from public schools and welfare programs, and other acts of bias or repression.

Wisensale's citation of Generations United's guidelines for discussing generational equity questions is an especially welcome part of his essay. Generations United's calls for moderation and for going beyond sloganeering in discussing questions of intergenerational concern certainly bear repeating in our overcharged and much too partisan political atmosphere.

Few readers, I suspect, will come away from Wisensale's essay more hardened in their views than before they began it. Like me, they may come away thinking they have learned a great deal–an all too rare phenomenon where American political discussions are concerned.

FEMINIST RESEARCH OF WOMEN'S EXPERIENCES

Counter-Spaces as Resistance in Conflict Zones: Palestinian Women Recreating a Home

Nadera Shalhoub-Kevorkian

SUMMARY. Women's voices, roles, and contributions are the most misunderstood issues in the analysis of war zones and conflict areas. This paper brings the feminist lens into the analysis of Israeli policies in the Occupied Palestinian Territories. It examines the effect and legacy of policies inflicted by the doctrines of "no safe haven" and of "security reasoning" in relation to women, explores the way it shapes women's interactions with their family members, and discusses the ways in which continued and unpredictable political oppression creates an art of resis-

Address correspondence to: Nadera Shalhoub-Kevorkian, PhD, Faculty of Law and the School of Social Work, Hebrew University, Jerusalem (E-mail: msnadera@mscc.huji.ac.il).

[Haworth co-indexing entry note]: "Counter-Spaces as Resistance in Conflict Zones: Palestinian Women Recreating a Home." Shalhoub-Kevorkian, Nadera. Co-published simultaneously in *Journal of Feminist Family Therapy* (The Haworth Press, Inc) Vol. 17, No. 3/4, 2005, pp. 109-141; and: *The Politics of the Personal in Feminist Family Therapy: International Examinations of Family Policy* (ed: Anne M. Prouty Lyness) The Haworth Press, Inc., 2005, pp. 109-141. Single or multiple copies of this article are available for a fee from The Haworth Document Delivery Service [1-800-HAWORTH, 9:00 a.m. - 5:00 p.m. (EST). E-mail address: docdelivery@haworthpress.com].

© 2005 by The Haworth Press, Inc. All rights reserved.
doi:10.1300/J086v17n03_07

tance with therapeutic qualities. By using a collection of narratives, personal witnessing, and analyses of studies gathered since the onset of the second Intifada, the researcher reveals how women have managed to develop women-oriented strategies that protected the domestic space and produced innovative transcripts that created counter-spaces of safety to rebuild (actually or metaphorically) the family home. The paper concludes by showing how the processes of displacement and the attacks on the domestic sphere, nevertheless, engender agency and creative resistance and calls for front-line feminist activism. *[Article copies available for a fee from The Haworth Document Delivery Service: 1-800-HAWORTH. E-mail address: <docdelivery@haworthpress.com> Website: <http://www.HaworthPress.com> © 2005 by The Haworth Press, Inc. All rights reserved.]*

KEYWORDS. Feminism, security reasoning, house demolitions, gender, violence, conflict zones, Palestinian women, Arab family, counter-spaces, family policy, social policy, war

When they started demolishing the house, I hugged [my son] with his sisters . . . wrapped them all in my deshdasheh [long, wide housedress] and we all cried. To this day, the girls still remember how the whole family stood, wrapped in my dirty home deshdasheh . . . cried while our hearts were on fire.

Islah, a 28-year-old mother from a refugee camp near Jerusalem

INTRODUCTION

Unabated, the "national security reasoning" (Al-Haj & Ben-Eliezer, 2003) underlying Israeli military policies in the occupied Palestinian territories (OPT) has justified many violations of basic human rights and created a context in which the concept of "no safe haven" for the Palestinian Other has come to be accepted as a matter of policy. Such reasoning, a prevalent part of the colonial project, continues to affect Israel's perceptions regarding the survival of the Jewish state (Al-Haj & Ben-Eliezer, 2003; Bartal, Jacobson, & Klieman, 1998; Kimmerling, 1992).

Herzog (2003) discusses the effect of institutionalized security reasoning in the Israeli political and cultural system, stressing how it prolongs gender inequality. She shows that there has always been a clear Israeli consensus that the state is facing constant security threats, or what she calls "survival threats" (*i'yum kiyumi*). The effect of the survival threats and security reasoning has been found also to deeply affect the way the Israeli state perceives and reacts to Palestinian Israelis (Herzog & Shamir, 1994). Thus, notwithstanding Israel's military power, this perceived threat has become the foundational premise of its relationship with Palestinians (Arian, 1995, pp. 24-53, in Herzog, 2003; Samooha, 1989).

Such an approach to the Palestinians and to the OPT allows for the surveillance of, and attacks on, not only the public spaces in both Palestinian and Israeli society, but also the most private spheres of domestic spaces, particularly the home (Hammami & Johnson, 1999; Herzog, 2003; Johnson & Kuttab, 2001). Demolition and destruction of private homes has been one of the most strategic elements of containment practiced by Israel in the OPT. These attacks, particularly those into domestic spaces, have had tremendous implications on how Palestinian women and their families function, react, cope and survive in the face of ongoing struggles. In many instances, during these home invasions and demolitions, family members are unable to protect their own children and themselves from the Israeli military. Imprisonment, torture, injury, killing and other methods of abuse are often witnessed by their loved ones. Palestinian women, like their counterparts in other war and conflict zones around the world (Berger Gould, 2001), have created remarkable strategies of personal survival as a means of easing the continuing pain of living under occupation. Women in Palestine have taken a frontline position in introducing innovative methods for containing the effects of the trauma caused by violent conflicts and for resisting oppression.

This author examines the effects and legacy of policies inflicted by the doctrines of no safe haven and of security reasoning in relation to women. Furthermore, I explore how the dynamics of "securing one [the Israeli Jew] by terrifying the other [the Palestinian]" (to borrow the words of 16-year-old Luma) has shaped women's interactions with their family members, and discuss the ways in which continued and unpredictable political oppression creates an art of resistance with therapeutic qualities. In doing so, I examine how an environment of political violence activates existing resources that further acts of resistance, transforms gender roles, and calls for frontline feminist activism.

It is important to recognize that an epistemology of women's resistance and agency, in dealing with violent political conflicts and wars, is located at a juncture where different political powers, social norms, and rituals are entangled, be they economic, religious, cultural, or gender-inflected. What is of great interest to me is to observe how strategies of resistance adopted by women genuinely succeed in disrupting and redefining the preestablished boundaries of such powers. When looking at women-oriented healing circles and resistance, my previous work in the region has shown me that, despite the victimization of Palestinian women during violent encounters, women often redirect their energy into frontline activism. They take the specifics of their political context (replete with often capricious and arbitrary acts of violence) to develop an ideology of power and empowerment that stems from their national and personal victimization (Shalhoub-Kevorkian, 2003, 2005). Through my personal observations and interactions with these women, as well as my clinical efforts in the region, I have found that acts of political resistance, when they work in concert with the needs of a group seeking liberation from occupation or oppression, can attain the highest level of feminist expression and provide an instance of the transformation of gender rules and roles. This paper therefore examines how the processes of displacement and the fragmentation of selves and families, as a result of attacks on the domestic sphere, nevertheless, engender agency and creative resistance.

CONCEPTUAL AND METHODOLOGICAL UNDERPINNINGS

It is thrilling to think–to know that, for any act of mine, I shall get twice as much praise or twice as much blame. It is quite exciting to hold the center of national stage, with the spectators not knowing whether to laugh or to weep.

–Zora Neale Hurston, *"How it feels to be colored me"*
(in Trinh, 1989, p. 79)

This article is premised on a collection of narratives and voices of Palestinian women, gathered in the course of numerous studies conducted since the onset of the second Intifada. Much of the material comes from personal witnessing of the effects of violent conflict in the Jenin refugee camp (Shalhoub-Kevorkian, 2004): clinical intervention with 10 mothers of martyrs whose children were shot to death by the Israelis (Shalhoub-Kevorkian, 2003); voice therapy intervention with 52 women related to political prisoners (Shalhoub-Kevorkian, 2005); a study of 76 women living in Jerusalem and its surroundings and addressing the effect of the political conflict in general, and the Israeli Separation Wall (ISW) in particular (Shalhoub-Kevorkian & Abdo, in press); and a study of 58 college women who participated in focus groups and 80 high-school girls who wrote compositions exploring the displacement effects of the ISW (Shalhoub-Kevorkian, in press). All participants were directly affected by house demolitions, land confiscations, and military incursions in their living places and spaces.

My data is based on the discussions, writings, and photographs of these women, which specifically address the effects of the invasions into the domestic sphere and the consequence of the loss of home on gender relations and the construction of women-oriented, feminist counter-discourses. Following Scott's (2002) analysis of the relationship between power, hegemony, resistance, and subordination, I look at how, in the face of personal terror (arbitrary beatings, sexual brutality, insults, public humiliation), the "subordinate group creates, out of its ordeal, a 'hidden transcript' that represents a critique of power spoken behind the back of the dominant" (p. xii). In examining how Palestinian women living in continuing violence respond to particular sets of sociopolitical forces and oppression within a particular historical context, I hope to reveal how they have managed to develop strategies that protect the domestic space, producing innovative, if hidden, transcripts that create counter-spaces of safety to rebuild (actually or metaphorically) the family home.

It has always been my purpose as a scholar and researcher to advocate and promote politically progressive/liberating research methodologies. I am a citizen of the region I study, not a mere observer or an occasional visitor. Thus, my aim is to critically examine the process of knowledge production itself regarding colonized/oppressed people and try to give research subjects more power, offer innovative methods of inquiry, and consciously analyze and criticize the often colonizing, theoretical underpinnings of all research that one is in a position to circulate as "knowledge." My position as a Palestinian woman living and studying my society also aims at benefiting those who are studied. Thus, perhaps it will come as no surprise that I consider myself a feminist activist and therapist as much as I position myself as a researcher or scholar.

My methodology is based on what researchers, particularly feminists, refer to as unsettling boundaries by liberating the discipline from "the colonizing domination" of its past (Abu-Lughod, 1990; Behar, 1993; Collins, 1986, 1990). It is my conviction that "the master's tools will never dismantle the master's house" (Lorde, 1983). Therefore, I do not use the epistemological and other analytic tools of patriarchal militarism to examine women's reactions to political occupation, but rather I borrow meaning and learn from the women's own epistemologies, using the words and wisdom they themselves offer. By employing an anti-Orientalist mode of discourse that refuses the use of vocabularies, scholarships, doctrine, and other colonial and oppressive bureaucracies, I share women's voices, narratives, and ordeals so as to grant them the opportunity to express their history, culture, politics, and activism. My theoretical approach is based on varied decolonizing feminist methodologies which challenge the assumption that research can obtain outside of ideology, that it is culture free, and that researchers can occupy a kind of moral high ground from which they observe and make judgments without bias. Decolonizing approaches take into account the gaze of the colonized–in our case, the occupied (Tuhiwai Smith, 1999). Thus, my study is committed to voicing the voiceless, as a way of making a material difference in the lives of people for whom violence is an ongoing reality.

In my attempts to dismantle hegemonic perceptions, it is critically important to also look closely at the politics of representation that has hitherto inscribed the Palestinian Arab women in the cultural imagination, particularly her ubiquitous portrayal in the Western media as an unfit mother, terrorist, and backward-yet-seductive exotic female (see also Shalhoub-Kevorkian, 2003). It is my intent to juxtapose this Orientalist politics of representation with the voices of Palestinian women, their narratives, epistemologies, and the analytical tools they utilize to enable their own survival.

This paper studies Palestinian women's perceptions of and reactions to the safe home. I looked at these women through the matrix of the occupying context in which they were embedded. In this way, I hope that the Other will come to have a name, a face, a particular identity–namely, as the Palestinian woman. The study's focus entails more than simply collecting oppressed women's words, voices, and insights, but rather aims at helping us to better understand their experiences and acknowledge the way women's daily lives, bodies, homes, and communities became spaces of resistance and hope (Tuhiwai Smith, 1999). My analyses are grounded in particular, local feminist praxis, but also aim at understanding the local context in relation to larger, cross-national processes. Thus, an attempt is made to reconceive categories, such as "women as victims/survivors of political conflicts," within new definitions of justice. This mode of research challenges the hegemonic patriarchal and political powers that deliberately silence women by offering Palestinian women an opportunity to voice their experiences.

My point of departure is one of the foundational premises of feminism–the personal is political and the private is political and, consequently, our treatment of the home/family space is as a political domain. In analyzing women's agency and strategies of resistance in politically conflicted areas, we should keep in mind the often fluctuating visibility, invisibility, or even hypervisibility of political spaces–the legibility of the space itself and what epistemic strategies are used to read it. What must be accounted for is how the epistemology of the space then renders women's bodies, homes, families, sexualities, and so on as legible objects. For women living under occupation and violence, the need and desire to nurture, protect, and safeguard each other is not merely emotional or pathological, but rather redemptive. As many studies on women in conflict zones have shown, it is in such oppressive spaces that women's powers are more readily discovered and transformed (e.g., Alexander & Talpade Mohanty, 1997; Butalia, 2002; Talpade Mohanty, 2003).

HISTORICAL AND CONCEPTUAL BACKGROUND

Using Orientalist projections to fabricate the Palestinian Other, and understanding Arab emphases on the qualities of honor, shame, and family solidarity, as well as the importance of the social network, collectivism, and particularly the family home, the Zionist colonial project and later the state of Israel has worked to undermine this social structure. This has been reflected in a policy of confiscating homes, lands, and sources of living (see Khalidi, 1992, 1997; Morris, 1987; Said, 1997). Historian Benny Morris (1987) has written of how Al-Nakba (the Palestinian "Disaster," the exodus in 1948) created some 760,000 Palestinian refugees dispersed among surrounding Arab countries, and how the war of 1967 created another 400,000 refugees, leaving the rest of the residents of historic Palestine under Israeli military occupation in the West Bank and Gaza Strip (Farsoun & Zacharia, 1997). This has scattered Arab families across the region and gravely endangered their sense of safety and security, jeopardizing the rights and needs of family members, mainly the most vulnerable.

Since 1999, the Israeli military has destroyed more than 5,200 Palestinian homes, rendering 25,719 Palestinian women, men, and children homeless (see B'Tselem, 2005 a, b, c; Al Haq, 2004). These policies incapacitate the Palestinian family's ability to protect and nurture its members, further endangering their sense of safety and security.

One reason for the destruction of Palestinian homes is punishment for the acts of a family member. Israeli troops often storm the home at night with dogs, randomly shooting at walls, windows, clothing, furniture, and people, and imprisoning family members (see Al-Haq, 2004; Elfstrom & Malmgren, 2005). As women related to political prisoners explained, orders for house demolitions are imposed in addition to any sentence that the military court may later pass on the accused person. In 2004, there were more than 8,000 Palestinians in prison, 110 of them Palestinian women, and 80 Palestinian children under the age of 16 (Israeli Military Order No. 132 contravenes the internationally accepted definition of a child as anyone under the age of 18 by defining any Palestinian over the age of 16 as an adult; Elfstrom & Malmgren, 2005).

Construction of the Israeli Separation Wall (ISW) has also led to demolitions of homes, for reasons of "military necessity" (Al-Haq, 2004). In 2004, 1,399 Palestinian homes were destroyed for such purposes. Since 2003, more than 696,700 dunams of land (174,175 acres) have either been completely enclosed by the ISW, or effectively annexed by Israel. This land accounts for 12.4% of the total land mass of the West Bank (Al-Haq, 2004; B'Tselem, 2005 d, e, f; PENGON, 2003). Families living in homes destroyed for military necessity are given about 30 minutes to gather their belongings. This occurs under great duress, often in the middle of the night, with soldiers threatening to shoot into the houses, set houses on fire with children still inside, and other forms of intimidation (Al-Haq, 2004; B'Tselem, 2005 a, c; Elfstrom & Malmgren, 2005; PENGON, 2003).

Women and young girls have been particularly impacted by these policies, fearing specific violence directed at them by the Israeli occupation (Shalhoub-Kevorkian, 1994), including acts of rape and sexual harassment. Thornhill (1992) has discussed the way women security detainees have been treated by the Israeli security services. She has reported how detainees, once removed from their houses, have been subject to forced confession by interrogators who used tactics such as threatening to rape female kin. She has also shown how female detainees were sexually harassed, threatened, fondled, or raped, and mothers were pressured by threats of harm to their children (Thornhill, 1992).

The invasion of the domestic space, and approaching this space as a locus of security concern, has also resulted in forced restrictions on the mobility of Palestinians, often to the point of infringing on their livelihood. Thus, curfews, roadblocks, checkpoints, closure of entire geographical areas, deportation, and bypass roads, and lately the construction of the ISW itself, have all contributed to the ghettoization of Palestinians within closed enclaves and areas. Palestinians have experienced a spatial policy of separation that makes them reliant on countless permits from the military forces (which are arbitrarily assigned and regulated) to arrive at their workplaces, build homes, reach hospitals and schools and their land, meet relatives and participate in family gatherings, such as funerals. Such synchronized disruptions of the family's domestic space is indicative of the Israeli conception regarding the culture of the Palestinian/Arab–a continuing legacy of the Orientalist project. The policies and military tactics attempt to manipulate and ultimately destroy the Palestinian family structure.

This security reasoning and its uses and abuses in the deployment of state policy is reminiscent of what Brazilian historian and social philosopher Santos (2002) has labeled the fascism of social apartheid:

> [by which] I mean the social segregation of the excluded through the division of cities into savage and civilized zones. The savage zones are the zones of Hobbes' state of nature. The civilized zones are the zones of the social contract, and they are under the constant threat of the savage zones. In order to define themselves, the civilized zones turn themselves into neo-feudal castles, the fortified enclaves that are characteristic of new forms of urban segregation– private cities, enclosed condominiums, gated communities. (p. 454)

Similarly, Beck (1999) refers to this as the "risk society" or the "Brazilianization" of the world. These authors note that the earlier fascist order was based on a political regime, while the current social fascism is "a social civilizational regime" (Santos, p. 453). This fascism trivializes democracy, allowing the coexistence of democratic states within overall fascist societies. In the OPT, such social fascism is reflected in the consolidation of Palestinians into tight, restricted spaces and the Judaization of large areas (turning Palestinian/Arab-oriented areas into Jewish-oriented ones by building and settling more Jews than Palestinians), including Jerusalem (see B'Tselem, 1998, which described the situation as "systematic and deliberate discrimination against Palestinians in land expropriation, planning, and building," p. n5). This separation of Palestinians into discrete and manageable enclaves has immobilized many individuals and halted the economic and social growth of these communities.

SHATAT, SUMUD AND WOMEN'S HIDDEN TRANSCRIPTS

In numerous discussions, writings, and focus groups, Palestinian women shared the effect of *shatat* (dislocation, displacement) on their lives, and their constant need to search for a safe haven. For instance, Firyal (Shalhoub-Kevorkian, in press), a young college student from a village outside Jerusalem, witnessed "countless house demolitions" and "radical changes in the roads that connect us to other villages and cities in the OPT." She stated:

> Do you know what does it means to be *m'shatateh* [displaced] in your own home? When you leave not knowing whether you will be able to come back? When you will be back? And how? . . . At the checkpoint. . . I feel like I am uprooted [*zai il ma'toaah min shajarah*] . . . at home I feel unsafe. . . *shatat*.

Seventeen-year-old Shaden (Shalhoub-Kevorkian, in press) wrote the following:

> We were refugees, but my family managed to work hard and bought a piece of land and built our house. All my uncles built their houses in this area so as to feel we are not refugees anymore and to be together. Now, the wall [ISW] will divide us again, our house will be on one side of the wall, and my cousin's will be on the other. My other uncle's house is under threat of being demolished and so we hired a lawyer to prevent the demolition. Now, all the family savings will be collected to pay the lawyers and fight Israel in the Israeli court. My grandfather said that he might need to sell one of the family houses to fight them in court. My main fear is that we will lose the case, and then our house, and turn back to being refugees.

The voices of these women remind me of Said's (1990), mainly his remark that the exiled know that in a secular and contingent world, homes are always provisional. Borders and barriers which enclose us within the safety of familiar territory can also become prisons, and are often defended beyond reason or necessity. Exiles cross borders, break barriers of thought and experience. Shaden's experiences reflect this ambivalence: "Being at home doesn't mean you're at home. Look from the window and you see the ISW, you realize that no one in this house is safe. My home, my land, my school, and life became unsafe."

Through Shaden's narrative of displacement, we understand how experiences are deeply rooted in a sense of place. To be separated from the persons or location that one loves best or knows most intimately is to experience loss. Similarly, Firyal's concept of the home as *shatat* requires imagining distance in less binary and more complicated ways. Many of the young women felt that distance from the ISW–or proximity to it–carries one meaning and reflects only one interest: the interest of the dominant to turn all their spaces into unsafe terrains.

Firyal's story, as shared in the focus group, described her family's constant need to move from one location to another, in an attempt to find a safe place. She explained how they had moved to another neighborhood to avoid having to go through a checkpoint daily. But this move created great loss in terms of social support; when her sister became ill with a high fever, the family was unable to find someone to take her to the hospital. Later, the checkpoint was moved closer to their new home, making it impossible for her parents to reach their workplaces, causing them again to relocate. This internal displacement was painful to Firyal, who had to change schools, lose old friends, and make new friends only to lose them again: "Every time I felt I found a safe home and a loving environment, I ended up losing it. . . . *Shatat*. . . that's what Israel wants for us." Thus, the family home and the sense of security and privacy that it generally affords was turned into an arena that displays state power.

Women in my voice therapy groups articulated their increased sense of loss as a result of the policy of building Israeli housing projects on Palestinian land in the OPT. Hafiza stated (Shalhoub-Kevorkian, 2005):

> Every day I wake up, I discover again and again–as if I refuse to believe it–that I lost my home following the arrest of my two children, but I also see the new homes built for the Jewish settlers. . . . [Seeing] their homes being built in a modern manner, with large gardens and a playground for their children, while my children are either in the Israeli prison or here, in this *khusshe'h* [small, barely built, unsanitary room] that the members of the camp were able to give me following the demolition of my house–[it] kills me. So, the *khusshe'h* is my home and my children's home.

Hafiza's constant denial of the loss of her home became harder and more painful following the actual witnessing of Israelis building their homes, while Palestinians are displaced, even from their own homes built in a refugee camp. She constantly reiterated the question: "We are imprisoned in our own homes, and they are free to move. . . . Why do they consider us animals and themselves as human beings?"

Continuous and unanticipated hazards–as seen, for example, in Firyal's, Shaden's, and Hafiza's narratives–have affected the ability of Palestinians to preserve family ties and connections, and at the same time have shaped how they deal with countless acts of violence and military practices. Despite their feelings of *shatat*, many women also stressed that the most pervasive result of continued oppressions and occupation has been to preserve the bonds of social solidarity and family. Hafiza, for example, voiced her conviction that every Palestinian woman should work harder to safeguard her family and protect her home from invaders:

> In our neighborhood, we women divide the work between us. One helps by filling out the forms to register our children in schools, or get the needed official documentation and permits to obtain safe movement for our family members; another gets medication for the sick; and my sister in law–who works for the UN–informs us about any roadblocks or other restrictions, so we will all be aware. We also call other relatives and friends to check on them, and are ready when needed. I sometimes refuse to sleep in a nightgown.... The reality of Palestinian women differs from others. We have learned from our history of *shatat*... I am always ready... even when I am sleeping.

The results of such a reaction, as the women explained, have in fact created more *sumud* (steadfastness), strengthening and promoting the construction of a national and personal identity. In my observations, this sense of bonding, mediated through a national sense of belonging, was often found to transform gender roles.

Both a reliance on family and the awareness of a national legacy of oppression and denial have promoted the need for *sumud* and togetherness. Mothers of martyrs, for example, who repeatedly discussed the loss of their children and the related loss of their homes, often spoke of their home as a vessel of unity, love, care, and hope, expressed through the rituals of cooking, meeting together, and maintaining social ties. The loss of their children evoked memories of being refugees during the Nakba in 1948 (Shalhoub-Kevorkian, 2003), taking them back in history to other narratives of loss, cognizant of the recurrence of loss in the present. While these deep-rooted legacies of loss understandably create a sense of hopelessness, they also encourage women to search for a safe haven for their families as part of their *sumud*. As one mother stated:

> We won't allow them to kick us out of our homes, like in 1948. In 1948 they *shatatuna* [displaced us]. In 1948 they took our land,

our homes, and destroyed all family ties. My uncle Hafiz became a martyr, and his wife and family moved to Jordan; my uncle Mohammed (who was 14 years old at the time) was imprisoned by the British colonialists, and we lost all contact with him, while my father remained in Palestine. They turned our homes into a lamentation house . . . and each time we rebuild it, they attack us, kill our relatives, take our homes and leave us *m'shatatin* [displaced, dispersed]. Now, it is not '48, and they are much more powerful–now not only England supports them, but also America, and we never stopped resisting them . . . but we are afraid, and no one knows what the future holds for us. . . . (part of this quotation appears in Shalhoub-Kevorkian, 2003, p. 398)

The women repeatedly referred to Israel's practices of attacking the family's unity, sense of privacy, and integrity. Umm Riad, mother of a martyr (Shalhoub-Kevorkian, 2003), often reiterated the ways Israel and the Western world aim at destroying Muslims and shared narratives of Israeli soldiers who made sure to burn the holy Quran when destroying homes. Other women related incidents where Israeli soldiers humiliated Muslim women and disgraced Muslim clergy at prayer. Nora, a young participant in a focus group, stated:

We as Christians felt very threatened and hated. My family not only lost its land and property following arbitrary land confiscation in 1948, but we also lost many family members. Most of my family emigrated to the U.S. or to Chile. And do you think the Christian world feels with us Palestinians? America worries about money, and about their economy . . . no Muslims or Christians count.

The women's narratives of displacement and loss were constructed such that attacks on families can best be understood as part of a larger repertoire of hegemonic militarization of the Palestinian Other (Christian and Muslim alike). Women analyzed the wider process of attacking the family unit and family members as a way of undermining the stability of the social fabric. They traced an entire process that begins with dispersion of the family and destruction of the family home and continues with night raids, beatings, imprisonment, and shooting of family members, and pointed to the constant trauma and helplessness of not being able to safeguard loved ones. They constantly spoke of oppressive techniques aimed at disrupting or destroying the family, such as torture of family members (often with others present), and they focused on the sexual nature of the harassment and violation of the home. Zahira (Shalhoub-Kevorkian, 2003) stated: "How would a mother feel when soldiers invade her house while she is sleeping? . . . Every time they invaded my home, I felt totally naked . . . as if they raped me . . . they actually raped my home."

In our numerous discussions, the women and girls portrayed a ritualized military routine that sends a symbolic and practical message to all Palestinians: "there is no safe haven." Such a message was also sent during Sharon's forceful entrance into the Dome of the Rock–an act that triggered the onset of the second Intifada in late September 2000. Such a tactic attempted not only to subdue a rebellious population, but also to minimize the role of the Palestinian family to protect its members by the use of various means of dehumanization and oppression, including an incursion into such a sacred place–the Haram Al Sharif. (The violation of the religious space is also considered a corresponding violation of the familial, domestic space.) Whether such attacks have been aimed at religious places (spiritual homes), schools and universities (educational homes) or actual private one's (family homes), they all ultimately constrain the social/family unit and its members. Such attacks are aimed at reducing the individual body by materially reducing the confines of that body, consigning it to an ever more limited area, time, and space.

The young college women who shared their feelings about the effect of the ISW on their lives (Shalhoub-Kevorkian, in press) poignantly expressed their sense of loss and displacement. I asked them to take photographs of the Wall and write a caption underneath, telling me what they saw, thought, or felt when they looked at each photo. Some chose to take pictures of the ruins of a demolished house. For instance, Photo 1 shows a mass of rubble–demolished houses in front of a young woman's home, in preparation for further extension of the Wall. The photographer Himmat (pseudonym) said the Wall turned her house into a dark, dirty, imprisoning space. She wrote beneath the photo: "You defiled our environment, darkened our life. When will you get out of our war?"

Photo 2, in contrast, captures a scene of green fields and trees, of peace and serenity; the ISW is present peripherally, at the far end of the frame. This image expresses how the Wall's construction separates the land from its people. Referring to the verdant, but empty space, the photographer Shaden (pseudonym) wrote: "Even heaven is not a place to be in, if those individuals [we care for] are not there." She was quoting an

PHOTO 1

Arab proverb that is generally used to convey that we are social people and that we need each other's company.

In looking over the many images taken by these young women, I was struck by the absence of the photographers. It seemed as if the violation of space was strong enough to reveal the effect of the continuous uprooting on the women's sense of *shatat* and the *shatat* of their families. In almost every case, the images revolved around the spaces of their lives; whether ruined spaces that were nothing more than piles of rubble, or peaceful, verdant spaces where trees were growing and skies look serene, they are nevertheless landscapes that carry the effect of the political struggle. The emptiness is haunting. It is as if indeed no one does "live" here anymore, if we mean living a life with depth and breadth of emotion: joy, sorrow, family gatherings, laughter. In these photographs, the silence and screams tell a story of *shatat*.

Beyond sharing these photographs with me, the women also decided to hang them on the walls of their classrooms so that they could be seen daily, as if the photograph itself, however metaphorically, reclaimed the

PHOTO 2

space that had been taken from them. As Maha stated: "I need to enlarge the photo so as to never forget how my house looked before the ISW." Najwa said: "When I look at the photo, I go crazy, but then I promise myself to get good grades and find a job to help my family cope with the loss of our old home." The act of taking the photograph, of confronting it daily on the classroom wall, is also an act of healing and a reflection of agency.

Gendering and Sexualizing the Family's Sense of Security

Violation of the security of the family is usually sexualized and directed specifically at the women (see Al-Haq, 1988, pp. 40-41). This upsets not only family equilibrium, but also gender roles. Salma, who participated in one of my voice therapy meetings (Shalhoub-Kevorkian, 2005), shared the following story:

It was midnight, we were all asleep, and suddenly we heard someone at the door, a person who spoke Arabic very well, but seemed to us a Jew. They did not wait until we opened the door; they broke it down and came in like a storm. We were all in a state of shock. The soldiers asked for my 15-year-old son. When I asked, "Why? What did he do?" they said that he threw stones at a military jeep that morning. I explained to them that it is not true, that he was home all day because he had a cold, and that I took him to the doctor in the village. They did not care; they did not hear me at all. They pulled Muhammad out of bed . . . did not allow him to wear warm clothes, put the dirty bag over his head, tied his hands behind his head and pushed him into the jeep. It was so hard on me, the number of soldiers, the big dogs who looked like monsters in the middle of the night . . . and my son who did not say a word.

Then I saw one soldier who seemed to be listening, so I went to him, stood in front of the jeep, preventing them from leaving the neighborhood, and asked him to help me. I asked him, "Don't you have a mother?" And told him that I would do anything to help my son. Then he got out of the jeep and told me if I cleaned the street, he would leave my son with me and I could bring him to the police station the next day. I agreed, and for more than an hour I cleaned the street. When I told the soldier I was done, he looked at his friend and said something in Hebrew. I told him, "Don't say you're not going to release him. I beg you . . . I am not an animal . . . I am a mother with feelings." Then the other soldier told me that if our village would always look clean and we would be better and our kids wouldn't be terrorists, maybe we could be treated like human beings.

Despite Salma's plea, Mohammad was not released that night, and he remained imprisoned during the course of the group therapy. Her utilization of all her options to decrease the effect of such a traumatic attack and support her son backfired. She ended up being doubly humiliated, first in her own home space, then in the expanded home of her neighborhood, being degraded as a woman, a mother, and a member of the community.

The gender-oriented victimization and the sexist violations during a highly violent attack are well reflected in Umm Riad's words at the Jenin refugee camp:

> I did not know how to handle so much pain. Every hour we heard a new story, a new rumor.... It was terrible ... we were 36 people in one room that barely could hold 6 or 7 people. We were unable to breathe or move, unable to talk most of the time, unable to cry, unable to look outside ... all we heard was voices of the soldiers invading the house. They went into the house, broke all the furniture, the electric appliances, the doors, the windows, even my [eleven-year-old] son's schoolbooks were shot. Madness isn't it?
>
> Three weeks after she delivered her first baby, my daughter-in-law still had heavy bleeding because we never managed to take her to the hospital–the political situation prevented them from leaving the camp–and her health was in bad shape. She was with us in this small room, with three other women who started menstruating and four children with diapers. The room, the smell, was very bad. We were unable to open a window or a door, and going to the bathroom was a very risky task. The smell of the blood filled the room, and the old man [she refers to her husband] got very upset, and decided to ask all menstruating women and children who urinated on themselves or who had diapers to sit in the corner. On day eight I also started menstruating, and sat with the group of filthy women and children, the group that cried the most, cursed themselves the most. I personally knew that being a woman is a curse, but never imagined how much of a curse it is... (Shalhoub-Kevorkian, 2004, p. 74) (2004a).

Challenges to gender roles were apparent in the stories of women whose family members were imprisoned (Shalhoub-Kevorkian, 2005). Israeli military forces tend to detain men, which leaves many Palestinian women the sole heads of their households. In such a context, women with no previous experience were turned into the main breadwinners of their families. In many cases they needed to create a new home space following the demolishing of their old homes. Rana, whose husband was detained, shared the following:

> After my husband's arrest, everyone wanted to use me. I needed to find him a lawyer, but did not have the money, so I needed to ask for help from welfare and legal institutions. Being a woman made people believe that I am weaker without a husband.... I lost control over my own home, for the military forces prevented us from entering the house. I lost my support, for my husband was de-

tained, and his family never liked me anyway. I come from a good family, but we became very poor due to the economic hardships.... So, I needed to only count on myself, and God's support... that turned me from a housewife into an active woman. I found two rooms in the camp near my family, rented them and turned them into our new home. I became a teacher and even a lawyer. I think I knew the laws more than our own lawyer.

The feminization and genderization of the individual's and family's sense of security was more salient among Jerusalemite Palestinians who carry Israeli identity cards than those who hold Palestinian IDs. Those who are considered Jerusalem residents have blue cards, while the rest carry orange ones indicating they are ex-political activists/prisoners or the green ones issued to residents of the West Bank and Gaza Strip. (Note that many women and men who were originally Jerusalemites were not assigned blue IDs for a number of political reasons. In fact, siblings born in the same house may have different colored ID cards.) Carriers of blue IDs are served by the Israeli health, social security, and other state systems, while the rest are denied such medical, educational, legal, and social services. In addition, carriers of blue IDs are allowed to be physically present in Jerusalem; the rest need to obtain a special permit that is controlled by the Israeli military system and sanctioned by it. Thus, carrying different colored IDs means facing different restrictions of movements and having differential access to needed services. Families are divided between those members considered Jerusalemites and those considered West Bankers. The importance of Jerusalem for Palestinians, added to the Israeli state benefits given to Jerusalemite Palestinians, has created a new social, economic and political status and generated additional tension between members of the same family and community.

This tension is exacerbated when the beneficiaries of such a status are women. This Jerusalemite status changed and challenged certain gender roles, as is related by Nawal, the 26-year-old sister of a political prisoner (Shalhoub-Kevorkian, 2005):

The fact that I was the only one who carried the Jerusalem blue ID allowed me to work, turned my salary into the main source of income, allowed me to be more mobile than my own father (for the mobility of men has been extremely restricted) and brother (he was born a year before me, and his ID is orange).

Nawal and her sister explained that having to deal with Israeli state and non-state agencies, with national and international NGOs, has expanded their (and other women's) gender roles, functions, and spaces. Other women related how such additional demands have mobilized them and expanded their membership in the public/political space, making them more visible, but also more sexually and socially vulnerable.

The young women in my focus groups (Shalhoub-Kevorkian, in press) were more direct in stressing their sense of frustration, their ability (or lack of it) to expand their gender spaces. Twenty-year-old Byan, who got engaged seven months before our first meeting, said: "I am not sure where my home is anymore. Jerusalem is my home, the village is my home, and now I need to move to Hebron to live with my fiancée's family and turn it into my home. . . . I really do not know where my home is . . . . I feel like the nomadic Bedouin." Her identity was unclear and occluded, as she was uprooted and could not return to her family home in Jerusalem. Although she was born in Jerusalem, she did not legally belong where she was, due to the constant state of forced migration and imposed restrictions on her mobility. Accepting an early marriage proposal "helped" her, as she said: "to find some peace and safety, but . . . *min il illeh* (this was for lack of other options)." The search for a home with clear borders and a legal status of safety and security was also expressed in the other focus group participants' discussions. The girls were constantly in search of a space that could be clearly mapped, wherein a visible social and legal order was apparent. The lack of a definable space to call home meant death to some; as one stated: "We are locked in a prison . . . as my friend said collective graves . . . ."

Creating a Counter-Space and a Counter-Memory

In response to the physical and symbolic attacks on their families, demolishing homes and turning safe havens into potentially abusable spaces, Palestinian women spoke back with counter-discourses that created counter-spaces and safer spaces. Following Israeli incursions in April, 2003, which destroyed most of the Jenin refugee camp, the sight of women recreating a home from the rubble was not uncommon (Shalhoub-Kevorkian, 2004). Women I met with were reorganizing their homes and inventing sleeping places for their children and neighbors, cleaning up the litter of utter destruction. I found one woman hanging a long bed cover, turning a half-demolished room into a home, transforming the bed cover into the missing fourth wall of the room. I witnessed Suhaila making a basinette for her newborn daughter out of two plastic basins that had been cut in half, which she cushioned with some material and softened with handmade covers. She used the higher ends of the tubs to hang a piece of cloth that would protect the baby from flies and mosquitoes. I vividly remember seeing Nahil sitting on the remains of her balcony, looking at the scene of the destruction of the camp, while she held two pots in her lap and prepared dinner for the family. The fact that their homes were attacked by air-to-surface missiles and bombs and were demolished, cut in half, or partially destroyed, did not stop these women from immediately recreating what they could from the rubble to house their families and begin again.

Nadia, a young mother whose child had been shot by the Israeli military, was also striving to build a new home out of her suffering: "The problem is that our pain started with the loss of my child, but it never stopped afterward. We were harassed by daily night raids, imprisonment of my two brothers, and the demolition of the house. . . . I feel sometimes that they want to burn our hearts" (Shalhoub-Kevorkian, 2003, p. 400). Yet, Nadia's story does not end with such loss:

> After we moved on, to living with my family, I needed to be stronger, and to take more responsibility. I needed to find a job, work, and have some income. At first it was very hard . . . but then I started filling my time and handling my loss with my work. It was the idea of Nora, my sister-in-law. So, I first learned how to sew pants for a local factory. Now I am able to provide for my family without even leaving the house. It is hard to do such work, mainly because it messes up my family's house. I really hope that if I keep on working . . . I will be able to rent my own home, or even build a new house for my children. I am working very hard to rebuild my home. . . .

Israeli attacks on Palestinian homes have transformed the resistance strategies of Nadia and other women into counter-discourses to the hegemonic one. The creation of such counter-discourses opens up new venues and activates potential resources, turning women's acts of resistance, as Areen from the Jenin refugee camp stated, "from *niddal' a'adi* [normal acts of struggle] to daily acts of *muqawameh* [resistance], where everybody in the family, young and old, man and woman, participate." Women decorate their homes, or what is left of them, with remaining pieces of furniture, pictures, pots and pans, and shards and fragments from the lost home, or by adding new tokens of remembrance to the new space, such as pride in the fact that family members have managed to earn a university degree or high-school diploma despite all obstacles in their way. Thus, the determination of the military to destroy the safe haven is addressed by a counter-determination that stresses not only the importance of the home (be it the actual family home, the land that surrounds it, or the close neighborhood's "homeland"), but also the importance of recreating the home, creating a counter-space.

This was clearly reflected in young women's discussions of their photographs of the ISW. These women voiced not only their pain, but also their ability to create new venues when the old ones were blocked. Samah told the group that she discovered a new way to help her and her young brother evade facing the soldiers at the checkpoints, but she also revealed the sorrow she holds when looking at the temporary dividers that will soon be turned into a permanent part of the Wall. Her image (Photo 3, below) directly relates to her own home space, and the way the

PHOTO 3

ISW violates that sanctuary. In her caption, she wrote: "If they demolish my home ... I fear not. If they block my path, I won't crawl." Samah's counter-discourse, and particularly her words "I fear not" and " I won't crawl," were mixed with the sadness she expressed at the group meeting: "Every time I see [the ISW], I feel so *majroha* [hurt]."

Photo 4 (as seen below), taken by Rula, similarly shows how the ISW violates her home. The Wall, itself surrounded by rubble, surrounds her house halfway, and its shadow falls ominously on the home. Rula provided the caption in English and not Arabic: "To be continued." When I asked why she wrote this in English, she replied: "You plan to show the photos to people in the West, and write about it in English, and I want to say to everybody that no matter how much they keep on oppressing us, we will continue with our resistance."

The need to protect and preserve the home have turned some homes into political and ritualized spaces that are markers of something greater than an individual loss–into sites of a collective loss and symbols of resistance and political struggle. As Umm Riad stated:

PHOTO 4

> I wake up each day, and before I go to pray, I open the door between my bedroom and my son's room [the son that she lost], I look at the floor. . . he was the one who put the nice titles on the floor. He is the one that made us all feel that this is the family home, he turned the house into a beautiful, elegant house [*raqi*], in the middle of all the messed up houses in the Old City of Jerusalem. So . . . I go down, kiss the floor, and put my cheeks on the floor to feel his hands, I feel his hands. . . . I even see them sometimes. If you only knew how much I miss him. (Shalhoub-Kevorkian, 2003, p. 400)

Umm Riad's words contain not only her daily grief over the loss of her son, but also her counter-discourse that innovates ways to talk back and oppose injustice. Her need to remember her loss is juxtaposed with her need to utilize such loss to gain power and refuse, as she puts it, to "become weak."

The women related how constant fear and insecurity made them believe their children were never safe, at home or outside it, but this did not prevent them from creating, metaphorically, a sense of home when home did not exist or when its existence was laden with insecurity, political violence, and violations. Counter-spaces were constructed in many unexpected locations. For instance, Hunaida, whose daughter was a political prisoner, told of how she turned the prison visit and the prison field into a safe haven for her other children as they sat in the waiting room:

> I brought food from home; I got them some crayons to draw for their sister and write to her. After all, the land of this prison belonged to Palestinians from Ramleh. My family originally, before the Nakba, lived and had many many houses and owned a large parcel of land in Ramleh. I told them that every time we come to visit her, we bring the lemon from our tree, and we bring her food, we write her, and make sure to show her that we are happy. I told them that the soldiers are holding guns because they fear us, because it is our land and home. If we act in the visitation place as if we are home, they will surrender, and then allow us to see her. It is, after all, our home, our land, isn't it?

Another innovative instance of created counter-space can be found in Iqbal's narrative, as she tells of the night her home was demolished with only 30 minutes' warning:

> They came, with their big bulldozers, cars, police forces... many soldiers with their weapons directed at my children... and the noise... their voices, their Hebrew language which no one understood, made me feel like I was in a whirlpool [*dawameh*]. I was running like crazy, between calming down the kids, fearing they would be shot, collecting our papers, documents, birth certificates... collecting the gold the children got as presents from their grandparents.... I was trying to gather everything in such a hurry... and when they said that they are about to demolish the house, Salim, my four-year-old son [at the time he was under the age of two] was not around. I thought he was inside the house and started screaming... screaming without being able to stop. But he was right beside me, holding my *deshdasheh* [long, wide housedress].... When they started demolishing the house, I hugged him with his sisters... wrapped them all in my *deshdasheh* and we all cried. To this day, the girls still remember how the whole family stood, wrapped in my dirty home *deshdasheh*, crying like we have never cried before, cried and cried while our hearts were on fire.

The immediacy and urgency of Islah's words, agonizing long after the actual event, bring us to the heart of the matter: the material destruction that a demolition invokes, as well as the enduring trauma and emotional duress. Nonetheless, there is courage, both actual and symbolic, to be found in the way she repeatedly describes wrapping the children in her *deshdasheh*–a home of sorts surely, the children gathered and held close to their mother's body, indeed protected by that body.

Despite the strength these women convey, mainly through the power of turning an enemy space into one's own safe space, the choices of such women, living in such contexts, are very few. Turning a half-destroyed balcony, a prison visitation room, or the yard of a demolished home into a safe space is but an instance of the power of the oppressed. It is in this context of mass homelessness and displacement that many Palestinian women are attempting to recreate home spaces for their families that are not only physical, but also psychological and social.

It is as if these women are turning their spaces into large wombs that nourish, protect, and contain their children, creating a counter-discourse. Women like Suhaila, who turned broken plastic basins into a basinette for her infant daughter; like Nahil, who sat on the remains of her balcony, cooking for her family and watching over the neighborhood; and like Islah, wrapping up her children in a dirty *deshdasheh*, are trying, consciously or unconsciously, to declare that the actual demolished house will not stop them from creating a sense of home. Thus, the continuous traumas facing women and their loved ones emerge as a primary site locating the injustices endured, and hence a site of resistance to restore the love, connectedness, and unity of the community. Women's efforts are energized towards restoring the loss of home by whatever means is at hand. These counter-spaces are mosaics of the past, of things and acts and rituals remembered, but they are also places of refuge that secure a future. Within the realities of an ongoing present, these new spaces of the old and new recenter their dislocated world and create another "home," one that effectively preserves what the bulldozers have seemingly destroyed.

DISCUSSION

There is a paucity of research examining women's roles, contributions, and voices in war zones and conflict areas (Cooke & Woolacott, 1993; Lentin, 1997; Turshen & Twagiramariya, 1998). Despite studies of women in war from a psychological perspective (Butalia, 2002) or in terms of the effect of militarization on women (Enloe, 1983, 2000; Goldstein, 2001), little is written on women's own ways of dealing with such contexts (Peteet, 1991; Sayigh, 1998). Through the narratives and photographs of Palestinian women and girls, this paper has focused on the role of women in families during political conflicts and shown their gender roles, political resistance actions, and social and economic functioning in times of war. In listening to their voices, one recognizes the significance of gender issues and a pervasive sense of otherness for each woman's own acts of agency. Confronted by racism and oppression, these women create new spaces of belonging that are remarkably not solely about individual restoration, but also about healing the community.

McClaim (1995) has explained how women occupy different symbolic and actual worlds of intervention and healing and how women's lives are less understood than men's due to their structural subordination. Thus, anthropologies of gender have attempted to explain how women sometimes share men's conceptualizations through willing participation in men's worlds (Strathern, 1981), while others describe societies wherein the women's worlds depart from those of men (Collier, 1974). Women heal, intervene, create, and project images of themselves to support or to gain economic, political, or social power (Browner & Lewin, 1982).

As the narratives have revealed, the women are aware of the militarized colonial project that aims at turning Palestinian spaces into unsafe, dangerous places. The minimization of those othered, as Said (1997) has shown, has reduced the Palestinians to a nonexistent population, stripped down to the status of a coolie or laborer class. Unlike nineteenth-century European colonial projects designed to "civilize" and transform "natives" into a regime of the same via assimilationist policies, the Israeli project has been aimed at creating a Jewish "homeland," subordinating and negating the Palestinian Other–their language, culture, and legacy (Said, 1997). Through their stories, the women have revealed their understanding of how such policies are deeply embedded in complicated systems of political oppression and military occupation.

I would like to build upon Santos' (2002) analytical framework to consider whether the destruction of the Palestinian home, in the name of Israeli security, is a hegemonically approved form of fascism. The policies deployed for security reasoning, though insisting on rational thinking, are in fact dependent on the irrationality of the creation of fear. Women were manipulated to fear a threat that does not always exist–just like the facade of fear and weapons of mass destruction was raised by Israeli state officials and other Western supporters before the invasion of Iraq. This manipulation of people's sense of security, in the context of actual and threatened demolitions of homes, night raids, imprisonments, construction of the ISW, and the like, has led to further material oppression and displacement of occupied Palestinians, causing chronic anxiety and uncertainty. This paper has focused on what happens to women within such a patriarchal militarized context, particularly when displacement specifically affects the family body and the domestic sphere, both generally considered the province of women (Khamis, 1998). Despite the sense of fear, uncertainty, and injustice, we can see that women are able to act in unconventional ways, transforming their gender roles into new, more expressive and active ones (see also Khamis, 1995). By engaging in united acts to resist oppression, they turn into creators of power, hope, and social-familial energies of mutual support.

Some forms of feminism see political efficacy only in affirming the strength of the individual woman. It is my belief, however, that the women's ways of challenging various systems of domination in the name of security reasoning strengthen their commitment against injustice. They refuse to let the West culturalize their acts as merely the nurturing instincts of the less civilized, less liberated Arab woman. Nurturers they are, and I do not think any of them would wish to refuse the label, but if feminism accepts that the personal is political, then why can't acts of nurturing, particularly collective nurturing in the face of disaster, also be political acts?

I have hoped to show how women's own ways of resisting have evolved out of their constant trials, through destruction both social and psychological. Contrary to what the world may think, Palestinian women are engaged in understanding the implications and effects of the racist policies and political violence they are subjected to, and this understanding is characterized by a multiplicity of voices and modes of coping. Women not only maintain a sense of agency in the midst of hopelessness, a sense of family unity and protectedness, but also, through their acts of coping, they challenge the doctrine of "no safe haven." Under Islah's dirty houseclothes was a safe haven for her children, even if she did not explicitly view it as such. Rula's preparation of the family meal on a broken balcony, caring for her loved ones in the midst of destruction, can similarly be seen as a counter-haven. By utilizing very limited resources, they managed to defy Israeli policy, continuing to search for new ways of coping with the extreme sense of loss, fear, and sadness. In the absence of resources and globalized support, Palestinian women shared with us new epistemologies that created an atmosphere of re-gathering of the displaced by offering various healing circles in the family. The death of Nadia's son motivated her to search for a job to compensate her own loss and that of her family. In this way, boundaries and borders in politically conflicted areas were challenged, when the private become public.

Women were found to construct new counter-discourses and counter-spaces to cope with the constant and unpredictable changes affecting the family. These narratives can be roughly divided into the following:

a. *Traditional continuity narrative.* Here women included religious beliefs and traditional practices. This is apparent in the story of Hafiza, when camp members provided her with a small room, as a home, to help her cope with the demolition, as well

as in the cases of Shaden and Firyal, who showed how family support and ties helped them cope with feelings of *shatat* following the added restrictions imposed by the construction of the ISW.
b. *Historical-national legacy narrative.* By invoking the historical and political legacy of displacement and loss, women-oriented counter-discourses managed to turn loss into a source of power and encouragement. Women such as Umm Riad, Nora, and Hafiza used the nation's history to lift the morale of family members and inspired them to maintain their daily activities–to go to school, find a job, cope with imprisonment or loss, or move to a new location to better manage additional restrictions.
c. *Transformative narrative and the creating of counter-spaces.* Through their actions, reactions, and proactive actions, women offered innovative and transformative modes that created counter-spaces to address the policy of "no safe haven." The examples shared in this article, and the countless others that were not mentioned, showed how women turned bedcovers into walls, *deshdasheh* housedresses into safe havens, and plastic basins into a soft bed for a newborn.

Whereas literature on women in war zones generally attempts to reveal women's victimization in contexts of conflict, particularly in their private sphere, this paper has shown the confluence of the private family sphere and the larger political and politicized space beyond. Women's ways of resistance and coping reveal their ways of surviving and their modes of preserving their families and communities. Women's ways of investing in the recreation of the home, empowering the victimized and protecting society from desperation, call for a new feminist perspective into victimization and agency itself.

Women's ways of fighting back were not based on physical confrontation, but rather on using their own powers to protect their families. Such a study calls upon us to look closer at the way women negotiate what they can do, examine their own ways of resistance and support, and explore their own methods of survival. One clear conclusion is that women's ways of healing, helping, and resisting are not based on hegemonic logic, but rather are multiple and complex. One cannot understand the internal dynamics of women's acts, agency, and resistance in war zones without attending to meaning from women themselves, and without contextualizing one's analyses. Having privileged the voices of the women, let me conclude with Halimeh's words:

When they invade the camp, they ruin everything, they destroy windows, doors, roads, furniture, they even defecate and pee in our beds, on our clothing. When they see us, the whole camp community, helping each other, restoring the place and the damage, they go crazy. When they invaded my house, and ruined it all . . . and then saw me, my husband, and my mother-in-law holding the children around us, while breastfeeding the youngest, they became angry. . . and very upset. They hate seeing us loving each other. I am not an educated woman like you [she was talking to me], but I know one thing–if we keep on having hope that one day we will have a *wattan* [homeland], if we keep supporting and being an *izweh* [social connection and support] for each other, and if we rebuild everything they destroy, and love each other (and I am afraid we have started losing it lately), they will keep fearing us. See, our support and love for each other is very dangerous.

REFERENCES

Alexander, M. J., & Talpade Mohanty, C. T. (Eds.). (1997). *Feminist genealogies, colonial legacies, democratic futures.* New York: Routledge.

Al-Haj, M., & Ben-Eliezer, U. (2003). In the name of security: The sociology of peace and war in Israel in changing times. Jerusalem: Keter. (In Hebrew)

Al-Haq, Law in the Service of Man (2004). Four years since the beginning of the Intifada: Violations of human rights in the occupied Palestinian territories. September; retrieved June 28, 2005, from: http://asp.alhaq.org/zalhaq/site/books/files/intifada04_report.pdf.

Abu-Lughod, L. (1990). Can there be a feminist ethnography? *Women and Performance, 5*(I), 7-27.

Bartal, D., Jacobson, D., & Klieman, A. (Eds.) (1998). *Security concerns: Insights from the Israeli experience.* Stanford, CT: JAI Press.

Beck, U. (1999). *World risk society.* Malden, MA: Blackwell.

Behar, R. (1993). *Translated woman: Crossing the border with Esperanza's story.* Boston: Beacon.

Berger Gould, B. (2001). Rituals as resistance: Tibetan women and nonviolence. In M. R. Waller & J. Rycenga (Eds.), *Frontline feminisms: Women, war, and resistance* (pp. 213-234). New York: Routledge.

Browner, H., & Lewin, E. (1982). Female altruism reconsidered: The Virgin Mary as economic woman. *American Anthropologist, 9,* 61-75.

B'Tselem, The Israeli Information Center for Human Rights in the Occupied Territories (2005a). Punitive demolitions of Palestinian homes. Retrieved June 29, 2005, from: http://www.btselem.org/English/Punitive_Demolitions/Statistics.asp.

B'Tselem, The Israeli Information Center for Human Rights in the Occupied Territories (2005b). Demolitions of Palestinian homes for lack of permit. Retrieved June

29, 2005, from: http://www.btselem.org/English/Planning_and_Building/Statistics. asp.

B'Tselem, The Israeli Information Center for Human Rights in the Occupied Territories (2005c). Demolitions of Palestinian homes for military necessity. Retrieved June 29, 2005, from: http://www.btselem.org/English/Razing/Statistics.asp.

B'Tselem, The Israeli Information Center for Human Rights in the Occupied Territories. (2005d). Land expropriation in the West Bank. Retrieved June 29, 2005, from: http://www.btselem.org/English/Jerusalem/Land_Expropriation_Statistics.asp.

B'Tselem, The Israeli Information Center for Human Rights in the Occupied Territories. (2005e). Separation barrier statistics. Retrieved June 29, 2005, from: http://www.btselem.org/english/Separation_Barrier/Statistics.asp.

B'Tselem, The Israeli Information Center for Human Rights in the Occupied Territories (2005f). Palestinian minors in IDF detention. Retrieved June 29, 2005, from: http://www.btselem.org/English/Statistics/Minors_in_IDF_Detention.asp.

Butalia, U. (Ed.) (2002). *Women speaking peace: Voices from Kashmir*. London: Zed Books.

Collier, J. F. (1974). Women in politics. In M. Z. Rosaldo & L. Lamphere (Eds.), *Women, culture, and society*. Stanford: Stanford University Press.

Collins, P. H. (1986). Learning from the outsider within: The sociological significance of Black feminist thought. *Social Problems, 33*, 14-32.

Collins, P. H. (1990). Defining Black Feminist Thought. In P. H. Collins, *Black feminist thought: Knowledge, consciousness, and the politics of empowerment* (pp. 19-40). New York: Routledge.

Cooke, M., & Woolacott, A. (Eds.). (1993). *Gendering war talk*. Princeton, NJ: Princeton University Press.

Elfstrom, B., & Malmgren, A. (2005). Palestinian children behind bars. Report from the International Commission of Jurists, Swedish section, December 12-20, 2004, submitted March 31, 2005. Retrieved June 28, 2005, from: http://www.dci-pal.org/english/doc/ reports/2005/apr03.pdf.

Enloe, C. (1983). *Does khaki become you? The militarization of women's lives*. London: Pandora Press.

Enloe, C. (2000). *Maneuvers: The international politics of militarizing women's lives*. Berkeley: University of California Press.

Farsoun, S. K., & Zacharia, C. E. (1997). *Palestine and the Palestinians*. Boulder, CO: Westview Press.

Goldstein, J. (2001). *War and gender*. Cambridge: Cambridge University Press.

Hammami, R., & Johnson, P. (1999). Equality with a difference: Gender and citizenship in transitional Palestine. *Social Politics: International Studies in Gender, State & Society, 6*(3), 314-343.

Herzog, H. (2003). The warrior family: The effect of the Arab-Israeli conflict on women's status in Israel. In M. Al-Haj & U. Ben-Eliezer (Eds.), *In the name of security: The sociology of peace and war in Israel in changing times*. Jerusalem: Keter. (Hebrew)

Herzog, H., & Shamir, R. (1994). Negotiated society? Media discourse on Israeli Jewish/Arab relations. *Israel Social Science Research, 9*, 55-88.

Johnson, P., & Kuttab, E. (2001). Where have all the women (and men) gone? Reflection on gender. *Second Intifada feminist review, 69*(Winter), 21-43.
Khalidi, R. (1997). *Palestinian identity: The construction of modern national consciousness.* New York: Columbia University Press.
Khalidi, R. (Ed.). (1992). *All that remains: The Palestinian villages occupied and depopulated by Israel in 1948.* Washington, DC: Institute for Palestine Studies.
Khamis, V. (1998). Psychological distress and well-being among traumatized Palestinian women durng the Intifada. *Social Science and Medicine, 46*(8), 1033-1041.
Khamis, V. (1995). *Coping with stress: Palestinian families and intifada-related trauma.* Bethlehem: Bethlehem University.
Kimmerling, B. (1992). Sociology, ideology and nation-building: The Palestinians and their meaning in Israeli sociology. *American Sociological Review, 57*, 446-460.
Lentin, R. (Ed.) (1997). *Gender and catastrophe.* London: Zed Books.
Lorde, A. (1983). The master's tools will never dismantle the master's house. In C. Moraga & G. Anzaldua (Eds.), *This bridge called my back: Writings by radical women of color* (pp. 94-101). New York: Kitchen Table Press.
Mar'I, M., & Pujara, M. (1988). In light of the Israeli draft law on denying compensation to Palestinians: Accountability of the Israeli occupier for violations of Palestinian rights. Ramallah, West Bank: Al-Haq. (English translation published in 1998)
McClaim, C. (Ed.) (1995). *Women as healers: Cross-cultural perspectives.* New Brunswick: Rutgers University Press.
Morris, B. (1987). *The birth of the Palestinian refugee problem, 1947-1949.* Cambridge: Cambridge University Press.
The Palestinian Environmental NGOs Network (PENGON) (2003). *The wall in Palestine: Facts, testimonies, analysis and call to action.* Jerusalem: Author.
Peteet, J. M. (1991). *Gender in crisis: Women and the Palestinian resistance movement.* New York: Columbia University Press.
Peteet, J. M. (1997). Zionism from the standpoint of its victims. In A. McClintock, A. Mufti, & E. Shohat (Eds.), *Dangerous liaisons: Gender, nation and postcolonial perspectives.* Minneapolis: University of Minnesota Press.
Said, E. (1997). Bombs and bulldozers. *Nation, 265*(7), 4-5.
Samooha, S. (1989). *Arabs and Jews in Israel: Conflicting and shared attitudes in a divided society.* Boulder, CO: Westview Press.
Santos, B. (2002). *Toward a new legal common sense.* United Kingdom: Butterworths-LexisNexis.
Sayigh, R. (1998). Gender, sexuality, and class in national narrations: Palestinian camp women tell their lives. *Frontiers, 19*(2), 166-185.
Scott, J. (2002). *Domination and the arts of resistance: Hidden transcripts.* New Haven, CT: Yale University Press.
Shalhoub-Kevorkian, N. (1994). Fear of sexual harassment: Palestinian adolescent girls in the Intifada. In E. Augustin (Ed.), *Palestinian women: Identity and experience.* London: Zed Books.
Shalhoub-Kevorkian, N. (1998). Crime of war, culture and children's rights: The case study of female Palestinian detainees under Israeli military occupation. In G. Douglas & L. Sebba (Eds.), *Children's rights and traditional values* (pp. 228-248). Hanover, NH: Dartmouth Press.

Shalhoub-Kevorkian, N. (2003). Liberating voices: The political implications of Palestinian mothers narrating their loss. *Women's Studies International Forum, 26*(5), 391-407.

Shalhoub-Kevorkian, N. (2004). The hidden casualties of war: Palestinian women and the second Intifada. *Indigenous Peoples' Journal of Law, Culture & Resistance, 1*(1), 67-82.

Shalhoub-Kevorkian, N. (2005). Voice therapy for women aligned with political prisoners: A case study of trauma among Palestinian women in the second Intifada. *Social Service Review, 79*(2), 322-343.

Shalhoub-Kevorkian, N. (in press). *Palestinian children facing the wall*. Research report submitted to the World Vision, Jerusalem.

Shalhoub-Kevorkian, N., & Abdo, N. (in press). *Women and political conflict: The case of Palestinian women in Jerusalem*. Research report submitted to the Women Studies Center, Jerusalem.

Strathern, M. (1981). Self-interest and the social good: Some implications of Hagen gender imagery. In S. B. Ortner & H. Whitehead (Eds.), *Sexual meanings: The cultural construction of gender and sexuality*. Cambridge: Cambridge University Press.

Talpade Mohanty, C. (2003). *Feminism without borders: Decolonizing theory, practicing solidarity*. Durham, NC: Duke University Press.

Thornhill, T. (1992). *Making women talk: The interrogation of Palestinian women security detainees by the Israeli general security services*. London: Lawyers for Palestinian Human Rights.

Trinh, M. (1989). *Women native other: Writing postcoloniality and feminism*. Bloomington, IN: Indiana University Press.

Tuhiwai Smith, L. (1999). *Decolonizing methodologies: Research and indigenous peoples*. London: Zed Books Ltd.

Turshen, M., & Twagiramariya, C. (Eds.) (1998). *What women do in wartime: Gender and conflict in Africa*. London: Zed Books.

Puerto Rican and Dominican Women's Perceptions of Divorced Women

Joyce A. Arditti
Nancy P. López

SUMMARY. The purpose of this study was to explore Puerto Rican and Dominican women's perceptions of divorce with particular emphasis on divorced women's image and experience in these countries. An on-line survey was administered in Spanish to a population of 95 Puerto Rican and Dominican women. Most survey questions were open-ended and some demographic information was gathered. Results of a qualitative content analysis revealed a range of perceptions, cultural beliefs, and social stigma about divorce. Specifically, divorced women were perceived as either being successful and independent, or as failures and social outcasts. Women who were divorced were more likely to hold positive attitudes about divorce as were women from Puerto Rico. Implications for clinical practice are discussed. *[Article copies available for a fee from The Haworth Document Delivery Service: 1-800-HAWORTH. E-mail address: <docdelivery@haworthpress.com> Website: <http://www.HaworthPress.com> © 2005 by The Haworth Press, Inc. All rights reserved.]*

Address correspondence to: Joyce A. Arditti, PhD, Department of Human Development, 311 Wallace Hall, Virginia Polytechnic Institute and State University, Blacksburg, VA 24061 (E-mail:arditti@vt.edu).

[Haworth co-indexing entry note]: "Puerto Rican and Dominican Women's Perceptions of Divorced Women." Arditti, Joyce A., and Nancy P. López. Co-published simultaneously in *Journal of Feminist Family Therapy* (The Haworth Press, Inc.) Vol. 17, No. 3/4, 2005, pp. 143-173; and: *The Politics of the Personal in Feminist Family Therapy: International Examinations of Family Policy* (ed: Anne M. Prouty Lyness) The Haworth Press, Inc., 2005, pp. 143-173. Single or multiple copies of this article are available for a fee from The Haworth Document Delivery Service [1-800-HAWORTH, 9:00 a.m. - 5:00 p.m. (EST). E-mail address: docdelivery@haworthpress.com].

© 2005 by The Haworth Press, Inc. All rights reserved.
doi:10.1300/J086v17n03_08

KEYWORDS. Family research, survey, divorce, women's perceptions of divorce, qualitative research, Puerto Rican women, feminist family therapy

INTRODUCTION

"¿Yo? ¿Convertirme en una divorciada más? ¡Jamás!"
Me? Become another divorced woman? Never!

–Popular saying among Dominican women

Divorce can be a life-changing situation for women, bringing about a host of social, psychological and economic changes. Most studies of divorce have concentrated on the divorce experience of Caucasian Americans without fully considering how culture might influence the divorce experience of women (Chang, 2003). It is important to recognize that divorce does not occur in a vacuum, but that the experience is embedded in a cultural context that will influence one's understanding of the phenomena. Latin America is a unique multicultural area composed of elements inherited from Europe, the Caribbean, Asia, and Africa. Thus Latin America, broadly defined, because of the pattern of colonization and Spanish heritage, shares similar bases for cultural ideologies involving marriage, separation, and divorce despite its wide geographical spread. Historically, these ideologies have emphasized male dominance and traditional, subordinate childrearing roles for women (Stain & Stain, 1970). Traditional Catholicism has served to reinforce this type of familism whereby women have had little overt power relative to their husbands and religious institutions (Darlington & Mulvaney, 2003; Stroup & Pollock, 1999).

LEGAL AND SOCIOCULTURAL BACKGROUND

Following independence from Spain, divorce was introduced differently in each Latin American country and therefore has had a variety of evolutions. Despite whatever diversity exists within Latin America, divorce tends to be more heavily stigmatized than it is in Western Europe, Scandinavia, Canada, and the United States for several reasons. Divorce in Latin America typically has a negative connotation, and communities have considered divorced women as social outcasts (Muñoz

Vázquez & Fernández Bauzó, 1998). Attitudes about women's social location and the importance of marriage are bound to contribute to how one perceives divorce in general, as well as how one may navigate the experience. For example, there is some evidence to suggest that women in traditional cultures have a more difficult time adapting to divorce than do women in progressive cultures where divorce is considered more normative (Song, 1991).

It is worth noting that attitudes about divorce in Latin America, and specific to Puerto Rico and the Domican Republic, are tied in part to divorce's legal context and patriarchic origins (Rawson, 1991). After the Roman period (during which divorce was largely used as a means to circulate women and wealth among the male artistocracy), divorce passed through a series of conditions, procedures and legislation due to the Christian imposition of restrictions, the consequences of the Reformation, and the French Revolution. Divorce laws transformed from liberal to restrictive and were implanted in much of Europe by French armies during the Revolution and Empire. In 1816, divorce was described by the French legislature as "harmful to society, to religion, to women and to children," according to Roman Catholic principles (Rawson, 1991, p. 77).

Two main legal systems, the Civil Law system and the Common Law system, characterize societies and divorce has been conceived and regulated within these systems. Societies throughout the world have created and maintained their own divorce regulations to fulfill different goals. Specifically, the majority of Latin America is regulated by the Civil Law system, which is characterized by the use of Code, while the Common Law system (used in the U.S.) is characterized by the use of sentences or court decisions (jurisprudence) to set precedence. Puerto Rico's history has put it in the unique position of having a mixture of these legal systems due largely to its relationship with the United States. Therefore, Puerto Rican society has had a different and more westernized adaptation with regard to the process of divorce (Rivera Ramos, 2000). Because the judicial principles of the Common Law system are less abstract than those of the Civil Law system, the former regulates existing issues and solves conflicts in a more practical and timely way. In contrast, the Civil Law system is more abstract and subject to legislators' rule which provides the base of regulations and norms of conduct through legal Codes (as opposed to jurisprudence). Thus changes in these codes have to be made through the creation of new laws or executive ordinances, which take a very long time to process (Terrero Peña, 1984). Subsequently, in the Dominican Republic, a Civil Law society, the process of regulating newly arising issues as they pertain to divorce is expected to be slower and less responsive to the needs of women who undergo such a process.

PURPOSE AND RESEARCH QUESTIONS

The purpose of this study was to examine Puerto Rican and Dominican Republican women's perceptions of divorce with particular emphasis on divorced women's images and experiences. Although both countries are located in the Caribbean, we at times refer to them as "Latin America" for the purposes of this study and in recognition of their common Spanish heritage. Due to subsequent historical events and to the stronger political, economic, and cultural presence of the United States in Puerto Rico, we recognize that many issues now separate the two countries. For example, Puerto Rico's economic and legal systems have largely been Americanized (Rivera Ramos, 2000). Given the westernization of Puerto Rico, it is likely that gender roles are less rigid and traditional than in other less "Americanized" parts of Latin America. Indeed, Darlington and Mulvaney (2003) note that contrary to stereotypes, Puerto Rican women are "not completely subordinate to their husbands" (p. 118). Differences in the degree of westernization between Puerto Rico and the Dominican Republic were not directly assessed in this study; however, inclusion of women from both countries provides an interesting context for exploration, particularly as it related to women's perception of divorce.

The following questions created a framework for this research and identified the phenomenon under study (Strauss & Corbin, 1990). Two basic research questions guided this study:

1. What are Dominican and Puerto Rican women's perceptions of divorced women?
2. How do Dominican and Puerto Rican divorced women perceive themselves?

The qualitative approach utilized in this study was similar to a process described by Miller and Crabtree (1999, 2005) comprised of an exploring or *gathering* process (whereby data is collected), an understanding or *analysis* process (whereby data is described and organized), and an interpretive process, informed by research reflexivity and reflection, whereby *common ground* is sought in terms of possible explanations related to the phenomena in question.

CONCEPTUAL FRAMEWORK

While many theoretical traditions hold promise in terms of informing this study on divorce and Latin American women, feminism and ecological conceptualizations of divorce can be applied to the growing number of women affected by marital dissolution in Puerto Rico and the Dominican Republic. A fundamental goal of feminist theory is to analyze how gender relations are constructed and experienced (Flax, 1987). Feminist epistemology seeks to expose disadvantage and oppression, and to make visible the voices of women (Few, Stephens, & Rouse-Arnett, 2003). It is appropriately applied to Latin American women in terms of their experiences and perceptions of divorce, as sexism permeates virtually all of Latin American society (Browner, 1989).

Thus, a feminist consciousness highlights the limitations of cultural attitudes such as *marianismo, hembrismo* and *machismo*. The dialectics of machismo (the cult of virility) and marianismo (the cult of feminine spiritual superiority) helped to shape the idea that females and males, because of their respective particular natures, should have different status and roles in society (Pescatello, 1973). In *machista* society, the male is perceived as "aggressive, intransigent in male-male interpersonal relationships, and arrogant and sexually aggressive in male-female relationships" (Pescatello, 1973, p. 90). Marianismo, on the other hand, exalts femininity and women's childbearing capacity emphasizing women's long-suffering nature or hembrismo, as well as the qualities of "obedience, submission, fidelity, meekness, and humility" (Darlington & Mulvaney, 2003, p. 118). These two polarities, machismo and marianismo, along with religion, traditional values, and specific political situations, have to a large extent been the cultural boundaries within which men and women operate. For example, marianismo anchors women's roles securely in the private sphere whereby the traditional ideal is the female role of *"esposa-madre" (wife-mother)* (Bose & Acosta-Belen, 1995; Darlington & Mulvaney, 2003). Yet, it is important to recognize that the "ideal" may not, in fact, be the reality. Latin American women, despite their subordinate status, have a great deal of covert power in the home (Shertock, 1998). In Puerto Rico, for example, contrary to stereotypes, women are not completely subordinate to their husbands and have a long history of forging strong roles for themselves out of economic necessity (Darlington & Mulvaney, 2003). In the Dominican Republic, working outside the home seems less acceptable, except in cases of dire economic need (Muñoz Vázquez & Fernández Bauzó, 1998). Consistent with traditional gender role ideology, a wife's work in the paid labor force implies her husband's failure or inadequacy as the family's breadwinner (Bernard, 1981). Hence, one could speculate that machismo has less powerful implications for working women, based on their economic contributions to their families and that this may be particularly true in Puerto Rico where there is a long history of women's participation in the paid labor force.

Bringing a feminist lens to this research also recognizes Latin American women's ability to overcome obstacles and barriers, open new spaces, and shift perspectives in the face of traumatic life events (Shertock, 1998). Thus, feminist perspectives emphasize meanings associated with gender, power, and dependency, but always relative to specific cultural boundaries. Feminist theory informs this study by grounding the challenge of rigid stereotypes and paternalistic notions around marital dissolution. Our exploration is one method of making visible the experiences and concerns of Dominican and Puerto Rican women relative to divorce.

Like feminism, ecological models are sensitive to context. Ecological theory emphasizes the embeddedness of women in a sociocultural network that stigmatizes divorce. One of the implications of such stigma is the belief that divorced women are "different" and less worthy than other people. Aulette (2002) points out that when people are stigmatized, others see them as having something wrong with them. For women, any stigma that is associated with divorce itself will be intensified by sexism and rigid gender roles. Cultural prescriptions which define the main roles of women as wives and mothers coupled with the belief that a marriage and two parents (both present in the household) are necessary in order for a family system to be defined as "legitimate," serve to contribute to a macrosocial environment that is hostile toward divorced women (Guttman, 1993). In Latin America, stigma associated with divorce is further reinforced by codes of cultural conduct imposed by traditional Catholic influences and paternalistic cultural prescriptions like machismo and marianismo.

In summary, the conceptualization of divorce as a cultural threat dominates much of Latin America. Feminist and ecological theories are useful in highlighting the connections between macro-social forces, social stigma, and women's perceptions of divorce.

EXPLORING: RESEARCH DESIGN AND DATA GATHERING

The present study is essentially a reconsideration of thesis data collected by the second author in 2003. The research design used for the purposes of data collection, and for the present study, was qualitative in nature, in that it was exploratory and emergent. Methodologically, such a design can be characterized as useful in examining various instances of interpretative phenomena, in this case the meanings attached to the image of divorced women in Puerto Rico and the Dominican Republic (Nelson, 1990; Polkinghorne, 1989). The term image has been defined in different contexts. The definition that corresponds to its use in this study is: "a mental picture or concept" (Cayne & Lechner, 1992, p. 483). Meaning and image are investigated on several systemic levels in terms of women's image of other women who are divorced, divorced women's image of themselves, and women's cultural images of divorced women. The central elements of the present reanalysis involve small modifications of the original coding scheme utilized and the first author's reimmersion in the narrative data as derived from the original study's participants.

The main source of data collection was an on-line survey consisting of 19 questions in Spanish developed largely by the second author with input from her thesis committee. Questions gathered demographic information from the participants and were designed to tap into perceptions about the image and behavior of divorced women in their societies as well as women's direct or indirect experiences of stigma or discrimination.

This survey was completed by a group of Puerto Rican and Dominican women (n = 95), who were contacted via several networks of family, relatives and friends, and via announcements on public and private web-pages, public on-line forums and on-line newsgroups.[1] Consistent with Miller and Crabtree's recommendation (2005), our approach to gathering data was purposeful, and sampling provided data that was "information-rich" (p. 620). The survey was administered by the second author during the spring of 2002. The majority of the questions in this survey were open-ended to enable participants to have the opportunity to speak in their own words and to bring forth aspects of their personal experiences from their own perspective. The appendix provides a list of questions that deal with the present study's thematic areas of concern relative to women's views of divorced women, cultural images of divorced women, and issues pertaining to stigma.

Reflexive Considerations

The second author, who is a native of the Dominican Republic, translated all qualitative text into English. Question generation was informed by the theoretical and empirical literature related to Latin American culture, gender, and social stigma, as well as the second author's insider knowledge as a divorced, Dominican woman. Clearly, personal experience is a valued element of the qualitative research process (see, for example, Rossman & Rallis, 1998) and served as a key source of knowing in terms of the recruitment of participants, and informing the study regarding areas of concern. Similar to an approach utilized by Arditti, Lambert-Shute and Joest (2004; see also Schmid & Jones, 2001), the first author provided balance to the study in terms of being able to maintain a sense of detachment relative to the second author's personal experience, thus triangulating the data collection and interpretative process. The second author has written a fairly extensive personal statement describing her experiences as a divorced woman in the Dominican Republic (Lopéz, 2004). For the purposes of understanding the "researcher as instrument," the following excerpts of the second author's personal narrative are offered in order to provide transparency relative to the formulation of the original study and the gathering and interpretive process.

Personal Statement: N. Lopez

> My interest in this topic is twofold. The first reason relates to my own personal history and educational background. I was born in the Dominican Republic, where I was raised within a conservative society. I received a Catholic elementary and high-school education and graduated from college with a Law degree. Shortly after getting married I moved to the United States, where I lived for six years. After that period I separated from my Dominican husband and moved back to the Dominican Republic (where I initiated the divorce process). I stayed there for two years and returned to the United States to earn an M.A. in the History/Area Studies at Virginia Tech. On my return to the Dominican Republic as a separated woman, I encountered many different reactions from family members, relatives, and friends varying from negative to positive attitudes. I was amazed to see how people based their images and conceptualization of divorced women on cultural parameters, particularly paternalistic and *machista* ideas. Among the negative re-

actions I experienced, many were concerns of family members regarding how society would view me: a failure, an immoral person, a weak woman, and someone unworthy of respect. On the other hand, among the positive reactions, I received support and words of encouragement. All these reactions are direct indications of both cultural traditions and changes in Dominican society and therefore I considered the opposing attitudes interesting grounds for exploration.

I researched the evolution of divorce throughout history, starting with the Romans, paying attention to law and the conceptualization of divorce, and continuing through Christianity, Reformation, and the French Revolution while underscoring the role of the Catholic Church in different periods of time and the continuous influence that this religious institution has had in Latin America. Important sources were the works of Beryl Rawson's (1991) *Marriage, Divorce and Children in Ancient Rome*, Max Rheinstein's (1980) *Marriage Instability, Divorce and the Law*, and Roderick Phillips's (1988) *Putting Asunder*. I then explored the influences of *machismo* and *hembrismo* behaviors in Latin American societies to better understand how these behaviors help shape image and create common stereotypes. Primary sources include Stanley and Barbara Stain's (1970) *Colonial Heritage of Latin America,* Ann Pescatello's (1973) *Female and Male in Latin America*, and Christine Bose and Edna Acosta-Belen's (1995) *Women in the Latin American Development Process.* Then, I proceeded to gather information regarding divorce and women in Latin America and the United States (because of its influence on Puerto Rico), paying special attention to the situation of women after divorce. I found information on the consequences of divorce on women, children, and society but mainly referring to psychological, legal, or economical issues. I consulted many sources in English and Spanish, including books, articles, newspapers and Internet pages from the United States, Puerto Rico, and the Dominican Republic. Universities in Puerto Rico (because they follow the model of United States universities) have demonstrated an interest in the topic of divorced women and their contribution to society, as well as the causes and consequences of divorce. However, information on the image and behaviors of divorced women within a cultural context is scarce in Puerto Rico and virtually non-existent in the Dominican Republic. This lack of information is what prompted me to create an on-line survey to explore these issues and to create a documented source on the cultural topics that I wanted to investigate. (Lopéz, 2004, pp. 9-11)

Additionally, the first author, although not Dominican or Puerto Rican, is previously divorced and has divorced parents (see Arditti, 1995, for personal narrative and reflections on personal experience and divorce research). Thus our collective experience with divorce informed our interpretations and understanding of the data. In particular, we were sensitive to divorced women's marginalized status. The second author's Catholic upbringing and cultural heritage served as an important lens by which to consider Dominican and Puerto Rican women's images of divorce. Clearly, because of our divorce-related experiences, we were both "more than just researchers" (Kleinman & Kopp, 1993) in that we acknowledge that our identities and viewpoints as divorced women were not neutralized. Rather, we embraced the feminist notion of subjectivity (Wonders, 1996) as well as the feminist recognition that both researcher and participant produce the interpretations that are the data (Diaz, 2002). Indeed, Krieger (1991) points out that the self researchers take into the work is not a troublesome element but a set of resources.

Coding and Analysis

Quantitative data was analyzed using SPSS. Qualitative analysis procedures fell into the typical phases of generic analysis outlined by Rossman and Rallis (1998) and McCracken's (1988) five-stage process for analyzing interview data. Both approaches emphasize organizing the data, familiarizing oneself with the data, and the generation of categories, themes, and patterns of experiences among respondents. In its original iteration, the second author immersed herself in the data, rereading the transcribed Spanish and English versions of the interviews several times. The first author then read and discussed the English translations with the second author, and preliminary coding categories were developed that represented the content and the study foci. The purpose of the next phase of the analysis was to identify and organize themes within each coding category that illustrated the predominant aspect of participants' interpretations and images. Exceptions, variations, and ambiguities in themes were also noted in the margins of the transcripts and discussed. Consistent with an approach to qualitative analysis described by Strauss and Corbin (1990) and Gilgun (1992), coding, identification of themes, and subsequent interpretation were developed over time and reflected a series of modifications based on repeated readings of the data and discussion between the co-authors.

As noted by Wonders (1996), truth is transitory and multifaceted–thus continually reconstructed and rewritten. And it is in that spirit that the first author has reconsidered and modified the codes, originally put forth in the second authors' thesis project, and thematic content and interpretation of the participants' responses to survey questions. Table 1 summarizes the coding scheme which was foundational to the present study. This scheme suggests several substantive areas for thematic analysis. The first encompassed participants' general perceptions of divorced women. Here several themes emerged including polarized images of divorced women as either successes or failures and women's expected role in enduring marriage. A sub-theme which emerged as women discussed these issues involved divorced women's self-image and thematic content regarding the empowering, or crippling, aspects of divorce. Finally, qualitative text which related to participants' beliefs about the cultural attitudes of their respective societies toward divorced women was reanalyzed. Religious influences as well as the transmission of cultural stereotypes were discussed. Pseudonyms or initials, chosen by the participants themselves, were used for all participants' responses.

Participant Characteristics

Ninety-five participants responded to the on-line survey. The average study participant was approximately 32 years old ($SD = 8.43$). Fifty-one percent of the respondents were from the Dominican Republic, 34% were from Puerto Rico, and 16% were from other Latin American countries. Sixty-five percent reported that they were professionals, 21% were students, and 14% were homemakers or not specified. Twelve percent of participants reported finishing high school, 6% attended vocational school, 13% attended some college, while 48% finished college and 23% attended Graduate School. Fifty percent of the participants did not have any children. Of the 50% who did have children, 19% had one child, 18% had two children, 12% had three children and 2% had four children. Regarding marital status, 27% of the respondents were single, 45% were married, and 30% divorced or separated. Within the group of divorced or separated participants, the average amount of time since the divorce or separation was 2.1 years ($SD = 4.31$). Chi-Square tests revealed that for this sample there was no significant difference between female participants from Puerto Rico and the

TABLE 1. Summary of Coding Categories and Related Themes

Coding Category	Themes, *Subthemes**, and "Exemplars"
Perceptions of Divorced Women	**Heroic and Successful** "A strong woman determined to triumph" "A woman who overcomes" *Self-Image: Empowered by divorce* "(I am) someone more powerful" "free, constantly progressing in society" "Independent, capable, mature" **Divorced Women as Failures** "Divorced women generally are cowards" "Frivolous and weak" "She didn't know how to hang on to her husband" *Self-Image: Crippled by divorce* "Alone and without protection" "I see myself as a big failure" **Capacidad de Aguante (Capability to Endure)** "The woman must try to endure in order to not break-up the family"
Image of Divorced Women in Society	**Cultural Change and Tolerance** "Today, people are open-minded" "Before it was negative….now the image is changing" **Cultural Stereotypes and Stigma** "she is seen as one who goes to bed with whoever" "she is rejected" "as a person with a contagious disease" **Religious Influences** "divorced women disrespect God's rules" "cowards who do not comply with the rules of the church" **Transmission of Cultural Stereotypes** "Yes I have heard a lot…actually, too much"

*30 percent of participants were divorced or separated (n = 28). Thematic content pertaining to self-image pertains to divorced or separated participants.

Dominican Republic in terms of the likelihood of being divorced, although in the general population, it is almost four times likelier for women in Puerto Rico to be divorced than in the Dominican Republic. Puerto Rican divorce rates are 4.47 per 1,000 people and the Dominican Republic divorce rate is 1.17 per 1,000 people (The World's Women Trends and Statistics, 1999).

The demographic profile of participants in our study suggests that women with few or no children, who were highly educated and professionally active, and who had access to technology, completed the survey. Our participants were disproportionately divorced when compared to the general populations of their respective countries. Thus, it is important to remember that participants in the study were not necessarily representative of the larger population of Latin American women in their respective countries. Participants in our study had significantly more education and lower fertility rates than Latin American women in the general population (Weinberger, Lloyd, & Blanc, 1989). We would expect the nature of our sample to influence our study results in that women in our study may hold more progressive views than are held by the general populations. Previous demographic research on Latin American women indicates that better-educated women have broader knowledge, higher socioeconomic status, and less fatalistic attitudes about their family roles than do less educated women (Martin & Juarez, 1995).

UNDERSTANDING: DESCRIPTION OF FINDINGS

Individuals create meanings about their lives by sifting personal experiences through received social meanings and expressed interactions (Schneller & Arditti, 2004). Cultural context and personal backgrounds influenced women's image of divorced women. Participants' interpretations of divorce were shaped by familial and peer group attitudes towards divorce, as well as their social and religious influences. It was interesting to note that participants in this study often departed from traditional terms (filled mainly with negative connotations) when discussing divorce, and responses often reflected a more modern trend of attitudes reinforced by positive experiences. This is not surprising considering the demographics of the sample involved in the study (i.e., highly educated and professional) and the number of divorced or separated women who responded to the survey. The findings are organized by coding and thematic categories as summarized in Table 1.

Perceptions of Divorced Women

When asked their opinion on divorced women in their societies, participants described many images of divorced women and responded with a wide range of answers. Thematic content seemed to be either negatively or positively valanced with responses varying from condemnation to admiration.

Divorced Women as Successes: Images of Heroism

Several participants described divorced women in almost heroic terms. A key element of this heroism involved the ability to be independent and stand up to life's challenges. For example, a respondent from Puerto Rico, Io, indicated respect, admiration and acceptance towards divorced women: "A divorced woman is an independent woman with the courage to meet life head-on." Another Puerto Rican woman shared a similar sentiment: "A strong woman, determined to triumph."

CHP, from the Dominican Republic, also emphasized the perception of divorced women as courageous: "She is a strong woman with courage, who has decided not to be a victim of anyone, not even of herself."

Dwos, from Puerto Rico, emphasized that an element of courageousness was the divorced women's fighting spirit: She describes a divorced woman as someone who "fights to succeed in raising her family, and has to fight common stereotypes against divorced women."

The previous statements denote sympathy and admiration toward divorced women, exalting values like courage, freedom, strength, and dedication to succeed in society. These values are conceived to be the positive consequences of divorce and recognize the empowering aspects of divorce for women. Indeed, Arditti and Madden-Derdich (1995) found similar thematic content regarding the emotional benefits and empowering aspects of divorce in their study of divorced mothers in the United States.

Empowered by divorce. While the previous areas of content tap into generalized perceptions of divorced women from all participants, content pertaining to self-image was drawn only from participants who were divorced themselves (recall that 30% of participants in this survey were divorced or separated). Not surprisingly, most divorced participants saw themselves in a predominantly positive light, and responses tended to mirror generalized cultural polarities (i.e., divorce as success or failure). For example, Manolita's response (from the Dominican Republic) highlighted the empowering aspects of divorce in terms of how she views herself: "As a human being whose dreams were shattered, but not her life. . . . someone who has suffered, changed her principles, and someone more powerful."

Other women internalized the liberation that is achieved by being on one's own. CH, from Puerto Rico, explains how she sees her divorced self: "As an independent person, who hasn't needed a man to feel complete as a woman."

For some participants, divorce was the gateway to satisfying work or professional careers. For example, Yayi, from Puerto Rico, stated that divorce created "A professional woman, free, constantly progressing in society and therefore, happy."

Other divorced women emphasized benefits of divorce in terms of having greater control over their lives. SH, from Puerto Rico, stated that she was "A fighter, a non-conformist. I myself take control of my life to make it better; with God's help, of course."

It's Her Own Fault: Images of Failure

In contrast to the previous descriptions emphasizing the empowering aspects of divorce and positive qualities of women who persist in the face of marital dissolution, the majority of responses concerning how one saw divorced women were negative. Descriptions of divorced women that fit this category ranged from them being cowardly and weak for not persevering or "enduring" in the marriage (hembrismo), to being "whores" or irresponsible. In any case, the implicit message was that somehow a woman who was divorced was at fault.

For example, this woman's response from the Dominican Republic illustrated the perception that the wife who failed to persist in her marriage, and thus allowed it to dissolve, lacked courage: "Divorced women generally are cowards who didn't know how to maintain their marriages . . . they're insecure women who like the easy road in life." Jum, from the Dominican Republic, also judges harshly the woman who falls short of the hembrismo ideal: "The divorced woman is frivolous and weak."

Thus, the idea of divorce as the fault of the woman seemed to be preeminent. For the women in our study, there was no middle ground. Participant responses emphasized the negative connotation of excessive freedom (*libertinaje*) or frivolous behaviors and weakness of divorced women, and reflected the cultural belief that divorced women were considered "easy-prey" for free sex.

Several responses from women who resided in the Dominican Republic further reflected the "fault/failure" mentality and the stigmatized status of divorcees. A participant from the Dominican Republic explained the source of the stigma: "Unfortunately, the divorced woman has a bad image because it is understood that she has failed in her marriage and that she didn't know how to hang on to her husband. . . ."

Another respondent from the Dominican Republic, Francia, also points her finger directly at the divorced woman herself: "In the Dominican Republic the divorced woman regularly puts herself in a situation of hopelessness and tragedy."

In Puerto Rico, where we would expect more progressive attitudes given westernization and the use of legal divorce procedures similar to the United States, women expressed an awareness of the negative stereotypes, even if they did not espouse these ideas themselves. For example, Katia explains: "The image is that she is a woman that, even in our times, is seen with eyes of rejection, like someone worthless. I have to admit that in my country this is changing, but slowly. . . ."

Crippled by divorce. Unfortunately, some of the divorced participants in our study seemed to internalize cultural images that reflected the stigma and failure generally perceived to be connected to divorce. For example, Dominicana, a divorced woman from the Dominican Republic, admits, "I see myself very poorly, alone and without protection." LLL, from Puerto Rico, also shares a negative self-image, but perhaps it may only be temporal: "I see myself as a big failure, but I believe that since I got divorced, I have to move on."

Hembrismo and the Need to Endure

It is worth noting that the endurance ideology seems to be at the very heart of the divorced woman's failure. This idea, known as "*Capacidad de Aguante*" (Capability to Endure), is the core of hembrismo ideology. Enduring difficult situations and, in some instances, abuse, is considered an unavoidable part of marriage. Women endure to avoid divorce, and therefore, failure.

As Gitana (from the Dominican Republic) stated, "The woman is the one who knows how to run a marriage. She must try to endure in order not to break up the family."

The definition and limitations of "Capacidad de Aguante" are unclear: Exactly how much a woman has to endure and for how long may be a personal choice. Respondents were specifically asked if they thought a wife should endure violence or any other physical or psychological abuse in order to preserve the marriage and before opting for a divorce. M, from Puerto Rico, responded in a way that reflected her ambivalence about her own situation: "Truthfully, I had better not answer (this question) given that I am currently enduring them."

Still, in both countries the majority of respondents explicitly disapproved of abuse and seemed to reject this aspect of hembrismo. In fact,

85% of participants agreed that nobody should endure any type of abuse, while 12% believed that women should endure difficult situations in order to preserve a marriage and before opting for divorce. It is not surprising based on their demographic profile, that participants in this sample held a more progressive view which contrasted with traditional hembrismo values that encourage women to endure abuse in order to preserve marriages.

To summarize, most people tend to use a range of attributions to explain marital failure, perhaps to protect or enhance one's self-image (Grych & Fincham, 1992). It was not surprising then that divorced women seemed more inclined to perceive divorce in positive terms, and emphasized personal growth and autonomy relative to their own experience. Yet, negative social stereotypes and the persistence of endurance ideology were evident in many participants' descriptions of divorced women. Such negativity seemed particularly tragic for divorced women who held these views and potentially hampered their ability to explain marital failure in terms that would protect their self-image.

Divorced Women's Image in Society

Of theoretical significance was the exploration of the "micro-macro" link with respect to the issue of stigma. Polarized responses in the previous section highlighted women's view of other divorced women as well as internalization of stigma in their view of themselves. It seems that the cultural default in terms of social approval still involved familistic prescriptions regarding the importance of wives being willing to remain married instead of opting for a divorce, even under adverse conditions.

Societal attitudes about divorce tended to mirror those that respondents gave specific to their more personalized image of the divorced woman herself. Responses in this section broadly describe respondents' beliefs about their culture's (in their respective countries) views of divorced women. Again, participants' responses were polarized–there seemed to be no middle ground–women in the study discussed the culture of divorce in either positive or negative terms.

Cultural Change and Tolerance

Clearly, progressive change in terms of a more widespread tolerance of divorce was reflected in several participants' responses about their beliefs regarding cultural norms concerning marital dissolution. For example, NN from Puerto Rico stated:

> Before, people had the perception (mistaken in my opinion) that a divorced woman did not have any deep moral values and that the only thing she was interested in was "being on the streets." Today, people are more open-minded and understand that a divorced woman is and has been a fighter (especially if she has children).... she simply recognized that the relationship she had didn't work.

CR, from Puerto Rico, also describes cultural change in terms of "before" and "now":

> I think the image is changing. Before, it was very negative. Men did not respect these women... Now their image is changing into that of an independent and strong woman who is not willing to put up with anything from anyone.

Stereotypes and Stigma

Cultural tolerance was tempered, however, by respondents' beliefs that "nothing had really changed" in terms of divorced women's status. Participant responses reflected familial ideals about marriage and the intractability of the status-quo (i.e., marital dissolution as non-normative and negative). Dominican women in particular expressed a strong visible awareness of negative cultural stereotypes concerning divorce. For example, this woman from the Dominican Republic, when asked how her country might view divorced women, equated divorce with sexual licentiousness. Tabata stated, "The divorced woman is seen as promiscuous, as one who goes to bed with whoever."

Indeed, there seemed to be no distinction between how the individual sees the divorced woman and perceptions about one's culture, suggesting that cultural attitudes and stigma are fully internalized. Respondents described their country's attitudes in the same terms they used to describe their own beliefs, and emphasized negative outcomes and the image of divorced women as cultural outcasts. La India, from the Dominican Republic, reflects this cultural sentiment well: "Society sees the divorced woman as a desolate, desperate and abandoned woman who cannot take care of herself." Manolita, also from the Dominican Republic concurs:

> She is seen with abandonment and without compassion ... As a person with a contagious disease ... the divorced woman is always

judged without a "fair trial." She is viewed as a failure, incapable of completing the simple task of being a wife.

And while women are aware of the marginalized status of divorced women in their culture, they do not necessarily feel good about it. Interestingly, Manolita adds: "Many times society limits the possibilities of divorced women and closes the door to their progress."

Thus, divorced women were viewed as actively rejected by the culture in which they live due to their perceived failings. Divorce poses a cultural threat to marianismo and all that it represents. Mayimbita, from the Dominican Republic, expresses this viewpoint emphatically, "Society sees divorced women as whores, who don't deserve another chance; as failures, who don't know how to be women; as weak and selfish, not willing to sacrifice themselves for their families."

Women from Puerto Rico echoed these thoughts in terms of acknowledging cultural views that divorced women were failures or outcasts. However, negative cultural perceptions were more likely considered within the context of cultural change and improvement. For example, A.M. states, "Puerto Rican society unfortunately perceives poorly the divorced woman and I think that is due to a lack of education, because a woman shouldn't be measured by her status but rather by her values. Nevertheless, we have to admit that our society has improved a lot." Lulu also acknowledges the marginalized status of divorced women in Puerto Rico, but optimistically believes things are changing:

> Society perceives the divorced woman with some rejection, or maybe I should say fear. Actually the divorced woman is gaining recognition for her good work and as an example of maturity and capability. Society is learning not to judge divorced women by their personal lives, but as human beings with the same rights and capabilities as men. Today the numbers of divorced women in Puerto Rico are so high that people understand that divorce is not grounds for rejection.

Participant responses reflected images of common cultural stereotypes in Latin America as well as some awareness of cultural change–or at least the need for it–and more westernized perspectives of divorce as normative. It is unknown whether beliefs about greater tolerance toward divorced women reflect more diverse and flexible roles for women or is simply optimistic thinking. Regardless of whether social change is real or imagined, the majority of women (68%) believed that their respective society discriminated against divorced women. Despite modernization, similar to findings from divorce research in traditional Chinese culture (see, for example, Lau, 2004), women who depart from the traditional gendered norms of wife/mother via divorce still appear to be heavily stigmatized.

Religious Influences

In Latin America, norms regulating marriage and divorce arrived along with the Spanish and the Catholic Church. Thus, in both countries a traditionally strong relationship existed between women and the Catholic Church (Miller, 1991). Although both Puerto Rico and the Dominican Republic were colonized by Spain, Puerto Rico has been in the possession of the United States since 1898 (Darlington & Mulvaney, 2002). It is interesting to note that in Puerto Rico, women's relationship with the Church shifted in the 19th century from the Church's earlier view of women as dangerous and sinful to viewing women as virtuous and innocent (Rodriguez, 1994). Regardless of this shift, Catholicism served to reinforce traditional gender roles, whereby women were victims of Spanish machismo and the family structure was based on absolute male authority.

Participant statements reflected the Catholic religion's influence on society and the perception of divorce, and how this perception connects with women's responsibility for the marriage. As La Beba, from Puerto Rico, stated:

> Society has been changing with time. In my country, several Latin traditions remain alive. Because the Church considers marriage as indissoluble by men, and the same Church tends to be stricter and assigns more responsibility to women, divorce is therefore seen as "woman's big failure." Society has considered divorce the "illness of the new century" and divorced women as "incapable of maintaining a family." In general, society thinks divorced women are disrespectful of God's rules and therefore rejects and looked upon them poorly. It is worse if a divorced woman tries to remarry or does not have any education or a job.

Naomi, from the Dominican Republic, also acknowledges the powerful influence of the Catholic Church in terms of social stigma connected to divorce: "Society sees divorced women, as well they should:

as cowards who do not know how to comply with the rules of marriage, nor the rules of the Church."

These statements illustrate the intertwining of religious and cultural beliefs. Even more, participant responses reflect the "power-over" of the Catholic Church in Latin American society. Starhawk (1987) defines this type of power (e.g., power-over) as inherently oppressive to women and reinforcing obedience in patriarchy. The issue of Latin American women's subordination and their seeming acquiescence to male dominated religious tenets is not necessarily new (Darlington & Mulvaney, 2003). Thus, religious doctrine obviously contributes to the idea that divorce is objectionable and shameful. Latin American women who divorce are, in a sense, defying the position of the church–either by default or by their own initiative.

Woman to Woman: The Transmission of Cultural Stereotypes

In an attempt to explore the transmission of cultural attitudes, one of the survey questions asked participants if they had heard negative or derogatory comments about divorced women. Because of the cultural similarity between Puerto Rico and the Dominican Republic, it is common for both countries to share idiomatic expressions and popular sayings that became part of the cultural tradition and general knowledge. By collecting some of these expressions, one can recognize stigma and stereotypes prevailing in each society.

From Puerto Rico, participants expressed a variety of responses and the use of very strong language. For example, PCH stated, "I have heard: 'that woman is a bitch.' 'She is an irresponsible woman.' 'She's crazy.' 'She doesn't care about her children.' " ZSR, also from Puerto Rico, states:

> I have heard: "X got divorced"... now we have to be careful with her because she's going to have her vagina on her forehead. She's going to be like a bitch in heat." This is mainly said by married women who are afraid of losing their husbands to a divorced woman.

Another participant, Dominicana from the Dominican Republic, also recounted negative comments she had heard from others in her social circle:

> Yes, I have heard a lot . . . Actually, too much . . . "Divorced women are not trustworthy. . ." (said mainly by wives). "I don't want my son to marry a divorced woman," "I'm sure she doesn't deserve him and that she will make him unhappy . . ." "I don't want people to see me as just another divorced woman" (said by a recently divorced woman). The unbelievable part is that the majority of prejudice against divorced women comes from women themselves. Ironic, isn't it?

Indeed, survey results seemed to support Dominicana's opinion, in that it appeared that women themselves tend to be most likely to perpetuate negative images of the divorced woman. Certainly this form of "woman bashing" runs counter to feminist ideals of a supportive sisterhood amongst women. Derogatory comments against divorced women in Latin American societies seem mainly connected to deviation from marianismo and traditional women's roles. For example, it is common for mothers to object to the marriage of their sons to previously divorced women, fearing the marriage can be easily dissolved, or that the Catholic Church cannot bless the marriage. Married women criticize divorced women and consider their status as immoral or with a tendency to licentious behaviors. They also fear that divorced women will endanger their marriage, because these women have already departed from traditional marianista prescriptions which would otherwise keep their sexuality "in check." Thus divorced women are perceived as likely to lure other husbands away from their marriages with their sexual wiles. Such views of divorced women's behavior perpetuate stereotypes of divorced women as sexually dangerous and socially threatening.

INTERPRETATION: CONCLUSION AND DISCUSSION

This study explored women's perception of divorce in Puerto Rico and the Dominican Republic, with particular attention to the image of divorced women in both societies. It is important to point out, however, that participants in this study may not be representative of all Latin American women. Most notably, this was a highly educated group with a high percentage of divorced participants. One can expect that the more educated people are, the more progressive their gender role attitudes will be (Scanzoni & Szinovacz, 1980). Yet, despite the characteristics of the sample denoting the group's likely progressiveness, it is interesting to observe the persistence of very negative stereotypes about divorced women.

Additionally, we continue our reflexivity with an awareness that there is no detaching the cultural self from our interpretations and discussion of the findings (Oleson, 2005). Obviously, we approached the interpretive work of this study with background, conviction, and perhaps with biases or agendas of our own (see, for example, Anderson & Jack, 1991). In particular, the second author's social location as a Dominican, professional divorced woman, and her Catholic upbringing makes salient the ways in which structures and cultures may typically disadvantage most women (Reinharz & Chase, 2001). We have represented the women's voices as they are, yet the interpretations are ours relative to the social processes, ideologies, and structures embedded in interviewees' narratives (Chase, 1996).

Divorce as a Cultural Threat

Divorce appears to threaten cultural boundaries in both countries for a number of reasons. Foremost would be the challenge it presents to religious doctrine. For example, Catholic Church doctrines have centered on Ecclesiastical laws which maintain that ". . . Divorce, by dissolving the family unit, jeopardizes fundamental values essential to the well-being of individuals and society" (Halem, 1980, p. 9). Beyond the abrogation of a religious covenant, an additional threat posed by divorce involves the departure from traditional family roles and the likelihood of labor force participation as divorced women attempt economic self-sufficiency. Divorce and subsequent labor force participation potentially transform the main structure of marianista behavior and at the very least may create new possible avenues of empowerment for women. Indeed, given the more likely scenario of economic risk after divorce, the positive consequences of women's breadwinning are generally not understood or emphasized (Arditti & Madden-Derdich, 1995). Centuries of marianismo and idealistic notions of women's long-suffering nature still shape marital behavior and influence perceptions of divorce. However, we recognize that marianismo may be articulated and understood in a number of different ways, depending on one's economic situation, and one's involvement in various social and political movements (see, for example, Steven's, 1973, and Ehler's, 1991, commentary). Specifically, there is feminist discourse which embodies a more positive evolution of marianismo to describe the feminine moral superiority and spiritual strength of modern Latin American women (Bocchi, retrieved 12/03/04 from http:www.lclark.edu/~woodrich/Bocchi_ marianismo.html).

Stigma and the Meaning of Divorce

Despite the strength-based possibilities of marianista ideals, our qualitative analysis provided rich text revealing that prejudice toward divorced women existed in Dominican and Puerto Rican societies. For example, thematic content related to divorced women's sexual nature reflected one facet of their marginalization. The belief that divorced women were promiscuous, especially compared to married women, originates in part from marianista ecclesiastical notions of purity and virginity that have prevailed in the Dominican Republic and in all of Latin America since the conquest (Muñoz Vázquez & Fernández Bauzó, 1998).

In addition, content related to divorced women's cowardice revealed another facet of their marginalization: divorced women were perceived as not having "what it takes" in that they did not fight long and hard enough to save their marriages. Thus, ideas about women's long-suffering nature ("La Capacidad de Aguante") reflected the persistence of hembrismo, a cultural philosophy which may contribute not only to marital unhappiness but also to domestic violence. In Puerto Rico, for example, more than half of all murdered women were victimized by their own husbands (Cintrón, 1981). Centuries old notions of romantic love, which differentiates "pure love" (characterized as noble, spiritual, and loyal) from "sexual love" (associated with men), serve to reinforce "La Capacidad de Aguante" as a cultural ideal in Latin America (Muñoz Vázquez & Fernández Bauzó, 1998). Thus, divorce presents an interesting duality as it is both a woman's failure and a cultural threat.

Overall, results highlighted that images of divorced women are influenced by macro forces such as culture, history, and religion. Indeed, there is a popular old saying in many countries of Latin America used mainly by women: *"Matrimonio y mortaja, del cielo bajan"* (marriage and funeral come from the sky), meaning that marriage is in store for everyone, especially for women, the same way death is: no one can, or should, escape. This idea of marriage as a necessary and natural phase of life is intergenerationally transmitted, and is influenced by Catholicism and the cultural ideals that perpetuate marianismo. Cultural and religious emphasis on marriage and patriarchic gender role ideology contribute to the stigma and shame associated with divorce and prejudicial attitudes toward divorced women.

Social constructionism, an interpretive approach that emphasizes social context, provides a useful lens for considering the findings in this study because of its emphasis on the centrality of people creating knowledge and meaning through languaged interactions (Gergen, 1985). Language in this study plays a revealing role in terms of how participants interpret and internalize images about divorce. Overall, participants expressed themselves using very dramatic and sometimes profane language. Strong direct commands and expressions were used, specifically when participants repeated derogatory comments commonly heard in their particular society. Some of this language was quite strong and sexually charged.

Because divorce is a well-known, disruptive life event as well as an experience filled with social meanings, it motivates people to interpret and make sense of their personal experience (Riessman, 1990). For participants in this study it seemed that the personal experience of divorce was a force in shaping self-image. Divorce, despite its stigma, also seemed to be a pathway for women to transcend stereotypical gender roles and marianita ideals. It is important to remember that the apparent likelihood of successfully navigating marital dissolution may be enhanced for our sample given their high levels of education and professional status.

Implications for Clinical Practice

In conclusion, it is essential to address the mental health needs of divorced women and, similar to recommendations emerging from research on divorced women from traditional Asian cultures (Chang, 2003), practitioners must acknowledge and openly address issues of cultural stigma and the marginalization of divorced women in Latin American society. Prejudicial images of divorced women are likely rooted in the machista traditional culture of Latin America as well as patriarchic religious doctrine. Women were quite explicit regarding the negative stereotypes associated with divorce. Marginalization of divorced women could lead to negative mental health outcomes in that some women may internalize cultural ideology which conceptualizes divorced women as failures. Women in both the Dominican Republic and Puerto Rico were quite explicit in assigning the fault of marital dissolution to women. Additionally, stigma was illustrated on several attitudinal levels. The result of this "layered" stigma and any subsequent internalization among divorced women could be social isolation, negative self-concept, and mental distress.

Although women in the study seemed quite aware of negative stereotypes, there was no real evidence of any active participation to create change in the situation of women. We did ask participants if they believed special services were needed in their respective societies to accommodate divorced women. Many who responded to this question seemed reluctant to have divorced women classified as a different group or to have special consideration from society. We speculate that women in the study may be ambivalent about intervention due to a lack of confidence in public social institutions, and fear that intervention will somehow intensify stigma by drawing even more attention to one's divorced status. Indeed, there is some truth to this fear as interventions aimed at marginalized groups, in this case divorced women, can in fact be stigmatizing (Gottlieb, 2000). Thus, interventions must be ecologically sensitive to Latin American culture. Effective community education, which offers alternative images of divorce, and the provision of easily accessed services are particularly important. It also would make sense to explore faith-based initiatives with regard to this population whenever possible. While not reflected specifically by the voices of our study's participants, we acknowledge that women's involvement in Christianity can become a means of social activism and empowerment through their base communities and the Catholic Church–especially for working class and peasant women (Randall, 1994). Mental health and social service agencies should partner with churches, and practitioners working with divorced women should seek the support of progressive priests and ministers, as religious life is particularly influential in shaping women's perceptions of divorce. It may be that compassionate church-based interventions can facilitate adjustment, provide much-needed social support, and empower women through social activism in many types of family situations.

NOTE

1. This survey was advertised on: Soc.culture.puerto-rico, soc.culture-dominican-rep., www.dr1.com/forum, www.quisqueya.com/forum, soc.culture-caribbean, soc.culture.latin-america, www.unibe.com.dr, www.reddominicana.com, www.borinquen.com, alt.culture.hispanics, and www.puertorico.com/forums.

REFERENCES

Anderson, K., & Jack, D. (1991). Learning to listen: Interview techniques and analyses. In S. Gluck & D. Patai (Eds.), *Women's words: The feminist practice of oral history* (pp. 11-26). New York: Routledge.

Arditti, J. A. (1995). Noncustodial parents: Emergent issues of diversity and process. *Marriage & Family Review, 20,* 283-304.

Arditti, J. A., Lambert-Shute, J., & Joest, K. (2003). Saturday morning at the jail: Implications of incarceration for families and children. *Family Relations, 52,* 195-204.

Arditti, J. A., & Madden-Derdich, D. M. (1995). No regrets: Custodial mothers' accounts of the difficulties and benefits of divorce. *Contemporary Family Therapy, 17,* 229-248.

Aulette, J. R. (2002). *Changing American families.* Chapel Hill, NC: Allyn and Bacon, 264-284.

Bernard, J. (1981). The good provider role: Its rise and fall. *American Psychologist, 36,* 1-12.

Bocchi, S. *The meaning of marianismo in Mexico.* Retrieved Dec 12, 2004 from http://www.lclark.edu/~woodrish/Bocchi_marianismo.html.

Bose, C. E., & Acosta-Belen, E. (1995). *Women in the Latin American development process.* Philadelphia: Temple University Press.

Browner, C. H. (1989). Women, household and health in Latin America. *Social Sciences and Medicine, 28,* 461-473.

Cayne, B., & Lechner, D.E. (1992). *New Webster dictionary and thesaurus of the English language.* Danbury, CT: Lexicon.

Chang, J. (2003). Self-reported reasons for divorce and correlates of psychological well-being among divorced Korean immigrant women. *Journal of Divorce & Remarriage, 40,* 111-128.

Chase, S. (1996). Personal vulnerability and interpretive authority in narrative research. In R. Josselson (Ed.), *The narrative study of lives, Vol. 4, Ethics and process in the narrative study of lives* (pp. 45-59). Thousand Oaks, CA: Sage.

Cintrón, I. (1981). Cincuenta por ciento de mujeres asesinadas son víctimas de sus esposos. *El Mundo Newspaper,* pp. A1, A5.

Darlington, P., & Mulvaney, B. (2003). *Women, power, and ethnicity: Working toward reciprocal empowerment.* New York: The Haworth Press, Inc.

Diaz, C. (2002). Conversational heuristic as a reflexive method for feminist research. *International Review of Sociology, 12,* 249-255.

Ehlers, T. (1991). Debunking marianismo: Economic vulnerability and survival strategies among Guatemalan wives. *Ethnology, 30,* 1-16.

Few, A., Stephens, D., & Rouse-Arnett, M. (2003). Sister-to-sister talk: Transcending boundaries and challenges in qualitative research with black women. *Family Relations, 52,* 205-215.

Flax, J. (1987). Postmodernism and gender relations in Feminist theory. *Signs: Journal of Women in Culture and Society, 12,* 621-641.

Gergen, K. J. (1985). The Social Constructionist movement in modern psychology. *American Psychologist, 40,* 266-275.

Gilgun, J. (1992). Definitions, methodologies, and methods in qualitative family research. In J. Gilgun, K. Daley, & G. Handel (Eds.), *Qualitative methods in family research* (pp. 22-30). Thousand Oaks, CA: Sage.

Gottleib, B. H. (2000). Selecting and planning support interventions. In S. Cohen, L. Underwood, & B. Gottlieb (Eds.), *Social support measurement and intervention: A guide for health and social scientists* (pp. 195-221). New York: Oxford University Press.

Grych, J. H., & Fincham, F. D. (1992). Marital dissolution and family adjustment: An attributional analysis. In T. L. Orbuch (Ed.), *Close relationships loss* (pp. 157-173). New York: Springer-Verlag.

Guttman, J. (1993). *Divorce in a psychosocial perspective.* Hillsdale, NJ: Lawrence Erlbaum Associates.

Halem, L. C. (1980). *Divorce reform.* New York: The Free Press.

Kleinman, S., & Kopp, M. A. (1993). *Emotions and fieldwork.* Newbury Park, CA: Sage.

Krieger, S. (1991). *Social science and the self: Personal essays as an art form.* New Brunswick, NJ: Rutgers.

Lau, Y. (2004). Nonresident parents' participation in nonresidential parenting in a Chinese context. *Journal of Divorce & Remarriage, 40,* 149-159.

Lopéz, N. M. (2004). *Latin American women's perceptions of divorce: An exploratory study of the situation and image of divorced women in Puerto Rico and the Dominican Republic.* Unpublished master's thesis, Virginia Tech, Blacksburg, VA, United States.

Martin, T., & Juarez, F. (1995). The impact of women's education on fertility in Latin America: Searching for explanations. *International Family Planning Perspectives, 21,* 52-57, 80.

McCracken, G. (1988). *The long interview.* Newbury Park, CA: Sage.

Miller, F. (1991). *Latin American women and the search for social justice.* Hanover, NH: University Press of New England.

Miller, W. L., & Crabtree, B. F. (1999). The dance of interpretation. In B. F. Crabtree & W. L. Miller (Eds.), *Doing qualitative research* (2nd ed., pp. 127-143). Thousand Oaks, CA: Sage.

Miller, W. L., & Crabtree, B. F. (2005). Clinical research. In N. Denzin & Y. Lincoln (Eds.), *The Sage handbook of qualitative research* (pp. 605-639). Thousand Oaks, CA: Sage.

Muñoz Vázquez, M., & Fernández Bauzó, E. (1998). *El divorcio en la sociedad Puertorriqueña* (Divorce in Puerto Rican society). Puerto Rico: Ediciones Huracán.

Nelson, J. L. (1990). Phenomenology as feminist methodology: Explicating interviews. In K. Carter & C. Spitzack (Eds.), *Doing research on women's communication: Perspectives on theory and method.* Norwood, NJ: Ablex.

Oleson, V. (2005). Early millennial feminist qualitative research: Challenges and contours. In N. Denzin & Y. Lincoln (Eds.), *The Sage handbook of qualitative research* (pp. 235–278). Thousand Oaks, Sage.

Pescatello, A. (1973). *Female and male in Latin America: Essays.* Pennsylvania: University of Pittsburgh Press.

Phillips, R. (1988) *Putting asunder: The history of divorce in western society.* Cambridge: Cambridge University Press.
Polkinghorne, D. E. (1989). Phenomenological research methods. In R. S. Valle & S. Halling (Eds.), *Existential-Phenomenological perspectives in psychology: Exploring the breadth of human experience* (pp. 41-60). New York: Plenum Press.
Randall, M. (1994). *Sandino's daughters revisited: Feminism in Nicaragua.* New Brunswick, NJ: Rutgers University Press.
Rawson, B. (Ed.) (1991). *Marriage, divorce, and children in ancient Rome.* Oxford: Humanities Research Centre: Clarendon Press, 31.
Reinharz, S., & Chase, S. (2001). Interviewing women. In J. Gubrium & J. Holstein (Eds.), *Handbook of interview research: Context and method* (pp. 221-238). Thousand Oaks, CA: Sage.
Rheinstein, M. (1980). *Marriage instability, divorce and the law.* Chicago: University of Chicago Press.
Riessman, C. K. (1990). *Divorce talk: Women and men make sense of personal relationships.* London: Rutgers University Press.
Rivera Ramos, E. (2000). *The legal construction of identity: The juridical and social legacy of American colonialism in Puerto Rico.* Washington, DC: American Psychological Association.
Rodriguez, R. (1994). *Bienvenida al club del divorcio* (Welcome to the divorce club) Mexico: Editorial Diana.
Rossman, G., & Rallis, S. (1998). *Learning in the field: An introduction to qualitative research.* Thousand Oaks, CA: Sage.
Scanzoni, J., & Szinovacz, M. (1980). *Family decision-making: A developmental sex role model.* Newbury Park, CA: Sage.
Schmid, T. J., & Jones, R. S. (2001). Ambivalent actions: Prison adaptation strategies of first-time, short-term inmates. In C. Pope, R. Lovell, & S. Brandl (Eds.), *Voices from the field: Readings in criminal justice research* (pp. 182-201). Belmont, CA: Wadsworth.
Schneller, D., & Arditti, J. (2004). After the breakup: Interpreting divorce and rethinking intimacy. *Journal of Divorce & Remarriage, 42,* 1-37.
Shertock, T. (1998). Latin American women's experience of feeling able to move toward and accomplish a meaningful and challenging goal. *Journal of Phenomenological Inquiry in Psychology, 21,* 175-174.
Song, Y. I. (1991) Single Asian American women as a result of divorce: Depressive affect and changes in social support. In S. S. Volgy (Ed.), *Women and divorce / men and divorce: Gender differences in separation, divorce and remarriage.* London: The Haworth Press, Inc.
Stain, S., & Stain, B. (1970). *The colonial heritage of Latin America.* New York: Oxford University Press.
Starhawk (1987). *Truth or dare: Encounters with power, authority, and mystery.* San Francisco: Harper & Row.
Stevens, E. (1973). Machisimo and Marianismo. *Society, 10,* 57-63.
Strauss, A., & Corbin, J. (1990). *Basics of qualitative research: Grounded theory procedures and techniques.* Newbury Park, CA: Sage.

Stroup, A., & Pollock, G. (1999). Economic consequences of marital dissolution for Hispanics. *Journal of Divorce & Remarriage, 30,* 149-166.

Terrero Peña, P. (Ed.) (1984). *Código Civil de la República Dominicana* (Dominican Republic Civil Code). Santo Domingo, República Dominicana: Editora Taller C. por A.

Weinberger, M., Lloyd, C., & Blanc, A. (1989). Women's education and fertility: A decade of change in four Latin American countries. *International Family Planning Perspectives, 15,* 4-28.

Wonders, N. A. (1996). Determinate sentencing: A feminist and postmodern story. *Justice Quarterly, 13,* 613-648.

The World's Women Trends and Statistics (1999). In *U. N. Demographic Yearbook.* Retrieved 07, 09, 1999, from *www.divorcereform.org.*

APPENDIX
Questions and Probes Pertaining to Images of Divorce

What image do you have of the divorced women? Please describe . . .

In your opinion, how does society in general perceive divorced women?

Have you ever heard negative comments about divorced women? Please specify. . .

Do you think today's society discriminates against or treats differently divorced women?

If your answer is yes, please give examples:

Do you think divorced women constitute a different group that deserves a special consideration from society?

If so, why?

Do you think that a divorce affects the personal development of the woman in terms of work, children's education and sociocultural activities?

If so, how?

Do you agree that women should endure difficult and humiliating circumstances like infidelity before opting for a divorce?

If so, why?

Do you think that your country and culture have old and mistaken concepts about divorced women?

If so, please explain.

Do you know if your society has programs to help divorced women?

Would you attend those programs?

Why or why not?

Additional comments:

Index

Adoption
  closed, 31
    anti-therapeutic nature of, 35
    severing of parent-child
      relationship in, 32-33,35,37
    lack of preventive law approach in,
      32-33
  open, 31
    of African-American children,
      37-38
    among African Americans, 37
    family systems theory principles
      of, 35
    preventive law approach in, 33
    therapeutic jurisprudence approach
      in, 33
  transracial, 37-38
African-American children
  in foster care system, 37
  open adoptions of, 37-38
African Americans
  childrearing practices of, 37
  families of
    "deficit view" of, 37–38
    extended, 37,42
  open adoptions among, 37
"*Aged as Scapegoats, The*" (Binstock), 83
Agee, William, 83
Age or Need (Neugarten), 83
Al-Nakba, 115
American Association for Retired
    Persons (AARP), 85
Apartheid, social, 117
Appell, Annette, 38
Arditti, Joyce A., 152
Asia. *See also specific countries*
  birthrate in, 49
Australia
  birthrate in, 49
  immigration policy in, 91
  work-family policies in, 50
  benefits for single mothers, 56
  tax systems, 54
  working hours, 59
Austria, work-family policies in, 50
  working hours, 59
Autonomy
  of adults, 29
  of children
    relationship to self-constructed
      identity, 30
    as right, 27

Baby-boom generation, intergenerational
    equity and, 83,84
Barbier, Christophe, 88
Becker, Gary, 84
Belgium, retirement age in, 90
Benefits systems. *See also* Welfare
    benefits
  effect on women's labor force
    participation,
    50-56,61,68,69,70
Berlusconi, Silvio, 94
Birthrate
  decrease in, 80
  effect of women's employment on,
    49-50
  in social-democratic countries, 53
"Brazilianization," 117
Bread and Chocolate (movie), 107
Bush, George W., 85,96,106
Business Week, 84

California, paid family leave legislation
    in, 86
Canada

birthrate in, 49
work-family policies in, 50
  childcare, 51
Caregivers, children's attachment bonds with, 68-69
Caregiving. *See also* Elder care
  shared responsibility for, 62-63
  by women, 61-62
Catholic Church, in Latin America
  condemnation of divorce by, 145,165
  influence on perceptions of divorced women, 144,145,162-163, 166-167
  influence on women's empowerment, 168
  influence on women's gender roles, 144
Child, definition of, 116
Childcare
  effect on women's labor force participation, 97
  gender disparities in, 89,90
  governmental provision of, 49,50-52, 61,63
    in conservative countries, 51
    in liberal welfare countries, 51-52
    in social-democratic countries, 52
  shared responsibility for, 62-63
  unsubsidized, 52
Childcare workers, exploitation of, 52
Childrearing, in African-American extended families, 37
Children
  African-American
    in foster care system, 37
    open adoptions of, 37-38
  attachment relationship with caregivers, 68-69
  Palestinian Arab, as political prisoners, 116
  state's primary responsibility toward, 28
Children's rights
  autonomy, 27,30
  free expression, 29

interdependent *versus* individualistic approaches to, 27-28
self-constructed identity, 27-28,29-31
  definition of, 29
  relationship to autonomy, 30
United Nations Convention on the Rights of the Child and, 26,27, 28-29,30
Child welfare system
  anti-therapeutic nature of, 35
  in Israel, 38
  lack of preventive late approach in, 32
  poor and minority-group children in, 38
China, birthrate in, 49
Civil law, application to divorce, 145-146
Common law, application to divorce, 146
Cultural competence, role in child and family policy, 36-39

"Daddy leave," 54
Defense spending, 82,84
Democracy, relationship to social fascism, 117
Denmark, work-family policies in, 50
  benefits for single mothers, 56
  childcare, 52
  gender-based pay gap and, 58
  paid parental leave, 53
Dependency ratio
  in France, 86-87
Dependency ratio, 85,97,98
  definition of, 98
  in France, 86-87
Dispute resolution, non-adversarial, 39
Divorce
  in France, 145
  gender inequity-related, 69-70
  Puerto Rican and Dominican women's perceptions of, 143-173

Divorced women, Puerto Rican and
    Dominican women's
    perceptions of, 143-173
  ecological theory of, 148
  effect of cultural change on, 159-160
  feminist theory of, 148
  gender roles and, 147-148
  hembrismo and, 157,158-159
  legal and sociocultural background to,
    144-146,151
  marianismo and, 161,165-166
  negative perceptions, 157-158,
    159-160
    cultural influences on, 166-167
    as cultural stereotypes, 160-162,
      163-165,167
    divorced women's promiscuity,
      157,160,161,163,166
    hembrismo concept and,
      157,158-159,166
    implication for clinical practice,
      167-168
    influence of Catholicism on, 144,
      145,162-163,166-167
  positive perceptions, 156-157,159,160
  research study of
    conceptual framework of, 147-148
    data coding and analysis in,
      152-153,154
    data collection techniques in, 149
    design of, 149-155
    findings in, 155-168
    gender roles and, 147-148
    participants' characteristics in,
      153-155
    purpose of, 146
    qualitative research approach in,
      146-147,149,152-153
    reflexive considerations in,
      150-152,165
    research questions in, 146-147
    social constructionism analysis of,
      167
Dome of the Rock, 122
Domestic Purposes Benefit (DPB), 55-56

Domestic relations law, individualist
    approach in, 26-28
Domestic violence
  family group conferencing approach
    to, 40
  family systems theory approach to,
    35-36
  in gender inequity-based
    relationships, 69-70
  preventive law approach to, 33
Domestic violence perpetrators,
  prosecution of, 25-26
Domestic violence victims, othering of,
  38-39
Domestic workers, immigrants as, 95
Dominican women, perceptions of
    divorce and divorced women,
    143-173

Eastern Europe, birthrate in, 49
Elder care, 79-103
  corporate support for, 85
  dependency ratio and, 85
  provided by families, 85-86
  in France, 88-90
  monetary compensation for, 92-93
  women's responsibility for,
    89-90,92,93,95,105
  provided by immigrants, 95-96
  in the United States, 85-86
Elderly population
  in developing countries, 80
  in Germany, 90,93
  heterogeneity of, 98
  increase in, 80,105
  in Italy, 93
Europe. *See also specific European
    countries*
  elderly population in, 80,81
European Union
  social policy of, 3
  work-family policies in, 51
Express, 88

Familism, Latin American concept of, 144
Family
　African-American
　　"deficit view" of, 37-38
　　extended, 37,42
　family systems theory concept of, 34
　gay/lesbian-headed, 70-71
　individualistic concept of, 26
　Latin American concept of, 148
　mutual interaction within, 34-35
　nontraditional, 5
　nuclear, 4-5
　shared responsibility within, 34
Family and Medical Leave Act of 1993, 85-86,96,99
Family group conferencing (FGC), 16-17,39-40,42-43
Family law, adversarial individualistic framework for, 26-27
Family planning, in Germany, 92
Family systems theory
　application to child and family policy, 34-36
　definition of, 34
Family therapy
　as couples therapy, 5
　culturally-competent methods in, 5
　feminist, in the United Kingdom, 2-3,4-5,7-8,16-19
　as individual therapy, 5
Fascism, of social apartheid, 117
Fathers, paid parental leave for, 54
Federal deficit, "generational accounting" approach to, 84
Federal Reserve Bank, 83
Feminine Economy and Economic Man, The (Burggraf), 86
Finland, work-family policies in, 50
　paid parental leave, 53
Flint, Jerry, 83
Forbes, 83,84
Fortune, 84
Foster care system
　African-American children in, 37

　closed adoptions and, 31
　minority-group children in, 38
　open adoptions in, 37
　poor children in, 38
France
　birthrate in, 86,97
　elder care policy in, 96
　elderly population in
　　heatwave-related deaths among, 88,89
　　suicides among, 89
　history of divorce in, 145
　intergenerational equity in, 81,86-90
　　dependency ratio and, 86-87
　　family-based elder care and, 88-90,92
　　pension systems and, 86-88
　life expectancy in, 86
　pension system in, 86-88,96
　retirement age in, 90
Free expression, as children's right, 29

Gender discrimination, in the workplace, 63
Gender equity, in paid employment, 49, 56-58,69,88
Gender roles
　of Latin American women, 147-148
　of Palestinian women, 120,124-128,135
Generations Unlimited, 97-101,107
Germany
　Agenda 2010 in, 91,92
　birthrate in, 90,97
　dependency ratio in, 90
　elder care in
　　effect of intergenerational equity on, 92-93
　　government policy for, 96
　elderly population in, 90,93
　"guest worker" policy in, 107
　immigration policy in, 91,92,94
　intergenerational equity in, 81,90-93

implication for family-based elder care, 92-93
life expectancy in, 90
pension system in, 90-91
projected population decrease in, 90
retirement age in, 96
retirement policy in, 90
reunification of, 90,92
Social Dependency Insurance Program in, 92-93
women's labor force participation in, 91,92
Gilligan, Carol, 28
Glendon, Mary Ann, 27
Golden Rule, 25
"*Graying of the Federal Budget, The*" (Hudson), 82,83
Green Party, 91
Grossberg, Michael, 26-27
"Guest workers," 107
Guthrie, Woody, 107

Head Start, 13
Healthcare rationing, age-based, 84
Health insurance, denial to gay/lesbian-headed families, 70
Hembrismo, 147,148,157,158-159,166
Heterosexist bias, 70-71
of therapists, 74
Homosexual-headed families, 70-71
feminist family therapists' interaction with, 74
Household work
by men, 88-89,90
shared responsibility for, 62-63
by women, 61,88-89,90
Hurston, Zora Neale, 112

Identity, self-constructed, of children
children's right to, 27-28,29-31
definition of, 29
relationship to autonomy, 30

Immigrants, as elder-care caregivers, 95-96
Immigration
to Europe, 3-4
as solution to labor shortage, 107
Immigration policy
in Australia, 91
in Germany, 91,92,94
in Italy, 95,96,107
Income gap, gender-based, 57-58
Infants, attachment relationship with caregivers, 68-69
Interdependence
as child and family policy principle, 23-46
children's self-constructed identity and, 27-28,29-31
cultural competence perspective on, 36-39,42
family systems theory perspective on, 33-36,42
versus individualist approach, 26-28
preventive law perspective on, 32-33,42
procedural justice perspective on, 39-40,42-43
therapeutic jurisprudence perspective on, 31-32
United Nations Convention on the Rights of the Child and, 26,27,28-29,30
between generations, 98
Intergenerational equity, 79-103,105-107
as class war, 84-85
dependency ratio and, 85,86-87,97,98
in France, 81,86-90
dependency ratio and, 86-87
family-based elder care and, 88-90,92
pension systems and, 86-88
in Germany, 90-93
guidelines and recommendations for, 97-101
in the United States, 82-86

women's participation in the labor force and, 90-93
International Labor Organization (ILO), 53,63
International Monetary Fund, 61
Iran, birthrate in, 49
Ireland
 birthrate in, 49
 work-family policies in, 50
 welfare, 55
 working hours, 59
Israel. *See also* Palestinian women, responses to Israeli Palestinian policy
 child welfare system in, 38
 family group conferencing use in, 40
Italy
 birthrate in, 49,93-95,97
 elderly population in, 93
 immigration policy in, 95,96,107
 intergenerational equity in, 81,93-96
  dependency ratio and, 95
  implication for family-based elder care, 94-96
 pension system in, 93-94
 projected population decrease in, 93
 retirement age in, 90,93,94,96
 women's labor force participation in, 95

Japan
 birthrate in, 49
 elderly population in, 80,81
 work-family policies in, 50
 working hours, 59
Justice, procedural, 39-40
 family group conferencing (FGC) concept of, 39-40,42-43
 mediation concept of, 40
 non-adversarial dispute resolution concept of, 39

Korea, birthrate in, 49

Labor force, women's participation in
 in Dominican Republic, 148
 effect on birthrate, 49-50
 in Germany, 91,92
 implication for family caregiving, 85-86
 intergenerational equity in, 90-93
 in Italy, 95
 in Latin American society, 165
 OECD *Babies and Bosses* reports recommendations for, 47-65,105
  childcare policies, 50-52,61,63
  critiques of, 60-63,67-77
  family-friendly work, 50-51,56-60,69
  flexible working hours, 58-59
  gender equity in paid employment, 56-58,62,63
  paid parental leave, 50-51,53-54,61,63,68-69
  single mothers' welfare benefits, 55-56
  tax and benefit systems, 50-51, 52-56,61,68,69,70
  work/life balance issues, 59-60
 in Puerto Rico, 147-148
Labor shortage, projected, 49,50
Lamm, Richard, 83-84
Latin America, perception of divorced women in, 106,143-173
Law
 preventive, 32-33,35,36,39,42
 as therapeutic agent. *See* Therapeutic jurisprudence
"Legal soft spots," 32
Lesbian-headed families, 70-71
 feminist family therapists' interactions with, 74
L'Express, 88
Life expectancy
 increase in, 80
 pre-World War II, 105
Lopéz, Nancy P., 150-152

Machismo, 147,148
Maoris, 16
Marianismo, 147,148
Mediation, as procedural justice concept, 40
Medicare, 84,96,97
MetLife Foundation, 85
Metropolitan Life, 85
Migrant laborers, 107
Minimum-wage legislation, 57
Minow, Martha, 28
Mobility restrictions, on Palestinian women, 116-117,118,119,120
Mutual interaction, within families, 34-35

National Alliance for Caregiving, 85
National Social Security Institute, 95
Netherlands
　pension system in, 87
　work-family policies in, 50
　　childcare, 52
New Republic, 84
Newsweek, 84
New York Times Magazine, 84-85
New Zealand
　birthrate in, 49
　work-family policies in, 50
　　benefits for single mothers, 56
　　childcare, 51
　　paid parental leave, 53,54
　　tax systems, 54
　　welfare, 55-56
　　working hours, 59

Office of Management and Budget (OMB), 82
Organization for Economic Cooperation and Development (OECD), *Babies and Bosses* reports of, 47-65
　clinical implications of, 71-74
　　awareness of diversity of family structures, 73-74
　　awareness of gender inequity, 73
　　culturally-competent therapy, 74
　　gender-sensitive therapy, 73
　　heterosexist bias, 74
　　self-awareness techniques, 72,74
　　systemic connectedness, 72-73
　context of, 49-51
　goal of, 68
　heterosexist bias of, 70-71
　recommendations of
　　childcare policies, 50-52,61,63
　　family-friendly work, 50-51,56-60, 69
　　feminist therapy-based critiques of, 60-63,67-77
　　flexible working hours, 58-59
　　gender equity in paid employment, 56-58,62,63
　　paid parental leave, 50-51,53-54,61,63,68-69
　　tax and benefit systems, 50-51,52-56,61,68,69,70
　　work/life balance issues, 59-60
Organization for Economic Cooperation and Development (OECD) countries. *See also specific countries*
　birthrate in, 49-50
　pension systems in, 87
Othering, 24-25,27,38
　of domestic violence victims, 38-39
　of poor families, 38
Overpopulation, 106

Palestinian children, as political prisoners, 116
Palestinian refugees, 115
Palestinian women, responses to Israeli Palestinian policy, 109-141
　anti-family policies and, 121-122
　conceptual background to, 115-117
　conceptual basis for, 112-115

counter-discourses of, 128-134
   as historical-national legacy
      narratives, 137
   as traditional continuity narratives,
      136-137
   as transformative narratives, 137
counter-spaces and counter-memories
      responses, 128-134, 136-127
family connections and, 119-120
gender roles and, 120,124-128,135
historical background to, 115-117
house demolitions and, 111,115-116,
      118,128-129,133,135
Israeli housing projects and, 119
Israeli Separation Wall and, 112-113,
      116-117,118,119,122-124,130-
      131,136-137
methodological approach to, 112-115
mobility restrictions and, 116-117,118,
      119,120
"no safe haven" doctrine and, 111
political imprisonment and,
      116,127,132
religious oppression and, 121,122
sexual harassment and, 116,121-122
shatat (dislocation) and, 117-124
sumud (steadfastness) response,
      120-121
torture and, 111, 121-122
violation of families' sense of security
      and, 111,115,117-119,121-122,
      124-128
   sexualization of, 124-128
Paradine, Kate, 35-36,40
Parental leave, paid, 50-51,52-56,63,
      68-69,97
   for fathers, 54
Parent-child relationship
   adoption-related severance of, 32-33,
      35,37
   attachment bonds in, 68-69
   effect of family public policy on, 48
   role of children's rights in, 29

Part-time employment, of women, 59,62,
      88,89-90
Pay, gender inequity in, 49,56-58,62,63,
      88
   as divorce risk factor, 69-70
   effect on lesbian-headed families, 71
Pelton, Leroy, 38
Pension systems. *See also* Retirement
      age; Retirement policy
   in France, 86-88,96
   in Germany, 90-91
   in Italy, 93-94
   in OECD countries, 87
   private accounts, 106
Population, age structure of, 81. *See also*
      Elderly population
Portugal, work-family policies in, 50
   paid parental leave, 54
Prejudice, toward gay/lesbian families,
      70
Preventive law, 32-33,35,36,39,42
Privilege, masculine, 3
"Psycho-legal soft spots," 32
Puerto Rican women, perceptions of divorce
      and divorced women, 143-173

Raffarin, Jean-Pierre, 87
Rape, of Palestinian Arab women, 116
Rawls, John, 100
Religious oppression, of Palestinian
      women, 121,122
Resource allocation, age-based, 100. *See
      also* Intergenerational equity
Responsibility, shared, within families,
      34
Retirement age, 90
   in France, 90
   in Germany, 96
   in Italy, 90,93,94,96
Retirement policy, in Germany, 90
Robert Wood Johnson Foundation, 92-93
Ruddock, Joyce, 85

"Sandwich generation," 61-62
Schroeder, Gerhard, 91
Self-constructed identity, of children, 27-28,29-31
  definition of, 29
  relationship to autonomy, 30
Setting Limits (Callahan), 84
Sexual harassment, of Palestinian women, 116,121-122
Sharon, Ariel, 122
Singapore, birthrate in, 49
Single mothers
  poverty of, 69
  welfare benefits for, 55-56,61
Social Democratic Party, 91
Social justice, as feminist family therapy component, 75-76
Social policies, impact on women's personal relationships, 48
Social Security, 84,85,96,97
  as an intergenerational tax, 83
  COLAs (cost-of-living adjustments) in, 83
  proposed changes in, 106
Social Security Act of 1935, 105
Soylent Green (movie), 106
Stress, work-related, 60,62
Suicide, 89
Sweden
  birthrate in, 49,50
  work-family policies in, 50
    childcare, 52
    child poverty rate and, 57
    gender-based pay gap and, 58
    paid parental leave, 53,54
  working-age population in, 49,50
Switzerland
  "guest worker" policy in, 107
  work-family policies in, 50

Taiwan, birthrate in, 49
Tax benefits, denial to gay/lesbian-headed families, 70
Tax rates, lifetime, 84

Tax systems
  effect on mothers' labor force participation, 52-53,54-55
  effect on retirement age, 91
Thailand, birthrate in, 49
Therapeutic jurisprudence, 31-32,33,35,36,39
Thurow, Lester, 84-85
Trade unions, 63

United Kingdom
  family support services policies in, 1-22
    Children's Act of 1989, 11
    Children's Trusts, 6
    definition of, 7
    domestic violence issue and, 17-18
    early intervention and prevention, 12-16
    Every Child Matters program, 11
    family group conferences (FGC) and, 16-17
    family theory approach to, 2-3
    feminist family therapists' responses to, 2-3,4,6-7,16-19
    Framework for Assessment of Children in Need, 10
    Home Start, 7
    implication for child and adolescent mental health services, 9-18
    implication for family caregivers, 8
    nuclear family focus of, 4-5
    parental support and education programs, 12-15
    Quality Protects program, 11
    relationship to changes in family characteristics, 8-9
    relationship to family therapy, 7-8
    service design and delivery aspect of, 4-7
    Sure Start program, 13
    systems theory approach to, 2-3

voluntary sector and, 2,8
work-family policies in, 50
  childcare, 51-52
  flexible working hours, 59
  welfare, 55
  women's part-time employment and, 59
  working hours, 60
United Nations, anti-gender discrimination policy of, 63
United Nations Convention on the Rights of the Child, 26,27,28-29,30
United Nations International Year of Older Persons, 100
United States of America
  intergenerational equity in, 96
  work-family policies in
    benefits for single mothers, 56
    childcare, 51
University professors, working hours of, 59,60

Welfare benefits
  for older adults, 81
  for single mothers, 55-56,61
Western Europe
  birthrate in, 49
  elderly population in, 80
Wexler, David, 31
Winick, Bruce, 31
Women
  labor force participation by. *See* Labor force, women's participation in
  in war zones, 111-112. *See also* Palestinian women
Work-family policies, 47-56
  childcare policy, 50-52,61,63
  in conservative countries, 50,51,54, 55,57,59
  in Europe, 97
  family-friendly work, 50-51,56-60,60
  flexible working hours, 58-59
  gender equity in paid employment, 56-58,62,63
  in liberal welfare states, 50,51-52,53, 54,55-56,57,58,59
  paid parental leave, 50-51,53-54
  in social-democratic states, 50,52,53, 54,55,57,58,59,62
  tax and benefit systems, 50-51,52-56,61,68,69,70
  work/life balance issues and, 59-60
Working-age population, decrease in, 49,50
Working hours
  flexible, 58-59
  of men, 59,60,61
  of women, 59-60,61-62
World Bank, 61

Zero Population Growth (ZPG), 106